Clearing the Way to Awakening
A Nine-Step Practice from Tibetan Buddhism
Yudron Wangmo

ARROW OF LOVE

Arrow of Love Publications

Copperopolis, CA

www.yudronwangmo.com

No generative artificial intelligence was used in the writing of this work.

Copyright © 2024 by Yudron Wangmo

All Rights Reserved

No part of this book may be used or reproduced by any means, graphic, electronic, or mechanical, including photocopying, recording, taping, or by any information storage retrieval system without the written permission of the publisher except in the case of brief quotations embodied in critical articles and reviews.

ISBN 978-0-9969241-6-0 Paperback

ISBN 978-0-9969241-7-7 E-book

Table of Contents

Preface	VI
Introduction	1
1. Aspiration Why We Practice	11
2. Reorientation The Purpose of the Four Contemplations	25
3. Appreciation Step One—Contemplation of the Precious Human Life	38
4. Deterioration Step Two—Contemplation of Impermanence	50
5. Dissatisfaction Step Three—Contemplation of Suffering, Stress and Pain	63
6. Repercussions Step Four—Contemplation of Karma	74
7. Exploration How to Find a Spiritual Friend	91

| 8. Accumulation | 97 |

Positive Karmic Force and Non-conceptual Wisdom

| 9. Representation | 102 |

Creating Sacred Space at Home

| 10. Interconnection | 111 |

Practicing with your Body, Speech and Mind Simultaneously

| 11. Protection | 131 |

Step Five—Going for Refuge

| 12. Motivation | 149 |

Step Six—Generating Bodhicitta

| 13. Purification | 180 |

Step Seven—Purification with Vajrasattva

| 14. Multiplication | 201 |

| 15. Unification | 225 |

Step Nine—Guru Yoga

| 16. Integration | 250 |

Bringing the Ngondro into Your Life

| Conclusion | 266 |

So Long... for Now

| Dakini Heart Essence Ngondro | 267 |

The Khandro Tuktik Ngondro

| Centers to Consider | 281 |

Controversial Organizations	293
Beginner's Glossary	295
Further Reading	305
Acknowledgments	311
About The Author	312
The Mayum Mountain Foundation	313

Preface

Imagine you're strolling down a California beach, right at the surf line. To your left, you hear the fizzing sound of water sinking into the sand as a wave withdraws back into the ocean.

To your right, the red ball of the sun rises over the coastal mountains. In front of you, in the watery froth at the surf line, there is a thick glass jar in the sand, freshly tossed up from the Pacific. You uncork its top and find a rolled stack of paper strips, covered in a neat black script. You've never seen this alphabet before.

What would you do?

If it were me, I'd get the words translated into my language, to find out who sent it and what they had to say.

Mystery. Intrigue. I'm all in!

What if it turned out that the message was exactly what you needed to hear, a handbook on how to transform your life into something meaningful and truly satisfying? Maybe that bottle washed up as an answer to an urgent prayer inside you. An unspoken prayer for wisdom and realization.

That's how I feel about the nine-step Buddhist practice that is the subject of this book. While it didn't literally appear in the surf, when my initial Tibetan spiritual teacher first imparted it to me, it might as well have. It was that fascinating. That mysterious.

Written in Tibetan, the language of the high Himalayan mountains of central Asia, it promised an unburdening from the ceaseless inner hankering that had underpinned my life. It said I could free myself from that uneasy feeling in the pit of my stomach... the fear that the happiness I yearned for, and put all of my energy into finding, would slip away, always beyond my reach. And, then, it went above and beyond that and urged me to become a truly great being, a future leader and role model for others, who could—someday—guide all living beings to inner freedom.

Now that I have immersed myself in Tibetan Buddhism for thirty years, I have such gratitude for my teachers. I have had a close connection with three Tibetan lamas—spiritual guides. Under the guidance of one, I completed the traditional three-year, three-month, group retreat. Under another, I spent a cumulative three years of shorter retreats in personal isolation—six months here, a year there. My third teacher is a continuous inspiration in my heart, although he lives in an inaccessible monastery in Tibet.

When I started on this path, and for many years afterward, I was working as an R.N. and a Nurse Practitioner. Later, as a nursing home director, I wrestled with this very practice before and after work. It changed my life.

I threw myself into these practices when I was younger, with energy, diligence, and enthusiasm. Now, practice is a gentler process. I've come into a new way of being with my body, my life, and the people and animals around me. It's like my presence in the world is slowly coming to resemble the dignified, graceful, glide of a whale in the depths of a cool ocean.

In this book, I will do everything in my power to help you connect with the step-by-step process my mentors taught me. Known as the *ngondro*, this is the series of gateway trainings that I have found so satisfying. Thousands upon thousands of people in Tibet, and all over the world, have started their transformational process with this practice. Some continued working with it to their dying day.

One of my Tibetan teachers asked me to teach the ngondro and gave me a formal Tibetan teaching title. I've been teaching this material for twenty years off and on, and intensively for six.

As a result of this practice, people I knew in my young adulthood might not recognize my mind today. Most of the time I feel like that dignified whale; free and chill. Occasionally, I lapse into being the same as your typical American person—too concerned about how I look, about money, projects, politics, the ups and downs of my relationships... my aches and pains. But even at those times, I remember how ludicrous my scheming thoughts are. They're based on anxiety that bad things might happen to me or that good things won't.

How unnecessary. Yet how alluring!

My message is that the mental hardships you carry—all that anguish—can be set down, like an exhausted hiker lowering her backpack onto a trailside boulder. These nine steps, linked together into a whole, are the tried-and-true method for removing hindrances to your discovery of that experience. If you decide to embark on this path, to allow yourself to be touched by it, it will help you settle naturally into the experience of a clear and open sense of presence. First for moments, then for hours and even weeks and days, this unburdened experience of freedom can open up for you. And then, just like that, you can viscerally realize that the weight you've been carrying—since forever until now—is optional.

Serenity, love, wisdom, compassion, and other hidden abilities lie behind the swirl of our habitual thoughts. These hidden qualities resist being nailed down or put in a box, even the box labeled "the real me." Within us is an indestructible, naked, truth. Neither nuclear war, oceans of coronavirus, nor the fires and floods of our overheated planet can kill it.

The Tibetan preachers of this tradition—the lamas—always say that this hidden ability to dwell in the peaceful state of wakeful, present, clear wisdom and compassion is here with us right now. It pervades every atom of our bodies and even the space between them. We just don't know how to access it.

However, if you're like me, you're skeptical of promises like that. I'm sick to death of being marketed to. For that reason, I invite you to bring a sense of intelligent doubt with you as you read this book. I've done my best to stifle hype and write what I have confirmed in my own experience. And I'm not going to promise you instant results.

Tibetan people would undertake these practices after they found a consummately trained and realized teacher. They would sit down and listen with reverence to their exalted lama as they would go through a formal classic book about these practices, their purpose, and their meaning. People generally knew what qualities and training to look for in a teacher. They knew their reputation in the community. Young people were directed by their families to the very best mentor available.

You may or may not have access right now to great teachers like that, or to one who personally inspires you. I'll talk about how to find a good one (and screen out sketchy people) in later chapters. In the meantime, I will go through these practices in a less grand and devotional style than the Tibetan classics.

This practice impacts both our consciousness and our interactions with others. The set of trainings it contains was boiled down over the centuries from a wider array of exercises that Buddhist teachers gave their students. As the centuries progressed, stellar Tibetan adepts observed what was most effective for their students and unified them into an ordered arrangement.

Like other versions of Buddhist practice that evolved in different parts of Asia, Tibetan Buddhism invites us to examine what we think of as "me." All Buddhist practice systems challenge us to suspend our knee-jerk assertion of a real self or identity through contemplation and meditation. Practice allows us to take breaks from our obsession with thoughts of the past, present, or future. In that opening, natural compassion wells up toward everyone equally.

Meditation practice. Study. People who don't harm others. Buddhism is well-respected for these things. The ngondro answers the question, where do you go from there? Its exercises are intense, varied, energetic, and provocative. People change their fixed ideas of the world, and their place in it, by doing them. If that thought doesn't spark curiosity for you, you have the wrong book in your hands.

There is chanting and singing in this practice. We use words to remove our faulty perceptions and self-destructive habits and chart a new path forward. Through visualizing with our mind's eye, making new physical movements with our bodies (one of them is even aerobic!), whispering mantras, and, eventually, forging a relationship with a qualified guide, we set new goals. The point is to speed up our transformation by outsmarting our built-in resistance in various crafty ways.

How does this compare with the path of the silent meditator? There is more variety, more activity, and more intensity. This power-pack of effortful practices appeals to practitioners with drive and enthusiasm. They pose the question: what if I could reach the point of total awakening in this lifetime, rise to the caliber of a buddha who can deeply help all living beings?

Intrigued? Come with me on a guided journey through the practice that shaped the greats of Tibetan Buddhism, from the yogis and yoginis meditating in isolated mountainside cabins to the spiritual leaders of lavishly-ornamented, gold-roofed, monasteries. Learn how to clear away all obstacles to awakening, right in the middle of your own real life.

Introduction

Smiling groups of two or three people chatted with each other, filling the room with the murmur of conversation before settling into their seats. The most limber among them plopped down on meditation cushions in front. Folding chairs in rows behind them creaked under the weight of the older folks. As soon as everyone got comfortable, the revered teacher arrived, along with the people who'd greeted his car at the curb. Glowing as they entered the room behind him, their white silk greeting scarves still dangled around their necks where he'd placed them with care.

With his entrance to the room, everyone rose from their seats again, their hands pressed together at their hearts. This traditional sign of respect in Tibetan culture had become second nature to these Americans who'd come to love venerable Asian spiritual teachers, especially this one: Lama Tharchin. His toothy smile lit up that room, a meditation center in Palo Alto, a university town south of San Francisco. Everybody loved him. He was gentle and kind. Humble, yet willing to be the focal point, a representative of his line of teachers… for us.

All roads had brought me there that night. I'd been looking for someone who could not only talk about enlightenment but show me what enlightenment might look like in real life. I wanted them to hail from an unbroken lineage of teachers going way back through time to the Buddha so that I could do the same practices as they did with confidence. Someone trustworthy.

There he was.

Rinpoche (we called him by this Tibetan title of respect, meaning precious) found his seat in front. He took in the room, greeting the regulars. When he first spoke, he invoked his mentors with a prayer.

What I recall is the dance-like movements of his hands as he spoke. Spontaneous and unchoreographed, his beautiful gestures signaled that his mind, too, was smooth and light. He'd been trained in the dances and sacred hand movements used in tantric Buddhist rituals since he was a kid in Tibet. Looking back on that day now, it seems to me that the graceful and mysterious ways he used his hands hinted at that.

Since his physical gestures told me he was the real thing, in the months that followed, I navigated up a winding road to his center in the mountains above Santa Cruz, California. The sign at the entrance said *Pema Osel Ling, Lotus Land of Clear Light*. It was a large piece of hilly, redwood-studded land. At that early stage of its development, the remote retreat center was staffed by a ragtag crew of lovable misfits living in trailers, tents, and yurts.

Still uncertain whether my particular misfit style would fit in with this crew, I parked my car and found the small dorm building. I'd heard that Rinpoche would be speaking in the living room there, which served as a tiny temple back then. I squeezed in with about fifty people, this time all seated on the floor.

Lama Tharchin was sitting in front on a cushion with a row of large open windows at his back. The light that poured in from behind him obscured the details of his face. He spoke warmly and deliberately, illustrating points about the benefits of practice on consciousness with stories and jokes. While his body was 100% settled on his cushion, his undefended mind seemed to extend out infinitely, relaxed and open.

Rapt, I felt completely present with him in that warm, crowded, room. As someone with the spaced-out kind of ADHD, it was probably one of the first times in my life that I was undistracted. There was nowhere else I wanted to be. My perennial to-do list temporarily lost its seat in my mind.

Rinpoche had learned our English language in his fifties at a community college. He said it made more sense to him that one person should learn English instead of a hundred people needing to learn Tibetan to understand him. He had a good vocabulary, yet the order of his words resembled Tibetan more than English. That only made me listen yet more intently as he launched into his talk, peppered with jokes.

I was riveted to his every word. We all were.

Just then, whatever was supporting the open window behind him gave way, and the upper section of the aluminum frame dropped down in its tracks, closing with a deafening bang.

Everyone in the room was startled and somewhat alarmed. Except for one person; Rinpoche. He never stopped teaching. There was not even a hiccup in the flow of his words. He didn't jump. His body did not tense.

It was astounding to me.

Driving the narrow roads, then highways, back home to urban Oakland, I couldn't get it out of my head. What kind of human was this? Completely relaxed and at home in his body, yet sharp and focused. It was like his mind was the space inside an open-air football stadium. His words were like the music and crowd sounds from the game, precise, yet natural, floating out into the sky above.

I was a happy flower when he was teaching.

Rinpoche had been raised from childhood in a family of weighty Buddhist practitioners. When he was nine, he was placed under the guidance of (some would say) the greatest teacher of twentieth-century Tibet: Dudjom Rinpoche. He spent nine years in retreat under his guidance in Kongpo, Tibet.

This isn't a book about Lama Tharchin. This book is really about you. But I hope that through sharing the wow factor of my first Buddhist teacher, you are getting a feel for what it's like to let your heart open to someone. To let them become your personal Buddha.

Yes, I loved him. Non-romantically. But more to the point, I wanted to be like him with all my heart. Looking back now, I wonder why? What led me to love these qualities that no marketing campaign had sold me on? He never promised that I would be thinner, sexier, wealthier, or healthier from studying and practicing with him. I wasn't recruited. There was no cult.

The truth was, after a long period investigating the practice-oriented wisdom traditions of the world, I'd settled on Buddhism some years before. I'd already been practicing meditation and taking part in study groups, first at a small center in Massachusetts, and later in Berkeley.

When I'd started out, I'd been unable to settle down for more than a moment. I'll be forever grateful to my early meditation teachers, particularly one who encouraged us to work our way up to meditating for a whole hour. My personal practice at the time began with a calming meditation joined with insight gleaned from noting the dividing line between when one is focused (for example) on the breath, and when one's mind reasserts its old habit of thinking, thinking, thinking.

The senior students in those centers helped me a lot. They were good people. But, to me, they did not embody the Dharma in their entire being the way Lama Tharchin did. While he had good and bad moods like all of us, there was this fundamental quality of spaciousness and evenness—as though one part of him was always okay, no matter what happened. There was something smooth and seamless there, in every setting and every mood. I didn't see these next-level qualities at my local meditation center.

Sometime later, I got in to see Rinpoche in private before a talk he gave in Berkeley. I was shaking a little when I asked him if he would teach me. What I had in mind was doing the practices he had specialized in his whole life. This style of practice is called Vajrayana Buddhism, or Tantric Buddhism. It is practiced by people who live in the Himalayas.

Rinpoche looked at me in a friendly way. He paused before replying. (Or have I added that pause into my memory because I was so nervous with him that seconds seemed like minutes?) Finally, he said yes. Yes, he would help me. He asked me to help him, too.

Before I'd entered the room with Lama Tharchin, a new acquaintance, Josh, had cued me that I should take the little practice booklet that all of his students used into the meeting with me and ask for what is known as *transmission*. Now that I was in the room with him, seeing the text in my hand, I had the presence of mind to ask Rinpoche for that. I handed him the booklet. He read it to me at top speed and bonked it gently on my head. I later learned that the bonking part was unnecessary, but I freakin' loved it.

That booklet that Rinpoche read me was the *ngondro*. The word literally means "what goes before." It is the foundation of Vajrayana Buddhist practice, especially in the Nyingma and Kagyu schools. It is an orderly and efficient training system distilled from practices that arrived in Tibet a millennium and a half ago from India and Pakistan. A similar set of practices is done in the Gelugpa tradition after people have been practicing Buddhism for years and then want to do Vajrayana practices. In recent times, the Sakya tradition has introduced a ngondro as well.

Over the years, the best traditional Tibetan books about this practice have been translated into English. I've put a list of those in the back of this book. The truth is, though, that many folks don't feel comfortable reading thick books in translation that are heavy with technical vocabulary. Even back in the 1980s and

90s, when the old gurus seemed to have popped right out of their retreat caves and into our lives—still gleaming with inner light—the books they asked all their followers to read often sat gathering dust on shelves.

Who is This Book For?

This book is for you if you want to discover whether or not you have a passion for these practices. As you read, in the back of your mind you can wonder: could this be the start of the meaningful life path I've been looking for? Could it scratch some inner itch that lives in the deepest part of me... the part that has not been touched by relationships, parenting, sex, weed, or a hundred pints of Ben and Jerry's ice cream?

You can ask yourself: do I want to let myself be touched and changed by this practice, the legacy of the sages of the past? Do I have it in me to be that brave and self-motivated... both when it's hard and when it's easy? Do I yearn to eventually find a qualified, honorable, and loveable personal guide, a teacher whose advice I can grow to trust over the years?

As I've said, I've had three men who have played pivotal roles in my spiritual life. After meeting Lama Tharchin I couldn't deny that I also had powerful devoted feelings for Lama Pema Dorje and Adzom Paylo (all referred to by the same title, Rinpoche). No one was more surprised than me that I, an ardent young feminist, felt uninspired when I met the leading female teachers of my time. I happened to be touched to my marrow by these three men.

It may be that you have already launched into the ngondro. Each specific tradition has its own practice booklet, containing poetic words that bring all nine steps alive. You can chant or sing it, to integrate it with your mind, body, and nervous system. The text itself may have an inspiring origin story, about how it arose of its own accord in the mind of an awakened practitioner.

If you've already met your inspirational guide, that person or an assistant will formally transmit it to you and teach you the details.

Back in the day, we who became Lama Tharchin's students were simply handed that booklet, the one he bonked on my head, with some clarifying drawings. He got us started in simple ways that could work for earnest lay people with jobs. We dove into practice and, over the years, gained an understanding of the meaning.

Other Tibetan scholars and clerics might be appalled to hear that we jumped into the practice like that. Their training may have stressed that you would need to study for years and years before doing them. But, it was the other way around for us. Mentoring and practicing were followed by the gradual introduction of knowledge. It was a perfect approach for me because I saw myself change from the power of the practice, and that made me curious.

I write this book in the spirit of all three of my teachers, each of whom encouraged students to begin ngondro as soon as they could and put their whole hearts into it.

The traditional Tibetan style of communicating the Dharma—the teachings—is to be quite formal, detailed, and serious. Please *do* listen to ngondro instruction by Tibetan and Bhutanese teachers in that style if you want to go deeper. It's wonderful!

In this book, instead I'll share based on my own experience over the decades as an ordinary American woman whose mind and life have been turned around by engaging with ngondro repeatedly. Through this adventure, I've changed from a judgey, gloomy, anxious, sourpuss into something... else. As you get to know me through these pages, I hope you will get a different feel for who I am now.

I'll also share with you the voices of others about their experiences doing these practices, gleaned through surveys and informal conversations.

The Inner Calling

Why are some people strongly drawn to Tibetan Buddhism in the first place, and others feel nothing for it? Sure, we were raised with or without a religion. That could account for a lot. But is there more? After all, why would a girl like me, who grew up in a suburb of Washington, D.C. in the sixties have any interest whatsoever? The only Asian person in my school was the daughter of a South Korean diplomat.

When I was a kid, maybe twelve, I remember gazing up at a large scroll painting of an intricate mandala, a sacred circle, on a museum wall in Washington, D.C. Hundreds of figures, both humanoid and fantastical, were painted in nested circles and squares, in a rainbow of colors. Mom had brought me there, to the Sackler Gallery on the National Mall, to see Asian art. Once we were there, she merely glanced at this wondrous, enrapturing, image, and moved on.

I couldn't get that thing out of my head.

Looking back, I now know that the mandala, painted on fabric so that it could be rolled up and transported, represented an aerial cut-away view of the palace of a buddha. The artist had painted the mandala as an aid for people doing a meditation practice that included complex visualizations. I, myself, have now spent years in cloistered retreats, imagining my consciousness in the center of sacred circles like that.

At that time, I'd never seen anything like that painting before. Something was stirred in me. At the risk of sounding woo-woo, I wonder whether a similar mandala image had left an imprint on my consciousness in a previous lifetime, creating a resonance like the sound of a bell vibrating long after it was rung.

Practice, Practice, Practice

The other day, I was lined up in a mirrored gym in a bi-weekly Tai Chi Class. The teacher asked us, "Did any of you practice at home since our last class together?"

Five people averted their gaze from the studio mirror. Including me.

In that silent moment, I wondered whether it would be a good idea to tell her the truth. I was never going to commit to practicing Tai Chi at home. When it came down to it, I didn't want to. It wasn't my passion in life.

Tibetan Buddhist practice is like that. Unless you have a passion for it, you won't do it. There are millions of people out there who go to the gym every day or practice a martial art, or a musical instrument, regularly. A few people still go to church every day. Some folks devote themselves to locating and having sex with a new partner virtually every day. Others methodically stock up on alcohol to get drunk reliably every day, without running out. They all have their missions in life, whether constructive or destructive.

By the time you add up the minutes spent in these different pursuits, it's at least an hour a day. Often more than that, if you count the driving time.

The kind-eyed Tibetan clerics want you to fall in love with this multi-faceted practice like that. If you compare the time commitment involved in doing it daily for a few years, it's similar to earning a black belt in karate, gambling away your house, becoming a sex god, etc. Surely, there are peak experiences with any of these activities. Any of them would change you. But none of these other passions, all of which are aimed at getting what you want in this life, will give you the lasting benefit and satisfaction that practicing the ngondro intensively will.

Come with me, and I'll show you why, what, and how.

Chapter 1

Aspiration

Why We Practice

Thousands of modern people have immersed themselves in ngondro practice. Why on earth would they do that when they could be watching Netflix, partying, or building up a side hustle to make more money, instead? After all, there are only so many hours in the day.

In 2016, the occupational psychologist and independent researcher Jens Nasstrum surveyed fifty-nine people who'd practiced ngondro. He shared the completely anonymous replies to the questions in his survey with me. (I was one of the participants, but I can't recognize my answers now.) I'll be mentioning insights I gleaned from his survey throughout the book, as well as from my own surveys and conversations with friends.

People gave a variety of replies when asked what had inspired them to do this practice. Some folks already had a teacher or center they followed. In their system of training, this foundation practice was a prerequisite. Others surveyed put things more in terms of a gut feeling, an intuitive yearning to do the practice as soon as they heard about it. Another group of respondents wanted to follow a Tibetan Buddhist tradition in a way that felt complete. They wanted to walk the path that others had trod before them for hundreds of years. Some, having already studied Buddhism, used traditional words, saying they wanted to purify themselves or accumulate merit.

Enlightenment

What drew you to pick up this book?

Western teachers are shy to talk about the big promises of the Buddha, for fear of being considered too far out there. Let's face it, these days you'll see a much larger crowd at a talk about how to love ourselves better than one about total awakening.

We've all heard the word... enlightenment. To traditional Buddhists, the Sanskrit word translated as enlightenment means a lot more than becoming happy, peaceful, and wise. When India became a British colony in 1858, familiar English words were repurposed to describe and translate the principles of the religions the colonists came upon in their explorations.

We might imagine that the word enlighten comes from the old English word, *inlihtan*, meaning *to illuminate*. However, the founder of the Pali Text Society, Thomas W. Rhys Davids, was the first to propose the word enlightenment to translate the Sanskrit word *bodhi* in 1882. He was thinking of the Age of Enlightenment in Europe, from the late 17th to the early 19th century, not illumination.

I turned to a scholar, Dr. Aaron Weiss, to understand this better. He wrote of the Age of Enlightenment in personal correspondence, saying it marked "...the emergence of scientific rationality as the basis of intellectual, political, and cultural legitimacy. This involved the questioning of traditional authority and the advancement of individual liberty and rationalized forms of society, such as liberal democracy. Rhys Davids saw a parallel between the demythologized mentality of that period and the teachings of the Buddha. For better or worse, this has influenced many modern interpretations of Buddhism, both in the West and in Asia."

This is a classic example of how the agenda and misconceptions of translators can mislead us in our practice. We are straying far from the original meaning of bodhi if we approach a system of practice indigenous to Asia with an agenda that the enlightenment we are seeking is about becoming a hard-headed anti-authoritarian, stripping away myth and legend and getting down to 'just the facts and nothing but the facts.'

In Buddhism, *bodhi* is more precisely translated as awakened. The word buddha literally means woken up. A buddha is someone who has woken up. Like Jesus was "the Christ," meaning the "Anointed One," Shakyamuni, of the fifth century BCE, was "the Buddha," the "Awakened One." His tribe was known as the *Shakyas*, and he became a sage or *muni*. So, Buddha Shakyamuni means: "The sage of the Shakyas, who fully awakened." He's thought of as the main buddha of this present eon. But he is not the only buddha.

When Buddhism came into Tibet, 1300 years ago, the translators used a different metaphor when they brought the word into the Tibetan language. The term they created is *jangchub* in Tibetan, which means purified and expanded. The Tibetan word for buddha is *sang gye*. Both words stress the purity and expansiveness of enlightened beings, the first syllable of each of these terms refers to purification or elimination, and the second is development or expansion.

Purity and awakening both ultimately refer to the same thing. All the thoughts and painful feelings related to clinging, and longing—all painful thoughts and emotions, and the habits that underlie them—are gone. Everything that obstructed the Buddha's awakening was removed. That allowed for the expansion of wisdom qualities that are inherent to all living beings, such as omniscience (we'll get to that), uncontrived loving kindness, and the capability to successfully address the suffering of the world.

Long story short, Buddha Shakyamuni experienced a dramatic shift in his awareness one night while sitting in meditation on a pile of grass under a tree. Apparently, after that breakthrough, everyone else looked like they were asleep to him, slumbering in ignorance of their true nature and the truth of the universe around them.

What Would Awakening Be Like?

The Buddhist sages have reported that all those yearning feelings of wanting and needing will vanish when we wake up. We will feel utterly content, no matter what our situation. Our thoughts will dissolve as soon as they arise without growing into bigger and bigger constructs. That old habit of ruminating on ideas and feelings—like a cow regurgitating the last meal to chew on it over and over again—will be gone. We'll be able to see the world nakedly, with no interpretation… the way it really is. It will be as though our awareness is a bright mirror or a translucent crystal.

This bright, clear, quality is hidden from us, like a lost sock. You know that sock has to be in the apartment somewhere, but right up until the moment that you find it, it's impossible to locate. After finding it, it was completely obvious where it had been. Like that, once you've found your pristine consciousness, it can never be lost again.

At that point, the practices that you had done on the path—prayers, mantras, formal sitting practice—won't be necessary anymore. There will be nothing left to accomplish.

On the outside, your body would look like an ordinary person. You'd act naturally, feeling no need to force yourself to be like this, or like that. You wouldn't care in the slightest about what people thought of you, bad or good. Even pain and poverty wouldn't be the big deal they are now. It would be a level of relaxation and contentment you'd never experienced before.

From your point of view, you'd see the world utterly purely. You'd have tapped into a reality that is even and unchanging, with no beginning or end. In that ever-fresh state, there would be a fundamental sameness to everything, but things would also be clear and distinct.

The highly-esteemed fourteenth-century practitioner/scholar, Longchen Rabjam, likened the experience of awakening to having all the confusion that's clouded your perceptions disperse like mist. In perhaps his greatest work, *The Precious Treasury of Basic Space*, he wrote that when your mind awakens it will be like the orb of the sun in a clear sky without clouds.

What does Omniscience Mean?

There's a word in Tibetan that's usually translated as *omniscient*. That's a smart translation of *kunkhyen* if you took it literally. *Kun* means all and *khyen* means *knowledge*. Put together, this word means all-knowing, or understanding all. Those who have awakened are said to be all-knowing. That doesn't mean that they are like Einstein in front of a blackboard. Omniscience is not so much about things like being able to understand the math behind advanced astrophysics or other forms of schooled learning.

Longchen Rabjam explained that there were two kinds of omniscience, the knowledge of the true nature of reality and the knowledge of whatever benefits others. In that interpretation, Buddhas do not know every detail of the universe. They know whatever they direct their attention to. Since they manifest only to benefit beings, there is little need to direct their attention to anything other than how to guide others to awakening.

Buddha taught extensively about what awakening entailed in an early Buddhist scripture, called the *Samannaphala Sutta*. He is reported to have said that his mind became "concentrated, purified, and bright, unblemished, free from defects, pliant, malleable, steady, and attained to imperturbability." These are the beautiful translation words of Thanissaro Bhikkhu.

From that night of awakening under the tree forward, Shakyamuni Buddha could direct his mind however he intended. When he focused his mind on his senses, he found they were now unlimited; his eyes and ears could see and hear many things that were normally beyond the abilities of human beings.

Here are some of these abilities he told one of his students about: He could form an invisible mental body that could walk through walls and mountains, walk on water, and fly through the air. He could hear the voices of human beings, gods, and goddesses, near or far. He was able to assess the state of the mind of others, for example, whatever painful emotions were burning in them. It was as though he could encompass the awareness of others with his own.

Buddha could remember his own "previous homes," meaning hundreds and thousands of past lives, right down to his name, how he looked, his experiences and travels, what foods he ate, and how he died. He could remember universes expanding and contracting throughout time.

In that same scripture that describes this, he said he could see with his "divine eye" how the present lives of other people have been shaped by their past karma. Likewise, he could see people and events far away from him, as clearly as when you and I look down from a high perch and can see the people below coming and going.

Maybe you're someone who is drawn to Buddhist practice but can't accept claims that supernatural abilities come along with enlightenment. If that's a bridge too far for you, it's okay. If we subtract the supernatural aspects of this description of bodhi, we're left with awakening as a continuous state of non-referential awareness that is steady, focused, clear, flexible, bright, and free from a rigid sense of self. When free like that we naturally overflow with kindness for others and become profoundly capable of helping them.

Based on my experience, I recommend going out of your way to meet one or more of the lamas in the world today who are viewed by experts in the field as having qualities similar to the Buddha. Visit them in person if you can, and check out whether they seem to be able to read your mind and give advice that really hits the target like no one else has.

The awakened person can perfectly direct his or her omniscient attention however it will be of most benefit to living beings. They are filled with an all-encompassing love and compassion toward those who haven't yet awakened. The idea of intentionally harming anyone is inconceivable to them. Because they're no longer truly suffering they naturally want to help others who are.

What Do Buddhas Do?

So how do a bunch of content and awakened whales help anyone? It seems… passive. Right? As I said, a guide like that can match their advice to what is needed by a specific student. They can see exactly what's going on inside the people they meet, including all the deeply ingrained subconscious habits that are causing them unnecessary pain.

That's different than you and me. I'm compassionate, but that feeling is muddied by my subconscious judgments and personal needs. Regular people like us often think transactionally. A quiet voice inside whispers, 'I'll help, but what am *I* going to get out of it?'

Buddhas solely abide in effortless purity and peace. For them, natural responsiveness has replaced the ordinary human emotion of compassion, which is contaminated with our own subconscious needs and wants. I can't prove it scientifically, but from what I've seen, teachers on the various levels of awakening spontaneously pop up to help folks who have launched themselves into heart-felt practice. The practitioner's virtue and compassionate enthusiasm sets off a teacher's responsiveness.

In the traditional Tibetan books about the ngondro, little is said about what awakening is. For example, *The Words of My Perfect Teacher*, by Patrul Rinpoche, a brilliant and comprehensive manual, contains only a few sentences about awakening. I think that's because, in Tibet before the communist takeover in 1959, most people had personal contact with living exemplars of awakening, in their area or even in their own families. While the complete qualities of the Buddha were not manifested by all of these highly-regarded practitioners and teachers, they were palpably different than ordinary people. You don't need to tell people who live next to a pristine mountain spring what pure water tastes like.

Buddha-Nature

Most of the Buddhists in the world today—but not all—believe that each of us has the same nature as the Buddha. There are some differences between the precise beliefs of Buddhists from various Asian countries and traditions. Catholics, Protestants, Baptists, and Quakers might all seem to have similar beliefs to an outsider looking in at Christianity. Yet if you are a Christian looking out from the inside, there are big differences between denominations. The situation is similar in Buddhism.

The capacity to awaken, exactly like he did, is right here inside every living being. It's not only present in cute little animals, but also in cockroaches, snakes, and ghosts. Everyone. They all have this buddha-nature. Sometimes, it's likened to a seed or a tiny embryo that needs to be nurtured through many lifetimes to become actualized.

The way I was trained, though, by Lama Tharchin Rinpoche and my other beloved teachers from Tibet, was yet more optimistic than that. The way they talked about it, this potential is not buried that deep. It's right here all the time, ready to be let loose. There could be people who hear a few teachings that hit the main point for them and from that the veils are cast off by the roadside.

No one I know has described having that experience, though. We ordinary people develop over months, years, and decades, perhaps lifetimes. Slowly, slowly, the layers of veils obscuring our awakened hearts become thinner and thinner.

We are Ordinary People

How do we know if we are ordinary, unrealized, people? We know we are because we have thoughts and feelings related to clinging. We want all kinds of things! But, words like *clinging* and *grasping* are also pointing to the velcro-like quality of our thoughts. We can't let things go; the more we try, the worse things get.

From merely noting something going on in our personal experience, we move on to label it. We give it a name or category, such as *bird*. The next thing you know... boom. We come to all kinds of conclusions about it. The bird is labeled beautiful or noisy, breathtaking, or a pest. We are constantly drawing conclusions and forming opinions.

How can we experience a seamless state of evenness and peace when our brains and nervous systems are constantly working, churning up concepts, and strategizing how to get what we want? Our inner landscape is chaotic, dotted with peaks and chasms.

People who are inclined to be intellectual can create and justify ever more complicated and stubborn concepts. Earthy people can have simple and rigid beliefs. Brilliant, simple, or in-between, our thoughts create emotions. Emotions build and we act out our rages and passions on the world, sending out ripples of effects to others and creating imprints on our minds that are the cause of future pain.

The Storehouse Consciousness

These imprints stick around even after we forget them. They impress themselves on what Indian Buddhist sages dubbed the storehouse consciousness, the *alaya vijnana*. Like hidden seeds created by our past intentions and actions, they can mature into the current situation of our body and surroundings, along with our tendency to respond to those circumstances in certain ways, whether positively or negatively. They shape us without us knowing it.

It follows that almost all Buddhist practices can be thought of as purification practices, cleaning out impressions and patterns from the past in a profound way even therapy can't do. Cleaning house. The process of undoing these imprints could also be called transforming or liberating. Truly, whether we talk about purifying, clearing, transforming, or freeing... they are all metaphors for how different practices help us escape the deep ruts of our personal storehouse consciousness. In any Buddhist system, we are aiming for a fresh start, one that is un-programmed.

It makes you wonder how this idea of a storehouse consciousness might correspond in some ways to today's medical research into what consciousness is, how it functions, and where it lives. Great minds are weaving together new information from functional MRIs and other measures of brain function, the use of prescribed psychedelics in healing, and rarified theories of quantum physics, to locate consciousness.

There is one new theory of consciousness that intrigues me. In 2022, a neurologist, a psychologist, and a pharmacologist (Budson, Kensinger, and Richman) from the Boston University proposed a theory that consciousness evolved as a memory system that our unconscious brain uses to imagine the future and plan for it. Based on brain studies, they noted that human beings act and make decisions unconsciously. When we do something, it's a half-second later that we make a conscious decision to do it. Weird, right? But that's what the science is showing. We delude ourselves into believing that we thought up an idea in our noggin and then take action, instead it is an unconscious function of memory. Not what we thought it was at all!

"We experience the world progressing serially because our conscious memory system creates a linear, coherent stream of experiences from our unconscious, parallel brain processes," the researchers concluded in the journal *Cognitive and Behavioral Neurology* after looking at the existing brain research.

That's a pretty outrageous claim, isn't it? We believe we're acting from our conscious intentions. Yet, we've all seen that athletes and musicians make movements with their muscles that precede conscious thought. More and more, it looks like all of us are operating that way. Our brains snooker us into believing we have conscious control when we do not.

The storehouse consciousness idea from Buddhism is probably not 100% the same as the idea of an unconscious that emerged from modern psychology. But, painting with a broad brush, both similarly confirm observations that we've made in our inner laboratory. If you've ever tried to directly control your thoughts for even one minute, you know your effort was doomed to failure. Trying to force your mind like that is often met with blowback, as is your intention to not eat the fattening foods that you love. We have unconscious habits to manage our unconscious and unwelcome emotions, like a computer operating system silently running in the background.

The nine steps of the ngondro practice are a doable method to delete a lot of our human and individual programming, to empty that storehouse. And, they don't demand that we do anything weird or dangerous, give up our lifestyle or relationships, or run off to a monastery or cave.

Right from the get-go, though, the ngondro process does mean radically reorienting our approach to life, while remaining in it.

Uprooting Habits

If you commute to work in a car, day after day, it becomes so automatic that you could practically do it in your sleep. It's almost like someone else is driving the car.

More than once, I remember setting off out of my driveway on the weekend, heading somewhere fun. Suddenly, I'd regain conscious awareness and notice familiar and unwanted landmarks going by. I'd driven myself half-way to work by mistake! I was running on autopilot.

There were other ways that mornings used to be like that for me. Long ago, I would wake up with anxiety, except I didn't call it anxiety. It was like every little problem I faced was an existential crisis. I'd plan and strategize to try to keep bad things from happening, either fighting them head-on or avoiding them. Yet, unwanted events moved like an army of giants across my mental horizon. Clomp, clomp, clomp. They crushed my brain cells and ground me down to dust.

What a drama queen, huh? I was conditioned to wage war against daily life every bit as much as I was habituated to driving to my job. It was as though I was a greyhound still running in counterclockwise ovals in an open field years after retiring from the track.

How to Practice

If you are new to ngondro practice, start by feeling your way into each of the nine steps, one by one, as I introduce you to them. If you're already a meditator, take ten minutes of your session and integrate one of these trainings informally after sitting for five or ten minutes. If you're not a meditator, it would be good to learn how to do a silent sitting practice first. Many how-to mindfulness meditation videos on YouTube can help you get started, or a local meditation center can guide you.

Those who are doing the ngondro accumulations, please bear in mind that most Tibetan or Bhutanese lamas practiced ngondro as teenagers in a supportive family or monastery. If they have not worked with students from your culture before, they may expect you to reach certain landmarks more swiftly than you do. That's because they care about you, and practicing intensively is very effective. Your situation is different than theirs, though. Check in with them once a year or more about your pattern of practice and how it is going for you.

If you keep practicing regularly, you can never go wrong. Don't lose your momentum. In our modern world frittering away your time on meaningless things is common.

Katie, a middle-aged practitioner from California, told me, "It's a different experience doing the ngondro as a westerner, versus how the traditional texts say. So, I would say... to persevere... to try and be kind to yourself."

If you have been asked to do a formal ngondro practice by your mentor, I recommend that you enjoy your practice and don't push too hard. Most of the surveyed European and North American practitioners agree with me. It's common for new practitioners to push themselves beyond their limits and burn out in the first few months. If you decide to accomplish the ngondro, start with about five days a week of practice.

Begin by simply singing or chanting the booklet you've been given. Focus on falling in love with it. Familiarize yourself with it. Reorient yourself to its worldview. Stop the session a little before you get bored or antsy. If your teacher wants you to count numbers (more on that later), do it from day one. Also, study books, and listen to dharma talks for inspiration.

In the second year, you will want to practice seven days a week when possible. As you gain momentum—maybe after a year or so—you will naturally start practicing every day, and time for longer sessions may open up for you in ways you can't imagine now.

Chapter 2

Reorientation

The Purpose of the Four Contemplations

Why Change Our Outlook?

Have you ever read a novel that was written from a first-person point of view? The world, its inhabitants, history, and backstory are written as seen through the eyes of the central character. The characters then play out their drama in relation to the rules of the world as imagined by the main character. There is no bird's eye view.

The first four steps of the ngondro, known as the Outer or Common Ngondro, invite us to move to that big-picture vantage point. They help us to come to terms with four unspoken truths of this life and to prioritize practice.

Uprooting Habits

The Outer Ngondro helped me accept the real situation of us human beings on Planet Earth. Everything comes into being, stays for a while, and comes to an end… both rainbows and hurricanes. At the beginning of storms and the end of rainbows, I felt anxious, depressed, and resentful. Other people experience this pain from change differently, for example with envy or rage.

By training my mind through its first four steps I came to accept that this life as a human being was never going to meet all my hopes and expectations. They helped me to reconcile myself to the fact that both bad things and good things do happen. It sounds dumb when I put it that way. Let me put it another way; it's unlikely that the United Federation of Planets will be founded in 2161 in San Francisco and launch starships on peaceful missions to explore new worlds and new civilizations. Humanity is not like that. Beyond human tendencies, there are also natural disasters that change our best-laid plans.

The Outer Ngondro can help us shift from unrealistic expectations for our short life, to a long-term goal of awakening.

What Are the Four Thoughts that Redirect the Mind?

The four steps of the Outer Ngondro can inspire us to move beyond our hopes and fears. Compare this approach with the more common practice of sitting down and meditating to relax in order to be a little happier and healthier. Meditation changes the balance of chemicals in your brain. It subtly increases pleasure (via the neurotransmitter dopamine), happiness (via serotonin), and calm (via GABA). If everyone meditated daily, it would be a game-changer for society.

As soon as you start ngondro, however, you're going to realize that the Buddhist sages are asking more from you. They call upon you to reflect on four axioms that will reduce the relentless thoughts of personal pain avoidance, and obsession with creating pleasant situations. Practiced deeply, they will also reduce your sensitivity to criticism and your wish to protect an untarnished reputation. For Buddhist practitioners, hopes and fears are downgraded in importance to merely "worldly concerns."

Of course, you need to look out for your own welfare. That's a given. But I've found that there are great benefits to limiting the number of schemes and tactics I've got running about this mundane life. I started flipping my priorities, gradually abandoning the alluring swirl of the human hamster wheel. That naturally happened when I took a conscious look at the big picture—our human condition.

The Four Thoughts, paraphrased:

1. This life offers a rare opportunity for awakening.

2. Your life, the lives of all sentient beings, and the world around you are temporary.

3. Suffering, stress, and dissatisfaction are features of being alive and unawakened.

4. Your thoughts, words, and actions all have consequences that will shape your future.

People I've known who remind themselves about these four principles daily have found that they influence their decisions, big and small. Many things that seemed critically important to them in the past, they now view as inconsequential. The endless projects of this life lose their grip on them. Instead, the pure and sublime teachings and practices of the Buddha light them up from the inside. You can see it in them.

Re-examination and Replacement

To have an expansive, bright, clear mind, a mind that naturally responds to everything that happens with love and compassion, I'm convinced that we've got to free ourselves from the dark jungle of thoughts and strategies that fill up our heads.

You and I each have a batch of recurring thoughts, rigid opinions, and emotions. We were born with basic psychological patterns, like raw material. These were plopped onto an assembly line and further shaped as they sped along the belt, impacted by the events and conditions of this life.

Listen to Yourself Read

To absorb the verses of the Four Thoughts, chant, or sing the lines of your practice text out loud. I've put a translation of the *Dakini Heart Essence* foundation practice in the back of this book as an example.

There is wisdom in saying things out loud. In 2016, two researchers at the University of Waterloo, Noah Ferrin, and Collin McLeod, compared reading out loud (while listening at the same time) to reading silently. The memory of the content stuck better when read aloud than when they listened to someone else reading it out loud or even listened to a recording of themselves reading it out loud. Their conclusion, in the journal *Psychonomic Bulletin & Review 18*, was that the process of using the muscles involved in speaking, coupled with hearing yourself address yourself, is a secret sauce that creates memories. It's personal and it is physical.

Go Slow

If you are like me, you're probably skimming or speed-reading these very words right now. You get the general idea from the first and last words of each sentence. This is the way most of us read in these busy, pressured, times. Or, perhaps you are skipping ahead to the parts that are new to you. We all tend to think, "Oh, I know that," and skip ahead. "I know that" can be a defensive reaction to the tough confrontation these practices pose to our values, priorities, and sense of self.

When you're working with an actual practice text, it will be more effective if you put down your phone. Read each step slowly. Let the tendrils of your consciousness entwine with the words.

Imagine you are a cup of hot water. Every verse is like its own teabag. Put that teabag into the steaming cup of your mind. Smell the musky leaves. Blow on it. Sip it. Feel the warmth. Taste the taste.

Recognizing Your Transformation

After I first started to take the Four Thoughts to heart, I noticed something new. I had a subtle feeling of contentment and peace that was unfamiliar to me. For the first time, I began to accept the fact that happiness and satisfaction will come and go, rather than battling change or trying to sustain the good times artificially. My Mom told me that her Indiana grandmother, Mary Stewart, was fond of saying, "Nothing is certain but change itself." The old me would think, what a terrible out-of-control thought! The new me finds it a fresh, and certainly honest, perspective. How can I live in the moment-by-moment acceptance of the truth of constant change? Not only live, but thrive.

A lot of my friends have also done this work. It's obvious when I think back on how they used to be, compared to now, that their thinking and moods have become more even. They've got more resilience and a firmer sense of purpose. By operating within a big-picture framework, they've become charming, chill, people, with sparkling eyes.

When you engage in these short contemplations regularly, you see yourself and the people around you through new eyes. Standing in line with strangers at the post office and in the grocery store you can feel how tightly wound some are. Their tense bodies tell a story of steeling themselves against anything that might thwart their goals.

I don't want to be presumptuous, but I think that by shifting to a more big-picture perspective you, too, may find that your body and mind become more relaxed. When we know that our ultimate goal, awakening, cannot be thwarted, we become more able to roll with the small stuff.

We could have the best teachers, meditate a lot, and have mystical experiences galore. But, if when some life problem comes up, we lose it, it's a sign. Drama and a "how could this possibly happen to me?" attitude mean that we haven't yet done this critical work.

How to Start Practicing

First, find someplace private and quiet. In an ideal world, you will have space you can use for practice where there is a door between you and the others who live with you. All of them, including your pets. You are going to center your focus within yourself, not on others. Try to claim a regular place in the home as your special place to practice.

When I was doing this practice for the first time, back in the nineties, I shared a little house in Oakland, California, that was divided up into tiny rooms. Miraculously, there was an extra room! It was quiet and pleasant most of the time. That kind of space is harder and harder to find these days. If you don't have a whole room, ask your loved ones if you can reserve and decorate a special corner of the bedroom.

Leave your devices outside the room. If your practice texts are on a tablet or phone, print them out.

When you go into that special place to practice, stop doing anything else. Yes, it is mission-critical to do positive things in our day-to-day lives. On the other hand, if you can't let them go during your practice time, they're going to mess up the quality of your session.

Enthusiasm

To have an effective practice session, you've got to come into it with some fire in your belly. Like anything else, it helps to have enthusiasm. So, even before you sit down, check in with yourself about whether you're fired up about it or not.

If you're not feeling it, think back on what inspired you to experiment with these practices. An author? A teacher? An idea? A story about a realized person? Sheer curiosity? Light yourself up by reminding yourself that this really is what you want to be doing. Apply some effort, like you've done before when you've pushed yourself to get up and get going when you had another big goal.

Faith is a big driver for people. I'm talking about faith in the practice here. Thousands of people have attained astounding levels of realization by doing these same practices. You're not fundamentally different from them. Whether for one session or a thousand, give it a real go.

Perhaps you already have faith in a person as your guide. If you have someone like that, a lama who recommends this practice, it is time to use that trust in their wisdom to motivate yourself. They know what they are talking about. Have they said that the ngondro is the right medicine for you at this time? If so, you can do some practice each day, like you are taking a medicine prescribed by a trustworthy doctor.

Sitting Down

The ideal seat to practice begins with a large rectangular mat on the floor. This protects your ankles and feet from the hard floor. This style of mat is known in the U.S. under a Japanese name: *zabuton*. Put a two or three-inch level cushion or folded blanket under your butt on top of that. Fold your legs in front of you. Sit with your spine upright and not tilted one way or another.

Most Western practitioners' bodies don't do well with the thick hard hockey puck-like cushions known as zafus in Japanese Buddhism. Good news! You can leave those for the Zen practitioners.

Your hands rest, palms down, on the thighs or knees. This reflects the attitude that buddha is within. Other spiritual traditions who worship an external entity, a god or goddess, like to put their palms facing up to receive their blessing. That's not the way we roll.

Your eyes remain open during ngondro practice. Blink normally. Generally, you are gazing softly at a point in space a few feet out in front and slightly downward. That is what the old texts mean when they say, "gaze in the direction of your nose." They don't mean you are supposed to cross your eyes to stare at your nose. The idea is relaxation without distraction. If your eyes are darting around the room, it means you aren't focused or relaxed. That's no big deal. When you realize you're doing that, bring your gaze back home without scolding or judging yourself.

Solving General Problems with Practice

Trouble Sitting

Floor sitting is common in some parts of the world, but you may not have sat like that since you were a kid. Your body has adapted to chair sitting. You can tell if your body is currently poorly suited for sitting cross-legged on the floor if you try it and your knees and thighs don't rest on the mat below. Initially, you will be comfortable when you sit down on a cushion to practice. After sitting for twenty minutes, though, something will start hurting or your legs will go numb. By the time an hour has gone by, all you can think about is the pain. What would have been a comfortable experience for our ancestors has turned into some kind of torture posture for some of us that does not get better from forcing the body beyond its pain threshold.

There are three ways you can work with the situation (presuming you're able to get down to floor level and back up safely.) You can buy different heights, shapes, and materials of meditation cushions to go on top of your base mat. You can do daily stretching practices to help your hips rotate externally, restore the range of motion in your hip joint, and loosen your pelvic floor muscles. You can visit a Physical Therapist for advice about your specific situation. Or, you can sit in a chair instead.

Truth be told, some people can't sit in a chair for long, either. It is possible to practice lying down or partially lying down if it is truly necessary.

The classic cross-legged posture is great if you can do it, but don't fuss too much about it if you can't. You aren't a failure, and it's not going to kill your practice to sit in a chair. Don't apply force to your mind or body to do anything truly painful in your practice. Be gentle. Put away the sledgehammers.

Agitation and Drowsiness

Quite soon after you start your practice session, you will notice how you're feeling. Is your mind racing, planning, ruminating on your problems and conflicts, nagging you to shorten your session because there is so much to do? In that case, you should touch base with that mental wildness.

Listen, it's not a crime to have a wild mind. It's just not very supportive of practice. I hate to bring up the subject of coffee, but drinking too much will make your mind race and scatter. They didn't have coffee back in Tibet. They had tea. Strong tea has a quarter the amount of caffeine as the same amount of coffee does.

In addition, a lot of tea has a natural chemical called L-theanine in it, to one degree or another. L-theanine mellows the stimulant effect of caffeine. If you find that you are jangled by coffee, make a mental note to reduce the amount you drink, or the strength, or to shift to green tea.

Sometimes we'll get mentally agitated when we aren't caffeinated. Try to negotiate with your busy mind.

"Hello, overactive mind! I would like to practice now for a while. I promise that when I am done, I'll remember the important things you are telling me." If the negotiation is unsuccessful, write down a to-do list, and tell your mind, "Don't worry. Now I can't possibly forget what I need to do. You can safely let it go until we're done with this session."

Lama Tharchin taught us a traditional, and sensible approach. When you sit in a low place (such as on the floor), darken the room, or eat heavier foods, your mind calms down a bit. Try that.

In Tibetan Buddhism, we practice with our eyes open. But, if your mind is wild, you can lower your gaze or only open them a sliver. See how that works for you.

At other times you'll find you're mentally drowsy and dull. Again, it happens to everyone. It doesn't mean you are bad or unsuitable for practice. Don't lay a trip on yourself, as we used to say back in the Seventies.

This is not a path of sleep deprivation or self-punishment. Isn't that a relief? If you are often sleepy in your sessions, it's probably a sign that you're not getting enough hours of quality nighttime sleep. If you're someone who tells yourself you are fine with five or six hours of sleep a night, your practice sessions are a time when you may discover that is not true. Nodding off when you relax and let go of your intense drive to do and accomplish things for a while may be a signal that you need to sleep longer at night.

If sleep deprivation is not the problem, you can try practicing in a high, bright place, and reducing the fat in your diet. Raise your gaze a bit. That will brighten you up somewhat.

Dissociation Because of Trauma

Some of the practices in the ngondro, such as contemplating impermanence and suffering, are specifically designed to bring up painful things that we would just as soon gloss over. Most people can easily handle them.

But, if you have had traumatic experiences in this life, you may be accustomed to dissociating when triggered. Dissociation means that you have a feeling of detachment from your body and what is going on around you. Please pay gentle attention to your body when you are practicing. Do you feel present in it? Looking at the big picture doesn't mean that your mind is out in space while you are play-acting the role of a practitioner on a cushion.

If you notice yourself dissociating, infuse yourself with warm love and kindness. Go light on those steps that trigger you. For example, you can sing them out loud without being intense about them. If that's not possible, you can skip over them for now. Focus on the first step, the appreciation of the rare opportunity for awakening you have in this life.

How to Set the Stage for Your Practice Session

For people seriously engaged with a traditional ngondro, your booklet will often include some short practices that you do, either in the morning upon waking or before the start of your session. These involve sound, visualization, and breathing. Since there are various details in accord with each specific tradition, I won't share most of these here.

Some common exercises are to recite the Sanskrit alphabet followed by the Mantra of Dependent Origination, a saying in Sanskrit that teaches one of Buddhism's core observations.

> ye dharma hetu-prabhava hetum tesaṃ tathagato hy avadat teṣaṃ ca yo nirodhaevaṃ vadi mahasramaṇa

The Tibetans pronounce it slightly differently and usually frame it as a mantra with the OM syllable before and YE SOHA after. Like this:

> om ye dharma hetu-trabhawa hetuṃ tekham tathagato hyawadat tekham tsa yo nirodha ewam wadi maha sramaṇa ye so ha

> All dharmas originate from causes.
> The Tathagata has taught these causes,
> And also that which puts a stop to these causes—
> This too has been taught by the Great Shramana.

Tathagatha means the *one who has thus gone*, another name for a buddha. *Shramana* means the great person who went forth from lay life and became a wandering spiritual seeker. This is a passage about the Buddha's teachings on dependent origination, that all things arise in dependence upon other things.

With this, you open purely into the practice that follows in a clear and uplifted state, a state of connection with the awakened ones of the past and present. Then, you earnestly wish that by doing this practice you will awaken, not only for yourself, but so that you will have the power to bring others to the same state. You focus on benefitting everyone equally, from the smallest insects to people, invisible beings, and even gods.

Next, imagine a pure source of blessings above your head, or in space in front of you. As you develop an affinity with Tibetan and Indian symbolism, you will come to feel inspired by visualizing this source as Guru Rinpoche, Yeshe Tsogyal, Troma Nakmo, Vajradhara, or another figure that symbolizes perfect awakening. They look at you with an expression of great kindness and care—so pleased that you are taking this time to practice. Many ngondro texts have a stanza that you recite at this time, but it can be done non-verbally as well.

> Essence of all the three times
> buddhas, precious guide, know me—
> I pray you bless my mindstream.

These are the opening lines of our example ngondro text, a treasure text from the extraordinary mind of the twentieth-century adept Dudjom Rinpoche called the *Dakini Heart Essence*.

They then melt into you, merging into your mind. This merging removes any lingering obstacles to your practice. Think that you have truly received transformative power from them.

Now that you have arranged your practice space and established your motivation to practice, the stage is set for the first of the Four Thoughts: how to appreciate the good fortune we have to be born in a human body and meet the Dharma.

Chapter 3

Appreciation

Step One—Contemplation of the Precious Human Life

> Appreciating one's life generates a courageous heart and a courageous mind.
>
> Khandro Rinpoche, This Precious Life

Why We Take Stock of Our Good Fortune

When a baby was born in Lama Tharchin's area of Tibet, the family would put aromatic cedar, barley, and sweet-smelling herbs on a low fire outside as an incense offering of celebration. Neighbors near and far would see the pillar of steamy white smoke rise into the atmosphere, and hear the breathy hoooo of a hollowed-out conch shell being blown. Everyone would rejoice, knowing that a precious baby had been born.

Nowadays many people feel that their life has no intrinsic value. At the very least, making a practice of mulling over the opportunities that this life presents, proves an ongoing counter-message to that viewpoint. It is one vital aspect of the process of changing a depressive mindset to a positive one.

Preciousness

On top of the inherent value of human life, only a small minority of people in this whole world have the chance to seek higher wisdom. You do. I do. But, most of us don't regularly touch base with how miraculous it is that we have the time, inclination, and ability to do so. Some people's entire lives are a struggle to survive. Others are uninterested in life's deeper questions, or are satisfied with the answers of theistic religion on the one hand or science on the other.

It's astounding what your human mind is capable of. You can ponder the great spiritual mysteries or meditate. Animals cannot. The first step toward awakening is a reflection on simply this.

If you pause for a little while throughout your day to consider the preciousness of your special human life, an urgent feeling comes up. You resolve to follow your true calling in life with your free time. Who would think that the first training of the great mystics would be about the need for time management?

Think about it, though. One of the reasons that some people succeed in business is their laser-like focus on building their wealth. Like him or not, Jeff Bezos was not a party animal while he was at Princeton.

Likewise, the great Tibetan lamas, including those who married or had jobs, were 100% focused on awakening. They spent as much time as they could in the first half of their lives listening to the teachings, reflecting, and practicing.

Later on, the practice is internalized. They can remain mindful while doing stuff. Sure, they may coach their kids' soccer team. While doing that, though, they are able to free their thoughts and feelings into wakefulness as they engage with ordinary doings. The great adepts are pros at that. They gained that excellence by never forgetting how fleeting this wonderful window of opportunity is.

I want to be like them. But you and I probably didn't start on this path when we were teens, with a strict schedule of study and practice set up and supervised by adults. We have to self-regulate, in this crazy world. These days, fascinating moving patterns of color and light in human shapes dance on command on our phone screens. And we have to work. We have to drive. Most of all, we have to tend to relationships (and to kids who need our love) with kindness.

People like me and you must be our own supervising adults to avoid frittering away our lives on superficial nonsense. We're bombarded with buy, buy, buy corporate messages every day. Romance is idealized. Sex is glamorized. Intoxication is normalized. If we are going to find our true nature, free and suffused with love... if we are going to discover the reality beyond our limited concepts, we need to affirm our intention over and over again. Positive. Compassionate. Determined.

Think: I will hike up to the mountaintop! I will not let myself flow downhill in the stream of my base instincts and negative, materialistic, values, to the polluted and stagnant quagmire below. I made that decision, and I have no regrets. I will not live my life like an animal running with the pack, never giving a moment's thought to where we are running to. I will not get to the moment of my passing and think, where did my life go?

Honor your spiritual calling. Whether or not you become some great enlightened being in this lifetime, you will have dedicated your life to an elevated purpose. You will die satisfied.

People talk about the Golden Age of this or that. This is your Golden Age! I mentioned that I felt like I received a special message in a bottle from the great teachers in the high Himalayas. Nowadays, there are thousands of messages in bottles from them all over the internet and at practice centers scattered throughout the world. It's never been easier to access the teachings of Tibetan Buddhism and apply them to your own life.

What We Appreciate

There are five different ways your situation is extremely rare and precious.

- You're a human being.
- You have access to authentic teachings. You can read, take in oral teachings, think about, and understand them.
- You're not so messed up on drugs or alcohol or mentally ill that you can't understand and take to heart what you're hearing.
- You aren't a sociopath with an uncontrollable compulsion to lie, cheat, rape, steal, injure, or kill others (which would make a life of kindness and compassion impossible).
- You admire, have an affinity with, and are drawn toward learning about the conduct, practices, and wisdom of these wonderful Buddhist ways.

I'm going to take some time here to go through all the ways you could have missed out on this opportunity. Think of it as a series of guided reflections.

Appreciation of the Availability of Dharma

The Buddha lived 2,500 years ago, and his teachings were eventually written down on palm fronds and the like. Later, the words were printed using inked wood blocks on paper. Today we have devices that can read PDFs and Kindle editions of the same illuminating materials. The ancient wisdom has never been lost. Over these millennia, people have mastered Buddhist practices and proved they work. They have passed on special oral instructions, from teacher to disciple, down to the present day.

Right now, there are about 400 million people in the world who follow various kinds of Buddhism. According to the 2020 census, one percent of Americans self-identify as Buddhists. Sounds small, but that's over three million people! There are 300,000 Canadian Buddhists, and between one and four million European Buddhists. It follows that there are people who practice Tibetan Buddhism right near you. In this period of Western history, we have the freedom to practice a minority religion. The situation has never been better.

Appreciation of the Eight Freedoms

In addition to the five aspects of our fortunate situation, there are traditionally eight freedoms that we should mull over. In order be free to make our life meaningful through dharma practice, we cannot be born:

- as a being in hell
- as a hungry ghost
- as an animal
- as a long-lived god
- in an uncivilized place
- with incomplete faculties
- among people with wrong views
- when buddha has not come

The first four are the relative freedoms that we have merely from being born human, not another kind of being. Neither vertebrates (fish, amphibians, birds, reptiles, and mammals) nor invertebrates (arthropods, mollusks, sponges, worms, insects, and jellyfish) study or practice the Dharma.

Do you believe in invisible life forms? Many traditional societies around the world do. To them, it's a given that hell-beings are living in agonizing states of burning heat or freezing cold. Ghosts also abound, and they suffer from hunger and thirst. Until recent times, people the world over believed in various levels of gods and goddesses who lived for eons, basking in pleasures and bliss we can barely imagine.

Whether you believe in unseen beings or not, the upshot is that it's best to be born as a human being if you want to pursue awakening. But all human situations aren't the same. We could be born someplace on earth where we wouldn't have access to these teachings, or be brainwashed by a negative religion, that teaches that bad is good. For example, we could think that animal sacrifice is holy.

If we had a mental disability that limited our understanding, or a mean negative mind, like a sadist with upside-down beliefs... we would be unable to practice the teachings of the Buddha, known as the Dharma.

Appreciation of the Era of Literate and Intelligent Homo Sapiens

We could have been born before the Buddha lived and taught. The birth of the Buddha was possible only after millions of years of evolution of our human brains and nervous systems. The 2,500 years since he taught is a drop in the ocean of time since hominins first evolved.

I don't know about you, but I can barely wrap my head around what a thousand years back in time means. A thousand years ago was thirty-three to sixty-six generations back. Minimum.

What, then, of our ancestors who lived more than 600 million years ago? For the first 100 million years, our aquatic ancestors did not have a centralized controller (a brain) to attend to all their senses. It wasn't until about 520 million years ago that vertebrates evolved, and with them came a primitive central controller that gave them a smidgeon of choice over where they placed their attention. I learned about this in an article in The Atlantic Magazine, in June 2016: A New Theory Explains How Consciousness Evolves by Michael Graziano.

Fish and amphibians were the first in our ancestral line who could control their movements in response to visual signals detected by their eyes. Another 260 million years passed before the first fish species with four hand-like flippers gradually transitioned from crawling around in the watery muck along a shoreline to living on land.

Among them were our ancestors, who I'll call Grandma and Grandpa Tetrapod (four foot). As evolutionary biologist Ben Otto from the University of Chicago told Sabrina Imbler from the New York Times (4/29/22), "While it was a dangerous time to be prey, it was also a place of mental peace—a time before self-awareness and embarrassment." He went on to say of Tetrapods, "Everyone is, like, only barely conscious of the idea that they're alive… It's great, just vibes."

From that Just Vibes period, the brains of our ancestor hominins evolved to use language about 1.8 million years ago, the same time they began to use fairly complex tools.

Our human species, Homo Sapiens, emerged only 200,000 years ago. For the first time, people existed who had the same brain and voice box as folks today. That equipment naturally led to the emergence of spoken language. The educated guesses of scholars about when people started using language vary between 50 and 180 thousand years ago.

Egyptian hieroglyphics and Sumerian hymns kicked off the earliest known written languages. Our ancestors started writing complete sentences in 2690 BCE. People back then wrote about communicating with the dead, casting protective spells, making divinations, and important news. They also kept lists.

You are so fortunate to have been born as a modern homo sapiens who can read and understand the lofty and transformative words of the buddhas and bodhisattvas. This era since the Buddha's birth has only existed for 2500 years, since the Buddha's birth around 563 BCE. The blink of an eye.

Appreciation of Rebirth as a Human Being

Belief in rebirth is not uncommon in various societies around the world, including non-Asian ones. Do you know a young child who says things or acts like they remember a past life? Some children seem to. Thanks to an acclaimed professor at the University of Virginia who conducted research on children who seemed to recall past lives, and a well-heeled funder, over a thousand cases were carefully investigated in the sixties and seventies.

Dr. Ian Stevenson visited parents in several parts of the world to record these statements by kids about who they were previously, where they lived, what they did, and how they died, and search for a person who matched that name and description. He confirmed hundreds of these young kids' stories, many of whom reported having died premature, traumatic, deaths. Of course, no amount of verification of past life claims by young children would satisfy skeptics.

He also compared the birthmarks on kids with the injuries, often mortal, of their purported predecessors. The location of marks on the body often appeared to correspond with that person's serious injuries. This is a fascinating field of study, which you can start to pursue with the curated shortlist of non-Buddhist contemporary books on reincarnation on the Further Readings list at the back.

I am inspired by the thought that our experience in the present is shaped by our past-life mental and emotional habits. Thinking about things that way, it is our emotional tendencies coupled with our latent habits from previous lifetimes that will lead to the conception of a new organism after we pass away. A new being with residual karmic traces carries forth from the old.

Buddhist scholars don't use the word reincarnation so much, favoring "rebirth." Reincarnation conjures up an idea of a real you that is reborn in a new body. This may seem like a difference so subtle that it is not worth mentioning. But thinking in a refined, precise, manner about spirituality was considered key by the Buddha. The reincarnation idea, which comes primarily from Indian thinkers before the Buddha, is one extreme on the continuum between a belief in no afterlife at all on the one hand, and a permanently existing self that takes a new body on the other.

Have you ever had an experience of feeling the presence of a loved one soon after they've died? I have. These can be written off as hallucinations, part of the grieving process. No one can convince me of that, though. Tibetan Buddhism proposes that there is a disembodied period between one life and the next.

Think the idea of rebirth through for yourself with an open mind. Reflect on your own experience.

My mom was a very spiritual woman. She was a minister of Spiritual Science who thought outside the box. Mom had been to see the great teachers from many spiritual traditions, including the Dalai Lama and the 16th Karmapa from Tibet. But even Mom, near the end of her life, told me that her own direct experience was all she truly believed. When it came down to it, she had a few breakthrough experiences that gave her faith in something beyond this physical reality.

Appreciation of This Stage in Your Life

Another way that you are very fortunate is that you are currently at a very special time in your lifespan. During the first eleven or twelve years of your life, you weren't capable of understanding symbolism, metaphor, or the subtle depths of poetry, art, and music.

Do you remember that time in your pre-teen years when you first came to both understand and love music and lyrics? I sure do. It was like fireworks going off in my head. I fell into the words of the singer-songwriters and the restless punk rockers of that time. They touched feelings and thoughts in me I'd never been aware of before. Turning up the volume, I sang along at the top of my lungs, cringing when my parents commented on it. I loved my records literally to death, wearing them out with the needle of my record player. The poetry of the lyrics on the large album covers of the era came with me to bed at the end of each day.

Whenever you were born, you had similar rites of passage in your teen years that marked your emergence into a full-blown capacity for deep thought and appreciation of symbols. They set the stage for an ever more refined and subtle level of understanding, and the ability to merge your mind with spiritual insights.

Your teens and twenties involved gradually learning the skills of adulthood; how to manage your life, your sexuality, your need for love, your education, and survival. While some extraordinary folks start following an inner yearning for matters of the spirit then, most of us are thirty years or older before our attentions turn to meaning-of-life questions. It is then that we realize we feel unfulfilled by the day-to-day script of our society.

By the time we discover that curiosity and a drive to find meaning at twenty-five or thirty-five years old, we already know trauma. We know disappointment. That time of life in which the fantasy of adulthood has met reality can be painful. The ground is then soft and ready to welcome the teachings of the Dharma, to soak them up like a gentle rain on moistened earth. That is the time to turn our priorities upside down. To find what will never hurt, what will never disappoint, but will instead take us to unknown heights of satisfaction and peace.

I invite you to lift your gaze from the haze of habitual worry and grief. Lift above the temporary giddiness of love, sex, and partying. See that blue sky? It symbolizes the 360 degrees of bright, free space, tinged with joy, that is your birthright.

How to Do the Practice

Here is how to do this first training on this precious human birth in a formal session:

1. Imagine that a wisdom being is sitting in front of you. Instead of being made of muscle and bone, they are translucent and comprised of colored light. They gaze at you with love and kindness. In our example ngondro text, the Dakini Heart Essence, a lithe and bejeweled representation of blue Guru Rinpoche, and a pinkish-white Yeshe Tsogyal (the mother of Tibetan Buddhism), are present in the space in front of us. They are in a seated embrace, representing the unity of wisdom and compassion.

2. Feel that the most profound source of wisdom and compassion in the universe is right there with you. What you are going for is a visceral sense of the experience of being in the presence of such majesty, such warmth. This is your witness. This is your guide. Try to feel the fullness of the experience so that it will have the power to transform your mind. If your practice is dry and technical, it will have little transformative power.

3. Ask this bright, loving, force to deepen your practice. Ask that you will come to realize how precious your life is. Ask for help in rousing the courage to do something meaningful and beneficial during this short window of time that you have available to you, by installing the Dharma in your heart.

4. Sing, or say out loud, a poetic verse about the precious human birth. For our purposes here, you can make up any melody you like. Sing it a few times, then relax quietly. It's that simple.

> This fine body, free time, and fortune
> will be hard to gain again.
> Now attain the unsurpassed
> Samantabhadra for other's sake.

5. Bring to mind how rare it is to have a human body, to live in this time in human history, this phase of your life. Treasure this chance to learn and practice transcendent wisdom. The sky's the limit on how far you can go on this path.

Samantabhadra means the state of ultimate awakening. The Tibetan version of the name—Kuntuzangpo—could be translated as total goodness or ever-excellent.

6. Finally, imagine blending the real wisdom symbolized by the visualized deity in front of you with your mind and rest in meditation.

That's the first step of ngondro practice, contemplating how precious your life is and the amazing opportunities it presents. But, there is trouble in paradise! The next step is to turn around and face it, to look it right in the eye.

Chapter 4

Deterioration

Step Two—Contemplation of Impermanence

Why Reflect on Impermanence?

Everything, animate and inanimate, comes into being because of myriad causes. Not only that, but like a seed needs sun, soil, and water to grow and survive, every single thing in the entire universe needs specific conditions to exist.

Eventually, those causes and conditions will cease to be. Everything we now see as permanent and reliable will deteriorate. When the sages speak of *impermanence*, that's what they mean.

For example, the City of San Francisco burned down suddenly in 1906 after an earthquake. Some families rebuilt their homes across the Bay in Oakland. I owned one of those houses a hundred years later. It must have seemed to the builders that that concrete foundation would last forever. But, by the time I lived there, it had largely turned to sand.

We've all known of the death of people in our circle. For example, while I was finishing this book, Christina Monson, a practitioner and translator who helped bring the teachings of the twentieth-century awakened woman Sera Khandro into English, passed away. I admired her so much, so it was hard to hear from her that the medical treatments for her cancer had failed. Younger than I am, and beloved by all, she knew the time to go was nigh.

Why do we think about such things so much in Buddhism? Although it seems harsh to focus on impermanence, we do this because we don't want to spend this precious human life in denial of how finite everything is.

We are more likely to decide to go deep when we remember that we only have so long to live. We stop pretending that we know when we will die, and that it will be far in the future. If we think that our death is far off, and it's better not to think about it, this life will slip away from us, like autumn leaves skittering away in the wind. Frittering away our time on temporary nonsense, we will never arrive at the permanent state of awakening.

Knowing that everything is changeable and impermanent loosens up our chains of attachment to people, places, objects, and circumstances. Living in awareness of impermanence reduces clinginess to your people. It decreases the hatred of people you see as adversaries. In the long term, it sparks a passion for doing good in the world while we can.

We can't know when we are going to die. It could be today or it could be decades from now. Mindfulness of the fact that nothing lasts is like a magic pill that stimulates the thought of doing something worthy with your life, as reliably as magic mushrooms make you see psychedelic greens and purples inside your eyelids.

Knowing that everything is constantly changing, you can understand how your brain's habit of creating a fictitious sense of order, predictability, and realness has colored your experience throughout your life. Once we can nakedly encounter the flux as it is, we can decipher why the Buddha taught that things are like an illusion or a mirage.

The Upsides to Awareness of Impermanence

What is it that creates our suffering then? A core message of Buddhism is that suffering comes from unwanted changes. It hurts to direct our mental focus to painful subjects. Yet, when I asked my friend Cate, a retired librarian and horsewoman, recently which of the Four Thoughts she found the most value in, she said, "impermanence" without hesitation. Ever practical, she said, "Reflecting on impermanence helps with depression because you know it's going to pass. But it also, I think, makes the current moment precious. Because if you're having a good time, you can't necessarily push it and extend it. In a way, if you try to do that, that's just going to fail. So it's more like… just enjoy it now."

Another friend, Lynne, a Canadian student of Tibetan Buddhism who describes herself as a wife, a mother, and a grandmother, mirrored Cate's sentiment. "The biggest aha moment for me was being able to see impermanence as my friend rather than something to fear. It changed everything."

Intense reflection on impermanence can also conjure up a vast encompassing view, like seeing the blue, green, and brown orb of the Earth from space. In watching the multitudes of sentient beings being born, living, getting old, and passing away something new can open up for us. Can we let go into the acceptance that all this is happening willy-nilly, everywhere, all the time? Everyone takes their little life story so seriously, yet none of their worldly victories and defeats amount to much in the big scheme of things.

You can only help others with the deep causes of their suffering after you have found stable, clear, and bright wakefulness in yourself. That one permanence surpasses the lifespan of the gods and goddesses of old, many of whom are now known only in history books.

Seeing this, we lose interest in everything but complete awakening itself. We reduce the dumb stuff we waste our hours and days on and increase our study and practice of Dharma. When the last moment of this life arrives there won't be much anyone else can do for us. We have to make our practice strong before then.

Start today. The benefits of reflecting day and night solely on death and impermanence are said to be boundless.

The old Tibetan lamas, with their kind eyes and loving manner, wanted people to break through denial and feel the reality that we are not going to get out of this life alive. With that gut feeling, our minds naturally turn to spiritual exploration. "What is birthless and deathless?"

This single practice of contemplating impermanence could itself lead to both recognizing your pristine consciousness and creating an intensely positive trajectory for your life.

Obstacles to the Practice:

Managing Fear and Anxiety

Anxiety is all about fearing that unwanted situations will arise in the future and that you won't be able to handle them. If your anxiety is high right now, in general, it's okay to put this practice of direct confrontation on hold until you feel ready. It may be too rough on you to dwell in uncertainty about the next hour, minute, or moment. And, if you can trace back your anxiety to alarming things that happened in childhood, it could be triggering. We don't want that, right?

If the full-blown contemplation on impermanence is too much, you could ease into a gentler form of the practice, and it will help garden-variety anxiety decrease over time. That could be one of the reasons why the Four Thoughts are balanced in the same sessions with meditations that include beautiful visualizations and sounds that bathe your nerves and brain in peace, love, and compassion.

Remember the deity in front of you bearing witness to the profound work that you are doing. You are laying the groundwork for awakening just as they did. They may give you a little nod, as if to say, "You go, girl. You can do this."

For now, just know that there are many styles of practice. If one feels like too much to you today, then think: Wow, practice is really powerful—look what it can do! But right now, I need to focus mainly on a different practice that works better for me. The nine trainings within the ngondro can be looked at as linear steps. But, in the bigger picture of a lifetime of practice, they are more like pieces of stained glass that come together to create a breathtaking stained glass window.

What is the Practice of Awareness of Impermanence?

When you think about it, our teachers, parents, and the world around us all taught us one thing. That one thing was how to get what we want and avoid what we don't.

Yet, the truth is that everything we encounter in our lives has a natural arc over time. The people, plants, animals, as well as non living things all come into existence, stay for a while, and then go. On the inside, random thoughts and feelings come and go. On top of that, you could say that all the encounters of our senses with sights, sounds, odors, and the touch sensation have a beginning, middle, and end.

We want the good stuff; the cute puppy, good health, great sex, success, money, and praise to come and stay. But, if we do obtain it, it's only temporary. Things won't always go our way. We will still experience the pain of change.

I know you know this. When you think about it, though, most of the people who have helped us set our goals in life and how to meet them have only taught us how to seek pleasurable experiences. It's understandable that when we get to the end of the arc, it feels like a terrible injustice.

As adults, although we have learned to control our temper tantrums at times of change, inside many of us are still terrible with transitions, like toddlers. Especially in early adulthood, left in the dark about the true nature of life as flux, we grope around blindly for a light switch.

When bad things happen out of left field, we make a big huge deal out of it, as though they, too, will last forever. For example, you and I have heard heartbreaking stories of teenagers who killed themselves over things that did seem harsh, but not that different than the bad stuff we suffered through when we were young. Things we barely think about today.

This is the first level of insight about impermanence, letting go of the half-truths and fairy tales we've been taught by unenlightened people that lasting happiness can be acquired with work, luck, or strategy. Living this lie is the source of frequent and recurring pain.

Awareness of Disease

> Life is short. Age and sickness gnaw away.
> I have no time for carelessness.
> Before this body breaks.
>
> Mittakali—an early Buddhist nun, 6th – 3rd centuries
>   B.C., The First Buddhist Women by Susan Murcott

I still remember the genetics counselor. After leading me to the consultation room, she pulled the door closed behind her and gestured for me to sit down, perched on a rolling stool. I said, "I had a dream last night that I was handed a piece of paper with the test results written on it, telling me I did have the mutation."

A "jigs up" expression flashed across her face. She didn't smile to reassure me that the dream was wrong.

I was in my early thirties and I'd submitted a blood sample some weeks earlier. In my small family, my grandmother, my aunt, and now my cousin, all had gotten breast cancer. The latest, my cousin, had been the first to be diagnosed in an era when it was newly possible to learn whether or not the cancer she had was hereditary.

That day I found out that I had a 50/50 chance of getting breast cancer, along with a smaller risk of ovarian cancer. I'd already been a Buddhist practitioner for a few years, but now the rubber hit the road when it came to impermanence. Did I or didn't I have the ability to greet the news with equanimity? I felt sad and scared. I tried to negotiate a solution by signing up for an early cancer detection study at a university.

And then there was anger—months later. I read something by the leader of a breast cancer non-profit group saying she didn't care about hereditary cancer. Looking back, people with hereditary cancer diluted the organization's message that environmental toxins are the primary cause of breast cancer. But at the time, I lost all perspective and flew into a rage, venting to my spouse at a bowling alley in Pacifica, California where we'd gone to have fun. I ranted on and on about it and ruined the outing.

My brother always says that I was born with a protest sign in my hand. I was always the kind of person who looked for a culprit for any problem. But until I heard that activist's uncompassionate stance, I'd had no one to be mad at for my genetic condition.

I'm embarrassed about that day, looking back on it now. I acted like a three-year-old. I'd supposedly been contemplating impermanence for a couple of years at that point. But I'd never really brought it home.

I never got breast cancer and my risk as the older person I am now is almost normal. But, I did learn something from thinking that I would. After throwing that fit, I made awareness of impermanence—changeability—my main practice for many years. Now, when I buy something, I naturally see the limited lifespan of the item. When I have a strong opinion, I remember that over months and years, the strength of that opinion will wane or change. Enemies may become friends, and friends become enemies.

Fast forward to 2020. Where were you when the news of the pandemic sunk in? At the time, I had a bedroom yurt in the back of my house in Oakland. I glamped every night, while I rented out the bedrooms inside my house. My place was located between two commuter interstates, and I came to love listening to the thrum of traffic starting up in the morning, along with the squeal of a BART public transport train, and occasional deep and powerful blasts from the horn of the long-distance Coastal Starlight train rumbling by.

But, one weekday morning in March of that year, like a dystopian novel in which one day the sun never rises, the reliable traffic hum never came. Instead, birds chirped and squirrels chattered playfully. Virtually everyone stayed home from work. The pandemic had taken hold.

Do you remember? We didn't truly know whether we would live or die. No vaccines. No medicines.

For a while, early on, I, a single older woman with no family in the area, decided to embrace the opportunity to practice like a Buddhist nun from the olden days. With each practice session of an hour or two, I strongly imagined that I would die when the session came to a close. By practicing like that, reminding myself of the key points I've learned about how to practice at the time of death, I essentially rehearsed so that I could be as ready as possible when the time truly does come.

Awareness of Aging

> Once my eyebrows were beautiful,
> like the contour lines drawn first by a good artist.
> Now, because of old age, they are bent out of shape by wrinkles.
> It's just as the Buddha, the speaker of truth, said,
> nothing different than that.
>
> Ambapali—an early Buddhist nun, Poems of the First Buddhist Nuns by Charles Hallisey

The most poignant awareness of impermanence is that this human body we think is the most important thing in the world will have spring, summer, autumn, and winter. This body will die. Everyone's body will die.

If you are over forty, you can use the mirror, like Ambapali did 2500 years ago, to come to terms with it.

In our cloistered group three-year retreat, one of my co-retreatants, in her early seventies, would speak of her expectation that she would live well into her nineties. After all, her mother was in her nineties, and her other ancestors had lived long lives. She does everything we oldies are supposed to do for longevity.

After our retreat ended, she traveled across the country to visit her mother. When she came back, she told me that she had changed her mind about wanting to live to be very old. She gestured with her hand showing me that she could almost close her fingers around her mother's upper arm. Her mother was fragile now, with papery skin.

The way I've handled aging is to call myself an "old girl" starting in my fifties. At sixty-five, I freely disclose my age to others. I never say things like "seventy is the new fifty." I'm intentionally running counter to magical thinking that not calling yourself old will prevent aging. I'm in the autumn of my life. My gums are slowly receding. I have to manage arthritis. There are good things, too, of course.

If you look at your body scientifically, during its lifespan the cells that make it up will almost all be replaced with copies. New copies of cells will replace skin cells and intestinal cells every few months. Liver cells will die and be replaced in three years. Bone cells in ten. The cells that replace the old cells are supposed to be identical to their ancestor, but there are often mistakes made in the process. That's why your body ages over the years and decades.

Think about that. This kind of reflection might lead you down the path toward the aha moment the Buddha wants each of us to have. Yes, there are a few types of cells that will be with us throughout our lives, but they will disintegrate or be incinerated when our body comes to its end.

If all the parts of the body are ultimately simply coming and going, what is it that your personal name refers to?

The continuous moment-by-moment consciousness of impermanence is very powerful. Some would say it is the most fundamental teaching of the Buddha.

This process of inner inquiry is a better offering to the buddhas, than a flower, a candle, or a burning incense stick on a shrine. By doing it, you are following in the footsteps of the Awakened Ones.

Awareness of Death

My mother used to warn me to wear nice underwear when I was a kid. "You never know if you might be in a car accident today and end up in the hospital," she cautioned. Do all mothers say that, or was mine just the best mother ever? I don't think she was referring to dying, but those underpants could indeed have ended up being cut off my corpse after a car accident. Young or old, death can come at any time.

Whether loved ones are beside you when you go, or not, you go through your dying process alone, because it is internal. There are practices that lamas will do for the dead that many people have faith in. Yet, one of the greatest meditation masters of the twentieth century, Dudjom Rinpoche, in his book about ngondro, wrote, "No one can help you when you die. Your body can't help you. Your possessions can't help you; your friends and relatives can't help you." We have to be ready to help ourselves.

The Kindness of the Buddha

Death, and all kinds of other changes, bring so much pain. If you have had a recent loss, it may be difficult to bring it to mind. Yet, at the same time, Dudjom Rinpoche, paraphrasing the Mahaparinirvana Sutra wrote:

> Of all the various kinds of cultivation, reaping the autumn crop is the best; Of all footprints, that of the elephant is the biggest; Of all thoughts, that of impermanence and death is the greatest: It stops all thoughts involved with the three worlds.
>
> Dudjom Rinpoche Jikdral Yeshe Dorje, A Torch Lighting the Way to Freedom

What are the *three worlds*? This is a way of referring to all sentient beings. Traditionally, there are two categories of unawakened gods' domains. The first of these worlds is the metaphysical locale of the formless gods. Akin to heavens, they have names like: *Nothing Whatsoever* and *Infinite Space*.

The second world is known as the *form realm*. Within it, are seventeen ascending heavens, in which gods and goddesses are born based on the virtue of their attainment of various levels of meditative absorption.

It might surprise you that wise sages see going to heaven as a god or goddess when you die as problematic. Let me clarify. Traditionally, gods were once people who meditated to attain ecstatic states, with no insight into the absence of a self that we can truly say exists as a real entity. We can all understand the allure of pleasure! This kind of practice, coupled with an enormous amount of accumulated positive force, can lead to a post-death transfer to a very long life as a god or goddess. Gods and goddesses don't have the discipline to study and practice a true path to awakening because they are not suffering. But, when their merit is exhausted, they are reborn as another life form. The suffering of leaving a state that felt like never-ending ecstasy must be excruciating.

I understand that you may only be able to see this metaphorically and not believe in unseen beings. The message, then, is to set our sights on awakening; not personal pleasure within cyclic existence. Gods and goddesses are not worthy of your worship.

There is a beautifully written book by Mitchell S. Jackson, called *Survival Math*, about growing up in a black family in Portland, Oregon. He describes his mother's first euphoric hits of crack as the beginning of a marriage (to the drug). How he wishes he could go back to tell his mother all the ways that this marriage would destroy every aspect of her life, including her capacity to mother. Euphoria is always unsustainable.

The third world that Dudjom Rinpoche referred to has all the rest of us sentient beings in it, from the residents of hell to ghosts, animals, humans, and warring low-level gods and goddesses. It's called the word of desire. All of us are cloaked with heavy cravings that obscure our true nature and prevent our awakening.

Awareness of impermanence is crucial training because it puts an end to our obsession with people, animals, ghosts, heaven, and hell.

How to Do The Practice

1. Regenerate the same visualization of the wisdom source in front of you as a witness and support.
2. Ask them to help you realize the nature of impermanence.
3. Recite the verse that follows from our example ngondro or use one from another ngondro text:

> Now this precious body is here, yet
> due to the foe, the evil Ruler of Death,
> the time of death is uncertain.
> View self and others as impermanent.

4. When you have become vividly aware of impermanence and death, stop and let your mind relax and open for a short while.
5. When you begin to come to terms with life's endings as being inevitable outcomes of its beginnings, the source of the stresses and pains of all beings gradually become more apparent. Let's look more deeply into this suffering and its causes.

In ancient India, the ruler of death, who is similar to the Grim Reaper in some Western societies, is called Yama. In Tibetan Buddhism, Yama has a bull's head and holds a skull and a lasso. Like an unexpected guest arriving at the door, death can come at any time.

CHAPTER 5

Dissatisfaction

Step Three—Contemplation of Suffering, Stress and Pain

> Samsara is like a putrid swamp, where we muck around in the sludge of insufferable misery. Think about this. Then go alone to the solitudes of the mountains and resolve your mind.
>
> Sera Khandro, Concise Spiritual Advice

The Problem with Cyclic Existence

Because of impermanence, the universal situation of all sentient beings means that we're going to be born, get old, get sick, die, and start over. During this lifetime, change is inevitable, therefore pain is inevitable. The Buddhist word for that endless circling is *samsara*, cyclic existence. It's like someone has put you in a dryer that never stops circling.

The point of contemplating this thoroughly is to ferret out all the hidden pockets of misplaced hope that you and your loved ones will be able to find permanent happiness in some little corner of samsara.

All the meditations, the contemplations, and the yogas that we practice are 100% about ending this repetitive pain, from the smallest dissatisfaction up to suffering in unbearable agony. If you don't accept this point, there is no reason to practice.

My friend Claire, a meditation teacher who lives in Canada and has a PhD in Religious Studies, wrote to me about this. "I feel that the Four Thoughts really do reorient me away from trying to get what I want, trying to play the game a little better, and toward the exit from samsara. We're never going to win! The Four Thoughts turn my mind in that direction and help me wake up a little bit from the trance of thinking this next samsara strategy will finally work."

Samsaric strategy will never work. But when we reduce our hopes that things like romance, sex, wealth, parenting, winning, being famous or highly regarded, and having personal or political power will bring lasting happiness, something else blossoms. Something beautiful.

Sera Khandro, one of the greatest female awakened ones of the twentieth century, told her rugged rural students in remote Tibetan valleys that they should drop everything and go practice in complete isolation from other people in a high-elevation huts. What would their practice be? Ecstatic blissful trances? 'Fraid not. She sent them off to do a mental inventory of all the different forms of pain and stress that various kinds of beings experience. They were to stay in retreat until they truly got it that samsara is like a putrid swamp.

What is the Practice of Recognizing Dissatisfaction?

There are classifications of different kinds of suffering in Buddhist psychology. Some translators feel words such as dissatisfaction, pain, or stress are better translations of the word we usually hear translated as suffering, *dukkha*. For example, this is how Jetsunma Tenzin Palmo described it on Facebook:

> Life is not all suffering, we may be happy at times, but there is still a basic 'dissatisfaction' as long as we continue with wrong views: even if everything goes right, we are afraid it will begin to go wrong, if everything is wrong, we want to put it right, hence the frequency of long-term conflicts.

When it comes down to it there is one root to our recurring dissatisfaction: we desire things to be a certain way, and they aren't. Or they are, but they change. Our desire itself is suffering. The times when we get what we *don't desire* are another kind of pain: Aversion. Ignorance of the true dynamics at play is the root of both desire and aversion. We think that we can find happiness in fleeting things. These are the three poisons: desire, aversion, and ignorance, the roots of our pain, our stress.

Take me, for example. Many people look at my life and feel envious of the freedom and opportunities I've had. But my relationships haven't lasted. For most of my life, I wanted an enduring relationship or marriage and it has eluded me.

Right now I could run a script in my head saying, "I am so lonely," or harbor resentful or wistful thoughts about my past lovers. Or, I could diagnose myself with some psychological condition that has prevented life-long bonding and intimacy. Or maybe there was something wrong with all the people in my dating pool! Once you go down that road, one anguished thought leads to another. My god, I could waste my whole life on a fantasy story about what a human life is supposed to look like!

The truth is that *anything can happen in a human life*. The above are just thoughts that create suffering. They begin with a mental habit of thinking things should be a certain way, and they build into a feeling of misery because they aren't.

This practice of reflecting on dukkha may surprise you. You might think it would be nothing but awful. However, it may transform into a concept-less mental space that—open and free—emerges, wet with compassion. That is your hidden gem, right there. The unity of compassion and emptiness. One of my teachers, Adzom Paylo Rinpoche, used to say that when we recognize the essence of suffering, we are freed from it. How could that be? In this third step of our practice, reflecting on the defects of cyclic existence, we discover how.

The Three Kinds of Dissatisfaction:

It's traditional to go through different forms of suffering, one by one. Let's do a concise guided tour of the three kinds of dukkha: dissatisfaction with dissatisfaction, dissatisfaction with change, and dissatisfaction related to our conditioning.

Dissatisfaction with Dissatisfaction

The first kind of dukkha is—I kid you not—the dukkha-dukkha.

The four biggest, most obvious, unpleasant circumstances that we will experience as sentient beings are birth, old age, sickness, and death. The suffering of suffering (the dukkha dukkha) is an aversion to those occurrences, based on denial.

It's not the painful incident itself that is the dukkha-dukkha, it is the compounding of suffering on top of suffering that happens because of our denial. We may say to ourselves, "This painful thing can't possibly be happening to me! I don't deserve it. This is a terrible injustice! People have let me down in my hour of need." Thoughts like that heap emotional suffering on top of the actual physical pain or loss. They are the stories we tell ourselves about the pain that can make the pain worse.

One of the coolest things about basic meditation practice is that you witness how your passing thoughts balloon into big concepts when you hold on to them. Concepts become judgments and opinions. Judgments and opinions become emotions.

Doing a solitary retreat allows you to slow down the unfolding of that process so you can witness it for yourself. I remember one time that happened to me. I was lying on my back in bed after a long day of practice. My thoughts, which had been streaming continuously, had slowed way down. The ceiling above was textured in a random swirling pattern. I noticed that the clear face of someone I didn't know popped into my head. It was probably the start of a dream. I thought, "Who is this guy?" I could feel a story or dream beginning.

Then I caught on to where he came from. There was a swirl in that ceiling plaster that was in his shape! My brain had popped out a mental image based on that and was subconsciously stewing up a tale about it.

We take our thoughts so seriously! They often lead to deeply held opinions about the world, the people and animals in it, and ourselves. Could it be that many of our thoughts are simply our mammalian brain making stuff up from random sensory input like that? The imprint of a workman's trowel spreading plaster on the ceiling above his or her head in 1982 became an imagined guy twenty years later.

Given that the minds of ordinary human beings like you and me work like that, how much more powerful will our thoughts and emotions be when we encounter real hardship? We need to do this inner work now in order to develop the ability to let go of thoughts as soon as they arise, before we face intense challenges.

Advanced practitioners, in addition to not heaping dukkha on top of dukkha, can transform suffering into joy. Take, for example, Lama Tharchin's uncle, the renowned Buddhist yogi known as Lama Sherab. He fell ill with what was described as "blood cancer." He had terrible bodily suffering. But the greater his pain, the more grave his illness got, the happier he became. After a lifetime of intensive practice, Lama Sherab prayed that through his cancer, the consequences of others' negative karma would ripen in him, instead of them. He believed he was exhausting the painful karma of others so that they wouldn't have to endure the repercussions. As his death approached, he got happier still.

It brings to mind the school slogan of the Tibetan Children's Village School in Dharamshala, India. Emblazoned in white above the soccer field there, where an American school might have a slogan about success or pride, is painted "Others Before Self" in huge white letters. What would it have been like to be raised in a culture like that?

Dissatisfaction with Change

> Arising, abiding, and falling away—
> this is all the Blessed One taught.
> This is all it is, she thought, this is it.
> All things arise, abide, and fall away,
> and we suffer only because we hold to what we are bound to lose.
> Pain is a given, but suffering—that we make.
>
> Teijitsu, 18th cent. Japanese Buddhist nun. Women of the Way, Discovering 2,500 Years of Buddhist Wisdom by Sally Tisdale

The second kind of dukkha is dissatisfaction with change; this refers to clinging to pleasant experiences. It is a less obvious form of dukkha. Our relationship with everyday life is oriented largely to keeping life smooth and avoiding nasty changes. Frankly, this is what gets most of us off the couch in the morning.

I've never heard the wise sages advocate that we become passive doormats who never intervene or manage things. You've got to do what you've got to do in order to take care of yourself and others. But practitioners mentally frame even good times within the enormous dance of many lifetimes. Just facing up to the inevitability of change can do so much to prevent compounding your pains. To prepare for changes, consider ways that you could accept them as they arise. Spend a short session on the cushion imagining sudden changes to your cherished plans. Rehearse acceptance.

The Dissatisfaction of Conditioning

If you take it as a given that consciousness will continue after your body dies, it follows that both the obvious habits that your mind has right now, and its dormant karmic tendencies, will continue too. This is called the "pervasive dukkha of conditioning." Your consciousness, laden with the three poisons, and related habits from time immemorial, is propelled forward into another body. Dukkha follows you like a shadow.

Intermediate States and the Six Realms

Within Tibetan Buddhist beliefs, after an ordinary sentient being passes away, its consciousness is massless. It moves around easily to whatever place comes to mind. Without a human brain and nervous system, this intangible 'body' is drawn to rebirth...

like a glutton is drawn to the refrigerator door. It is jonesing for samsara.

Unless we surface from our oceanic confusion and taste the fresh air of liberation in this life, our consciousness will join the zygote of a life form that matches its dominant emotional profile at the moment of conception. I'm using the word zygote because that's what the modern world calls it when the first two cells form from a fertilized egg, the moment most people think of as conception. The indigenous Tibetan tradition has its own concepts about how gods, ghosts, and hell beings are conceived.

The main point is that ordinary sentient beings have no control over what they will be reborn as, and it will be within cyclic existence. In Indian Buddhist cosmology there is a simplified scheme that categorizes all living beings into six realms characterized by their main afflictive emotion. It gives us a rough idea of what kind of sentient being we will become.

Class of Beings	Sanskrit Name	Afflictive Emotion
Hell Beings	Naraka	Anger
Hungry Ghosts	Preta	Miserliness
Animals	Tiryak	Stupidity
Human Beings	Manusya	Desire
Demi-gods	Asura	Jealousy
Gods	Deva	Pride

You may or may not believe that four out of the six broad categories of sentient beings above truly exist. We could go into the weeds here, exploring whether these are only mental states, or whether there are truly gods, goddesses, hells, and ghosts. People love to talk about that, but it is beside the point here. The point is that any sentient being that has not awakened is suffering in cyclic existence. If you believe in gods and goddesses, they may live for eons in states of bliss, but they will eventually fall to lower realms when their merit has exhausted itself. They are not worthy role models for what we are doing. Neither are spirits nor your beloved pet who you think of as a bodhisattva.

In the next chapter, I will tell of Buddhist-inspired shamans called *delogs* who tell of falling into death-like states for days, while they experienced vivid journeys to different realms. If you have faith in them, their visits with buddhas, bodhisattvas, and sentient beings suffering horribly in hell realms will be of interest to you.

Spoiler alert: You can learn to deeply transform or free your afflictive emotions and overcome intellectual veils through the practice and study of dharma and become a buddha. Only then will you have choice over your future parents and their location.

Suffering as Adornment

I'd like to conclude by quoting one of my teachers, Adzom Paylo Rinpoche, who I believe can speak from the point of view of ultimate truth. "In actuality, that which we call suffering is only a verbal appellation. An allegedly real sufferer, that which inflicts suffering, and the suffering itself, with all the causes and circumstances, is not something that has any genuine reality. Not even an atom's worth of existence."

Years ago, in teachings I helped edit and publish, Rinpoche went on to say: "With all this suffering, don't conceive of it as suffering itself. Instead, bring forth a realization, an engagement, that sees it as an adornment. Thus, a realization of the true nature of phenomena will surge forth, and these circumstances will become your allies. The nature of suffering then dawns as an adornment."

Let's aspire to that level of practice. In the meantime, let's at least cut through our denial about stress and pain being inherent to life as a sentient being in cyclic existence.

> Living beings for the most part don't know where their stress
> and pain comes from, because they've never studied them,
> never contemplated them,
> so they stay stupid and deluded,
> wandering on and on without end.
>
> Upasika Kee Nanayon, Pure and Simple

How to Contemplate Suffering, Pain, and Stress in the Ngondro

1. Imagine a wisdom source in front of you, as before.
2. Recite or sing a verse, such as this one from our example ngondro, out loud:

> The states of rebirth we wander through
> hold no chance of happiness.
> Don't look for worldly happiness.
> Take the path that leads past sorrow.

3. Contemplate the stress and pain that all living beings endure, and generate loving compassion for all those circling in samsara.
4. With the wisdom source in front of you as your witness, recognize the suffering, pain, and dissatisfaction that is inherent within the experience of all beings.

5. Knowing that there is nothing truly worth hankering for other than awakening, pray for the ability to free yourself from all attachment and clinging.

6. Make a firm decision to attain lasting satisfaction by transforming your body, speech, and mind into perfect awakening.

7. Merge your mind with the deity's mind, and then,

8. Meditate on open space.

When we come to accept that some level of pain and dissatisfaction is inherent to the lives of sentient beings in cyclic existence, we naturally wonder why—even within one species—the circumstances vary tremendously. That brings us to the last of the four contemplations, karma.

CHAPTER 6

Repercussions

Step Four—Contemplation of Karma

Why Reflect on the Causes and Effects of Karma?

Karma is a familiar word to us, even though it is originally from the Sanskrit language. We have a sense that it relates to the idea that "what goes around comes around." And it does. At root, karma means cause and effect.

In a majority Buddhist culture, people are mindful of karma. Whether they are good guys or bad guys, everyone knows they are planting the seeds for a positive or negative future through their acts in the present. Decent, good, people are always on the lookout for opportunities to do high-minded deeds in the course of their day.

For example, in Dharamshala, India, where the Dalai Lama lives, people allow extra time on their walk to work to reverently circle his house and temple a few times. Bringing him to mind as an embodiment of wisdom and compassion, and making some effort, sets up a fresh uplifted energy in their lives. Good karma. This is called merit-making.

On a larger scale, wealthy community members in Buddhist lands will sponsor the building of monuments commemorating the Buddha's life. Skilled clergy then direct volunteers in the building, filling, and consecration of these representations of pure positivity, called stupas. They fill them with many portrayals of awakening, such as small statues of Buddhas, and billions of printed mantras. Most importantly, they contain relics from great realized beings of the past. The relics are usually remnants of what remained after cremation. They think of this as the ultimate way to establish the Dharma in a place. With the thought that they are fostering peace and well-being, hundreds of men and women, of every status and income level, volunteer to make these large projects happen.

The Memorial Stupa in the capital of Bhutan, the only Vajrayana Buddhist country, is an example of this. Ever since it was built, people have risen before dawn to silently circumambulate it, or repeatedly bow down to the ground in its direction. Some do the very practices in this book there, actively turning their attention away from samsara, while still working a job and having families.

This is the people's dharma. And you can be a part of it! You can decide that you want to, then beautify your mind and your life.

There is so much to explore on the topic of karma! If you are intrigued by subtle questions about its workings, you can delve into this subject in Buddhist scholarly texts. For example, I highly recommend Traleg Kyabgon Rinpoche's masterful work on karma, listed in the Further Readings list at the back of this book.

For our purposes here, we are razor-focused on how we can use the power of karma to expedite our practice. After all, if we are in a bad situation, struggling with illness, drug or alcohol addiction, family strife, or poverty, there's no room for practicing and studying a wisdom tradition. The power of karma alone will not lead directly to enlightenment. But by fostering peace, safety, good health, and abundance, it supports the practices and the wisdom that can. A more positive outlook also allows you to see your personal spiritual mentor more purely, and that has wonderful benefits.

I think of karma like nutrition. If we eat a well-balanced diet of wholesome foods and don't overeat, while we could still die young from an accident or cancer, it's more likely that those nutrients will foster wellness and extend our lifespan by a few years.

Unlike nutrition, the effect of positive and negative actions is imprinted upon your consciousness and will go forth with it from this life to the next.

As Khandro Rinpoche from Mindrolling Monastery wrote in her book *This Precious Life: Tibetan Buddhist Teachings on the Path to Enlightenment*:

> Karma is simply the wholeness of a cause or first action, and its effect, or fruition, which then becomes another cause. One karmic cause can have many fruitions, all of which can cause thousands more creations. Just as a handful of seed can ripen into a field full of grain, a small amount of karma can generate limitless effects.

Let's Talk about Skepticism

This fourth practice, on the repercussions of karma, asks a lot of folks who grew up in non-Buddhist societies. It calls upon us to come to accept something on faith. We may have rejected faith when we moved away from the religion of our parents. Many of us are drawn to Buddhism because we want to discover spiritual truths that arise from our own practice and our own experience. We may resist what we regard as unverifiable dogma. Most people in our culture only believe in the most obvious effects of our actions on other people and animals.

If we look a little deeper we can see how our actions have larger effects that can spiral out of control.

A woman is arrested and went to prison for a crime. Her mother took her kids into her home. This grandmother fell into poverty from having too many mouths to feed. The stress took a toll on her, and before long, she had a heart attack. The kids went into foster care. They were abused by their foster parents, dropped out of school, joined the street life, became drug addicts, became teen parents, and so on. The effects of one woman's choice to commit a crime (itself based on causes and conditions) eventually affected hundreds of people indirectly. This extended way beyond the effect on the crime victims and herself.

It follows that a good person impacts the community in the opposite way. Positively.

In the ngondro, the focus is mainly on the imprints left by positive and negative actions on our individual consciousnesses. Because you may have doubts about this, let's dig into it.

Shaping Your Experience over Your Lifespan and Future Rebirths

Our primary consciousness is like an unbroken chain. Each link affects the next in a perpetual chain reaction that can continue infinitely, sequentially shaping one being after another. These mental, verbal, and physical ways of being are constantly conditioning our mindstreams. They can degrade or uplift it.

What if the effects of your conduct in this life continue as tendencies in future rebirths? It wouldn't necessarily mean that a karmic act will ripen in the next lifetime—it could happen many lifetimes out.

How would we test this karma theory, and how it might effect future lives, logically?

We could examine the past life circumstances of children who remember a previous incarnation. As I've said, many of these cases have been investigated and verified. But Buddhist karma theory does not claim that a lifetime of good deeds and minimal harm to others will result in a better situation in the immediate rebirth. Since karma is said to sometimes ripen lifetimes from now, an effect cannot be verified by a child's memory of their preceding life.

What if we went in the other direction, from the moment of death forward? With modern resuscitation techniques, many people have experienced death and been revived—with tales to tell of that brink.

Nowadays, people can be brought back minutes or hours after death, if the body is professionally cooled to delay the decay of their cells. Some intensive care units in hospitals use high-tech cooling beds that have extended the period after which people can return from death without brain damage. But, when the cells of the brain break down, and death is irreversible, people can't report to us how karma impacted their subsequent lives.

Tibetan Buddhist teachings agree with modern science that flesh and blood bodies cannot be successfully revived after what the Buddhist literature calls the "outer respiration" (the end of breathing) and the "inner respiration" (a subtle subjective experience that continues for a while after the heart stops) have ceased. After that point, consciousness is thought to leave the body and continue for minutes, hours, days, or weeks as a temporary intermediate state embodiment, a *bardo* body, while the mind grows increasingly detached from its old life and drawn to rebirth.

Buddhism doesn't have a tradition of seances with beings in the intermediate state before rebirth. Therefore nothing before or after the transition between lives can provide data about the effects of karma on our consciousnesses. Or can it?

Delog

There is a little-known corner at the intersection of Shaman Street and Buddhist Avenue. This is where the *delogs* of Tibet (known as *delom* in Bhutan) live. Certain special people, often—but not always—young women, claim to have died and spent longer periods before reviving. Afterward, they sometimes report that they've witnessed the karmic destinations of human beings.

Delogs can appear to people of their traditional society to be dead for days! From our modern medical perspective, and also in the classical tenets of Tibetan Buddhism, these people are not truly dead during that period. Without a heartbeat to circulate blood, their brain cells would have broken down over that length of time. As far as I know, no delog has been examined by a doctor of modern medicine during an episode like this. It might be considered by the community to be irreverent to do so. I assume that they fell into a deep coma and recovered. You can read about delogs in a couple of books on my Further Readings list and see what you think.

Similar experiences during coma or temporary death are not unheard of in our societies. Cross-culturally, some people whose hearts have stopped report a feeling of disembodiment, followed by meeting a guide who shows them beings in hellish or heavenly realms. Realms that seemed more real than real. In that state, they can easily intuit the mind-states and acts that lead those beings to land in that situation. These experiences end when they return to normal consciousness.

I also think of a non-Buddhist friend I had who had visions of long-gone relatives, pets, and scary fire in the semi-conscious final days of her life.

Whether Tibetan or not, people who have had these episodes share a common compulsion to broadcast the experience as a warning for others. People who were shown hell implore others to practice only virtue to avoid a torturous state. People who were shown a heavenly experience are compelled to reassure people that death is not to be feared.

Since there is no way to scientifically prove karma, let's consider the Buddha.

A Faith-based Approach to Karma

If you feel open-minded toward traditional Buddhist teachings, reflect on the abilities of the Buddha that I introduced earlier. After he achieved awakening, under the Bodhi tree in Bodhgaya, India, Buddha could "see" the whole unfolding of his own and other's previous lives, and the karma that was involved. Remember the Divine Eye? Buddha was able to see beings passing away and being reborn and what their qualities, joys, or miseries were. In other words, he could see beings' karma playing out. The divine eye is an inner, metaphorical, eye, that is not blocked by walls.

Many people these days are drawn to the earliest Buddhist practices and scriptures because they involve fewer supernatural claims. They see Buddha as a wise human role model for good ethics and good meditation. Yet, even in those early teachings, Buddha is presented as having this perceptual power.

So, there you go. The belief that the cause and effects of positive and negative actions shape your experience in later life or in a future life via imprints on your mindstream is a faith-based one, embedded in Buddhism from the very beginning.

Making a Decision

Here's my opinion. I think that, whatever your background, the belief in the transformative potential of karma is more powerful if you arrive at it intentionally. We all know righteous people who were raised in religious families who are total hypocrites. Following from that, it's important for your safety not to travel to Buddhist societies with romantic ideas that there are no thieves, rapists, or murderers there. Some Buddhist places have lower levels of violent crime than the U.S. In others, it is the same. In Myanmar, Buddhism has been used to justify political violence.

You can choose to think like a Buddhist about karma. It leads to continuously leveling up your good deeds, kindness, and generosity while protecting all living things from harm as best you can.

Traps

There are a few potential traps to embracing the idea of karma and committing to Buddhist ethics. One is that you could become holier than thou. You could turn into a rigid, judgmental, and uptight person.

A more common pitfall is passive-aggression. I'm embarrassed to say, I have fallen into that habit sometimes. It's subtle and hard to catch in oneself.

Passive aggression means that feelings leak out indirectly in what you do or say when you have failed to discuss a conflict with someone directly. You express brooding resentment through zingers, teasing, and resistance to doing what you promised them you would do. You may become a backbiter, smiling at someone when you're with them, and disparaging them while they're not around.

To prevent that, I believe we need to actively learn contemporary ways to deal with conflict with others directly, honestly, and without subtle aggression. The nine-step process of the ngondro itself does not explicitly teach the subtleties of interpersonal skills. Instead, it gives broad guidelines about how not to harm others.

Remember the alaya, the storehouse consciousness? If you are aiming to awaken, at the bare minimum you cannot plant new negative karmic seeds there. Otherwise, your future body and surroundings, shaped by unconscious tendencies, may be unsuitable for practice. A precious human life is like a Formula One racecar. It not only has all the components for victory already present in the design of its engine and body, but it also has a support team, drivers, trainers, a garage, and fuel. Continuing to harm others will downgrade future you to a rusted Hyundai with an expired AAA card.

The imprints left in our storehouse consciousness by harming others will eventually ripen into negative outcomes for us in the future.

Planting Seeds with Our Actions

Ethical conduct is classically broken down into ten specific ways to avoid harming others. These resemble the Ten Commandments, except no god is commanding or judging anything. The Three Jewels are not gods making moral judgments about us.

Instead of me going through the list of "don'ts," like a Sunday school teacher, let's look at our own experience. We already know how we've hurt the people and animals we've encountered. With our bodies, we've inflicted pain, sexual harm, or even death. We've taken the possessions of others without permission. There is no doubt that we have hurt people with our words, by lying, gossiping, speaking roughly to them, or pitting people against each other. Even the emotion-laden thoughts in our heads have had their noxious influence, reflecting the three poisons.

Working with our Conduct in Different Styles of Buddhist Practice

In early Buddhism, somewhat akin to Theravadin Buddhism of today, the practice of non-harming is focused on controlling your body. The ideal model is a peaceful monk with meticulous virtuous conduct based on numerous restrictive vows, including celibacy. There is also a large set of vows for nuns, and a smaller set that lay Buddhists can take. These vows prevent behaviors that could harm other beings.

A slightly different model of ethics arose with a later Indian Buddhist movement called the Mahayana which I will acquaint you with in Chapter Twelve. That's how we think about karma in Tibetan Buddhism: your motivations influence the karmic effects of your actions. What's more, the positive results of the actions undertaken with a benevolent motivation never end. They proliferate instead. Contrast that with the long-term effects of good deeds done with the thought of only benefiting oneself where the positive effects eventually exhaust themselves.

Perched on top of this compassionate model is Vajrayana Buddhism, which I will introduce you to in Chapter Fifteen. This training system came from practices developed on the Indian subcontinent around 500 AD. The practice of Vajrayana Buddhism rests on not clinging to polarized concepts. Rigid ideas of right and wrong, good and bad, angels and demons, are let go into a wide-open holistic headspace.

Killing

If you weren't raised by Buddhists, you may be unfamiliar with three points about conduct that are different than in our Judeo-Christian, Muslim, or secular upbringing. These regard killing, the multi-lifespan effects of karma, and obstacles to enlightenment.

There's no greater harm you can do to a living being than to kill them. Giving up intentional killing is right there in the first vow you take if you decide to commit to Buddhism. We'll talk about that process of commitment, known as going for refuge, in Chapter Seven.

People like you and I do not have great realization yet. We are simmering night and day in a soup of self-centered conscious and subconscious desires. Buddhist practice nudges us to humbly assess our thoughts, our speech, and our actions.

The number one thing that we must refrain from is killing. Deciding to commit to not killing involves some hardship. For example, instead of spraying insects or exterminating rodents, you could take the time and energy to block off their entry points into your house and relocate them to a place where they might be able to survive.

When someone does something harmful, like killing, there are four parts to it. First, they know that a being is alive to begin with. Second, they are awash with feelings of hatred or desire centered on that person or animal. They have no clue about karma. (That reflects ignorance.) Third, they kill. Fourth, they rejoice in the death of another at their hands. When all four of these aspects are in play, that is very heavy karma.

For example, a groundhog is eating up your garden, or ants are pouring into your house. Filled with disgust and rage, you think...

fuck 'em. You kill them. Afterward, you feel elated that they're dead. Good riddance!

The good news is that karma can be purified through confession and purification practices such as the Vajrasattva practice that we will be getting to in Chapter Thirteen.

You may find yourself in a situation where you are, for example, the manager of a restaurant, store, or rental property. You are legally required to kill pests yourself or call the exterminator. Most farmers raising animals also need to kill as part of their work.

First off, give some thought to karma before you take a job like that. Avoid being put in that position, if you can. If you're stuck, with no other option but to kill pests, think that you are regretfully taking on intensely negative karma of killing. Your motivation is for the safety of the larger community. Bring forth compassion for the creature beforehand, and intense regret afterward.

On to a more sensitive topic. Euthanasia of animals is the norm in our society. We tell ourselves we are relieving them of suffering. We tell ourselves they are crossing the 'rainbow bridge.' We need to be honest with ourselves. In our culture, it's expensive, inconvenient, and frowned upon to provide hospice care for a pet until the end of its natural lifespan. Having taken up the practice of remembering impermanence, we see the end of things at their beginning. Do we want to take on responsibility for nursing a pet at the end of their lives by buying or adopting a pet in the first place?

From a Buddhist point of view, after death, pets are heading into another life of suffering in cyclic existence. Their next rebirth may be worse than the illness they are now encountering as a pampered pet. There may be a rare situation where an animal is truly in pain that cannot be relieved by medicine, and you will feel the need to summon up all your love and compassion and take on the karma of killing through euthanasia. But, if we are honest with ourselves, those situations are rare.

There are two remaining subjects related to ending life: human euthanasia and abortion. These painful, fraught, and highly politicized topics are beyond the scope of this book.

The opposite of not killing is the Buddhist practice of protecting the lives of others. This is the cause of the greatest positive karma.

I didn't used to think that the possibility of saving a human life existed for me. More recently, I've found ways to be part of doing just that. I have sent dollars to sponsor rescue ships for refugees crossing the Mediterranean, or from Cuba to Florida, in overloaded unsafe boats. We can sponsor the groups putting out food and water for migrants crossing the desert to Arizona or California. This has nothing to do with a political position about immigration policy. Right now, corpses are being found by border patrol on the Mexico/U.S. border. It doesn't matter if the people were good or bad. Either way, we should do what we can to help save lives.

You can also save animals, even if you don't want to adopt them. You can send a dollar to a farm animal refuge or a no-kill shelter. You can buy worms that were destined to be used as bait and set them free in your garden.

Be careful though. Don't carelessly put a fish or turtle in the wrong ecosystem. I did that once when some Buddhist acquaintances bought live turtles from a Chinese market, where they were sold for eating. They had no plans as to what they were going to do with them. I took one home, but it did not survive in my yard. Set up a plan and a situation where the animals you rescue can survive.

The Buddha taught in his *Exposition on Karma* (*Karmavibhanga*) that karmic repercussions of killing can cause a shortened lifespan. He recommended that those who want a long life should not only abstain from killing but also speak out about how wonderful it is not to kill and encourage others to stop. Instead of killing, they can free both people and animals who are condemned to death. They protect people and animals from fear, and think kindly of the vulnerable, the sick, children, and the elderly. He told people to give food to the hungry and to think lovingly of them, to reject war, and to renovate stupas and monasteries. You can read this text in the Reading Room at www.84000.co, a growing library of translated Buddhist texts.

Maybe you're thinking that Buddha, here, was skillfully appealing to people's self-interest to persuade them to be good. But, I have to level with you. The Tibetan lamas I've known of who lived extraordinarily long lives, such as Chatral Rinpoche or Gyatrul Rinpoche, freed enormous numbers of animals from the fate of being used as bait or eaten.

I know. It sounds crazy. But, could Buddha be right?

What is the Practice?

The practice here is to be mindful of our physical and verbal actions and our thoughts as though they will inevitably have consequences. Most fundamentally, we avoid harming living beings like the plague, even when it is inconvenient or expensive for us. On top of that, we help others and keep them safe.

Reverend Angel Kyodo Williams, the Zen teacher, observed in the book, *Being Black: Zen and the Art of Living with Fearlessness and Grace*,

> The more aware we become of who we are, how our minds work, and how we really function in the world, the more natural the practicing of good feels to us. It is no longer something that we have to 'do'; it simply becomes integrated in the way we live our lives as a

result of awareness and experience. The moment we realize how connected we are to this world right now, the more obvious it becomes that there is nothing else that we can do but practice goodness.

Tibetan spiritual leaders stress that we should build on our small positive acts by summoning up the courage to increase the scale of our benevolence. As Dudjom Rinpoche wrote, "Train without respite, like a whirling firebrand going round and round." Remember whirling a sparkler around on a moonless night when you were a kid? It ceases to look like sparkling gunpowder. The red light creates a continuous circle in space. Dudjom Rinpoche was telling us that our good deeds should be so numerous and unabating that they look like one continuous circle of light. It is not enough to while away our hours in a passive neutral state, watching shows for example.

At bedtime, we can commit to doing only positive things in our dreams. When we wake up, if we remember our dreams, we can see whether we were beneficial or destructive and renew our intention to be of benefit for our lifetime. Never stop!

How to Reflect on Karma in the Ngondro

1. If you are doing formal ngondro practice, you picture the main figure of your text (for example Guru Rinpoche) in the space in front of you, or above your head
2. You then recite a verse on the effects of karma.

> While having this body, free time, good fortune,
> abandon afflictions, three poisons, non-virtue.

Cultivate dignity, strive in good deeds.
Guard vows and pledges of the three gates.

3. Ask him or her to give you the strength and clarity to be mindful of your actions and karma, and to create only positive karma.

4. After reciting this, we relax and meditate, allowing this intention to penetrate our minds.

Over time, you'll notice that you're changing. Goodness will start welling up from within. Take a moment to appreciate that. While the people who were drawn to the old you may not like it that you are not on the same wavelength with them anymore, new friends will come into your life who are harmonious with who you are becoming.

Wrapping up the Four Thoughts

I'm going to level with you. It's been twenty-seven years since I first started practicing the Four Thoughts. Back then, I felt frustrated that the Tibetan lamas spent most of their ngondro teaching time on this Outer Ngondro. Ngondro is famous for the five practices that follow them, which are energetic and uplifting. I was ready to burst forth into those practices like a racehorse zooming out of the gate.

Looking back, I was driven by my curiosity about what those other practices would be like. I was convinced that they would be transformative. I told myself that I was already convinced of the need for practice.

It's not easy to nakedly face up to impermanence, suffering, and karma. The purpose is to clear away shallow goals of romance, money, power, sex, fame, and reputation. It's easy to lie to ourselves that we have a deep feeling of renunciation for samsara when, really, we just want to run away and join the circus.

The arising of renunciation is a mission-critical transition point that ultimately defines what a Buddhist practitioner is. Feel-good meditations and going away on retreat are enjoyable, but we need to identify what samsara is in our personal experience.

For *that* big project, we need help and guidance to get beyond our conscious and subconscious desires. Have you considered connecting with qualified teachers of pure dharma? Whether they are good-looking and charismatic or simple and plain doesn't matter. Will you find him or her perched on a high golden throne in a monastery, or living alone in a trailer park in Oklahoma as a cat lady? Pure Dharma transcends title, status, and looks. Let's explore this.

CHAPTER 7

Exploration

How to Find a Spiritual Friend

Connecting with Teachers

At this transition point between the contemplative practices of the Four Thoughts and the active practices that follow, I'm going to jump in with a few words about who to rely on for personal or group instruction and guidance, and why.

Before Lama Tharchin, and my other teachers, came into my life, I couldn't see the forces in me that were working contrary to spiritual advancement. I meditated, read books, and leafed through Buddhist magazines. I took classes at the local Dharma centers. I went to talks by famous writers about Tibetan Buddhism on general principles and meditation.

Those things were beneficial. But, placing my trust in awe-inspiring, knowledgeable lamas who I knew in real life helped me more. Years of listening to, and interacting with, my three main guides, allowed me to see myself through their eyes. They saw the awakening potential inside me, at the ready. They could see the knots in me that blocked awakening from happening. Gently and kindly, over time, they helped me untie them.

I can't help but compare my experience with my lamas to my romantic relationships. When I was in my third long-term relationship, I noticed something that startled me. After the honeymoon was over, each partner would eventually level with me about things that they thought were flawed about me. For one partner, the way I laughed at my own jokes was repulsive. For another, it was cute. For one, my love of sitting at my computer for hours meant I was lazy. For another, it meant I was industrious.

I started to seriously question whether the people I'd been closest to were reliable sources of feedback about my strengths and weaknesses. Sure, they had opinions. But, those were based on their upbringing. Maybe they also had carryover likes and dislikes from past lives. They wanted what they wanted. They had no clue what was best for my unfolding, my blossoming.

These are speedy, materialistic, times. Yet, there are still Buddhist teachers available to you who don't care about any of that everyday human stuff (like my exes cared about). When teachers like that relate to you, they are only concerned about your spiritual development, in this life and beyond. It's a different kind of relationship.

I couldn't possibly know for certain whether any or all of my chosen lamas were fully awakened buddhas. Viscerally, when they were around me, I felt like each of them had an extraordinary presence in their bodies... a different way of relating to the world and their experience in it than us regular folks. How did all three of my lamas, who were raised by different parents in different places in Tibet and Nepal, turn out to have similar qualities after their thirty to fifty years of practice and study?

To me, it felt like they had a richness inside their chests, like a pool of bright, immaterial, golden nectar. When I talked with them individually, a rare treat, they were perfectly present, and centered, as though they truly had nothing from the past on their minds and no ambition for the future. They were 100% there with me in the present moment. Just me and them.

Buddhism has an idea of a spiritual friend, *Kalyana-Mitra* in Sanskrit. The idealized model is a monastic who can advise you about how to practice. These days, in most Buddhist systems, respected lay practitioners serve this function as well. The spiritual friend can be a gateway for you to become someone who is not just flirting with Buddhism, but (metaphoricly) married to it. Like I said, there is a commitment ceremony for this, called "going for refuge." They can perform that refuge ceremony for you.

This person may or may not turn into something more to you, a serious lifelong spiritual guide. We'll talk more about that important role, the guru, in Chapter 15.

Job Requirements of the Spiritual Friend in the Vajrayana Tradition

Although the first spiritual friend in your life can merely be like a wise friend, it's ideal that they have certain skills and qualities.

Pure Conduct

First, they must hold the universal vows of general Buddhism to do no harm. They also should hold the special commitments of a bodhisattva beautifully. On top of that, Vajrayana Buddhism has another level of more subtle pledges you should be able to see demonstrated in how they relate to you. They should spark the feeling in you that they see you purely. If they treat you like you are a bad person, worthless, or inferior, or as a dispensable servant, then they see you impurely. Not a good sign.

Knowledge

In addition to having excellent conduct, which is less common than we would hope, you need someone well-educated in the teachings of the Buddha and their interpretations within the specific lineage they hold. Often, they will have attended a formal school of higher learning in Buddhist studies. Those are usually monasteries. In the non-monastic yogi tradition, you will find wonderful teachers who got their education one-on-one or in small groups under the tutelage of a well-respected older lama.

Vajrayana Buddhism is very big on rituals. It is expected that lamas know them. To be honest, these days there are also fantastic teachers here in the West, both Tibetan and Western, who have seen the ambivalence a lot of us have about ceremony and pageantry and have largely abandoned it.

Compassion

As you are looking around for initial spiritual friends, look for people who are obviously compassionate. How the traditional Tibetan texts put it is that it should be plain to see that they love each being and every person 'like their only child.' That conjures up a wonderful image, doesn't it? This quality naturally emerges from realization.

Realization

The spiritual friend should also ideally have realization. The corresponding word in Tibetan has a range of meanings from having an epiphany about the nature of oneself and reality to a major, irreversible shift in one's consciousness. The shift is defined by having experienced reality itself as empty and beyond words and concepts, beyond what our thinking mind can grasp. This kind of realization is also called entering the Path of Seeing.

When you have crossed that threshold, Realization with a capital R, it is metaphorically like a light turning on in a dark room that never turns off again. With that new knowledge of the way things are, tremendous compassion arises for everyone mired in confusion.

This is not necessarily a full awakening. People on the Path of Seeing can have subtle blind spots. Still, they are more able to guide students and see how to teach individuals differently according to their personalities, understandings, and habits.

Encounters

Recently, I had the honor of speaking with a respected Tibetan lama named Chakung Jigme Wangdrak Rinpoche. He told me about his first encounter with a spiritual leader in Eastern Tibet decades ago, a relative named Kunzang Wangmo. He first met her at her unpretentious home in rural eastern Tibet. As soon as he entered the room and saw her there, he was blown away, moved by her sheer presence. He told me that he didn't go there seeking this or that specific teaching. Her presence *was* the teaching. She had all the qualifications of a Buddhist lama, but it was what she communicated through her being that moved him to great faith, and great devotion. Not her resume. You can see a video about her online called *Sky Dancer*.

I think my experience with Lama Tharchin was similar. He struck me as brilliant, but he was not an incredibly studious intellectual. He was an earthy man. An artist and father, he wouldn't always wear the religious robes of a lama when he went out in the world. In pants and a faded denim shirt, he probably didn't register to people at the mall as anything but an Asian immigrant... although exceptionally open and easy with a smile. He had a kindly way about him.

But when he donned his robes and sat down on an ornamented raised dais to teach us about the unique perspective of the 'Great Perfection' teachings of Tibet known as *Dzogchen*, it was like the sun had come out from behind the clouds. We were dazzled.

I wish I had the space here to talk about my other amazing lamas, but that will have to wait for a future book.

What is it about these great meditation masters? They fill the room... like you are swimming in their soup. The soup of bright aliveness. It's not like you can take out a vibe-o-meter and detect something measurable in the air around them. What they've got is immaterial.

Was it my trust and love for Lama Tharchin that made me feel as though blessings flowed from him? In part, I'm sure it was.

Therefore, it is important to not confuse charisma with qualifications. In Tibetan culture, people know who is a good teacher and who is not. They may personally know the lama's relatives, their teachers, and the center they were trained at. Villagers may know how that teacher conducts themselves when no one is looking. In other words, the community knows whether they walk the walk and talk the talk.

Evolving the Teacher-Student Relationship

Your relationship with the person you initially study with, and learn to practice from, may or may not evolve into a committed, lifelong teacher-student bond. If you want that kind of in-depth connection, viewed as indispensable in Vajrayana Buddhism, please take a good long time to get to know them. Be careful, friend.

Although you are not rushing into a heavy-duty connection with a "guru," you will still need help that goes beyond what you get as an anonymous practitioner in a large online class. If you decide to commit to the energetic process known as doing the "accumulations," that I will share with you in the next chapter, you will have lots of personal questions. Feelings of shyness can come up about asking someone you may not know well to be your support. It's important to nudge yourself forward on that. If they aren't able to help you, most likely they can tell you who is.

Chapter 8

Accumulation

Positive Karmic Force and Non-conceptual Wisdom

Preparing to Practice the Uncommon Ngondro

Having begun to reverse our priorities with the Four Thoughts, the practitioner then moves into the active practices known as the Uncommon Ngondro. To prepare for them, you need to know what you are accumulating and how to set up your physical space for practice.

The Accumulations

The amassing of positive karmic force and the recognition of non-conceptual wisdom together promote good life circumstances, joy, and a fertile field for waking up. The five steps of the Uncommon Ngondro will clear away mental pollution that obscures the buddha within.

Positive Karmic Force (Merit)

Positive karmic force, also known as merit, is straightforward. To create it, you go beyond being a decent person. You become someone who relentlessly bangs out generous acts, scrupulously practices good ethics, and has patience with everyone. You learn to persevere in virtue cheerfully, without burning out. You gradually develop a regular and stable meditation practice. You become a person who is not easily freaked out.

You accumulate merit by using your noggin. Neurons are firing when you carefully consider who you want to be in the world, and when you actively decide what kinds of thoughts and deeds you want to cultivate.

The Beneficial Effects of Making an Effort, According to Science

These days most of us have access to pleasurable things. When we encounter them our brains release dopamine, a neurotransmitter that juices up our brains. Whether we use weed, other drugs, alcohol, rich foods, sex, masturbation, internet gaming, or scrolling, the same reward pathways are activated. Only the degree varies.

Sadly, the amount of pleasure we experience from the same dose of any of these decreases the more we use it, requiring ever-increasing amounts of the substance or sensation to get the same effect. Once serious addiction kicks in, there is little to no pleasure, and lots of negative consequences.

Anna Lembke, a respected addiction expert from Stanford University wrote:

> Every pleasure exacts a price, and the pain that follows is longer lasting and more intense than the pleasure that gave rise to it. With prolonged and repeated exposure to pleasurable stimuli, our capacity to tolerate pain decreases, and our threshold for experiencing pleasure increases.

You can learn more in her book *Dopamine Nation*.

It's amazing how much this modern insight reflects what the Buddha said, that desire is the root of all suffering. In chasing happiness, we find sadness and turmoil.

Dr. Lembke goes on to make the point that some pain is necessary in daily life if you are going to experience true happiness. Like a child's teeter-totter, doing things that are somewhat effortful, difficult, or even slightly painful, resets your reward pathway, reduces anxiety and depression, and sets the stage for healthy joy. For example, taking a cold shower in the morning or exercising when you don't have to.

Doing the ngondro accumulations is like that. You may not wake up in the morning wanting to make an effort to do the twenty or more minutes of physical exercise involved, nor do you want to turn off your phone and bring your full attention to the process of singing or chanting the same text you have been using for one, two, or three years. But the discipline yields great rewards. You will notice feeling better later the same day, and over months you will see a lot of changes in how you relate to the world, and in your emotional life.

The changes will sneak up on you. If you used to get worked up quickly over unwanted situations cropping up in your life, you will find that you can let stuff go. "No problem," you hear yourself saying, or, "This isn't a big deal."

These are delayed rewards, and it takes a lot of strength to abstain from dopamine-stimulating things for the half hour or more of your ngondro practice period. Are you willing to put away the phone, the vape pen, or the porn for a while before or after work? An hour maybe? An hour and a half? More and more these days, that's the question. If you aren't willing, it's time to face facts. You have an addiction.

If you have an addiction, you will probably need to address it for at least a month before starting ngondro accumulations. Research shows that the most effective approach—for things that don't require medical management to withdraw from (such as alcohol, tranquilizers, opioids)—is to go cold turkey for at least a month. Remove everything you can from your home that lures you and put the phone and snacks under lock and key for long intervals. That will probably reset the numbness, anxiety, and depression from chronic overstimulation, and allow you to feel the full beauty and joy of your practice.

Wisdom

The second accumulation, non-conceptual wisdom, is called *jnana* in Sanskrit and *yeshe* in Tibetan. Jnana ultimately refers to the two kinds of knowledge of a fully awakened buddha. The knowledge that knows the nature of things, and the knowledge of things in their multiplicity. If we devote time, focus, and energy to the remaining five steps in the Uncommon Ngondro we will gain insight into dormant jnana within us and invoke it. You will hear this referred to as the 'accumulation of wisdom.' Among the five, the most powerful practice for this is the final step, unification with the guide.

Purifying the Two Veils

There are two ways our awakening is veiled. The first consists of the various feelings that suck us up in their obscuring clouds like tornadoes. The Buddha called emotions *afflictions*! If I may be so bold, I suggest you think deeply about that. Fortunately, when you grow your intentional acts of merit, the afflictions steadily diminish. Also, through meditation we recognize that this fable we tell ourselves about having a special eternal self is baloney. We can realize the wisdom of selflessness.

I don't know about your culture, but in mine, many people were raised with the idea that our emotions are like jewels we should hoard in a treasure chest. If you start thinking like a Buddhist, they are more like diseases in a germ bank.

The second veil has to do with our thinking, and also subtle emotions that we aren't fully aware of. It's jnana that will clear those out. As we begin to get glimpses of our pristine consciousness through our practice, we realize that we have misunderstood the whole universe. The filters that prevented us from "getting" reality just as it is, without labeling or judging, will be removed.

A bee's eyes are completely different than ours, right? They have five eyes and thousands of sight receptors. They can see 280 degrees, far wider than we can. The colors they see are all variations of three colors of light: blue, green, and ultraviolet. Wait! Ultraviolet? Yes, they can see ultraviolet light and we cannot. We can see red, and they cannot.

My point is that beings perceive reality differently from each other in millions of ways. Our karmic conditioning shapes our perception so diversely that, even within species, none of us can say that we share the same reality. (If you've been married for a while, you already know this.). Buddhism boldly claims that there are fully awakened beings who can see a true reality beyond all that. Boo-yah!

> All sentient beings are inherently Buddhas,
> temporarily defiled by gross emotional obscurations
> and by the subtle obscuration of habit.
> When these are removed, the Buddha within naturally manifests.
> Lama Tharchin Rinpoche, A Commentary on the Dudjom Tersar Ngondro

Chapter 9

Representation

Creating Sacred Space at Home

Although your pristine consciousness is veiled by lifetimes of conditioning, your innermost nature is divine. It follows, then, that your home—whether a van, an apartment, or a house—is a divine abode; a palace, a temple, a mansion. A home shrine is a physical representation of that. Every time you walk by, it can remind you of purity, love, and your higher purpose. It's an invitation to experience the presence of wisdom and compassion in your home and life.

A shrine set-up with symbolic objects of the Buddha's body, speech, and mind, is called a "field of merit." By sitting in front of these powerful objects of focus and exerting yourself in practice, positive momentum ignites, like getting into the driver's seat of a car and turning the key. If you actively engage with your shrine, by cleaning it and making offerings, it's like stepping on the gas.

Let's pause for a moment to appreciate how interwoven the daily life and culture of Himalayan people is with pure dharma. Imagine being raised in a family where Mom and Dad created a beautiful space to uplift everyone's mind and nurture generosity, a place to invoke your hidden qualities with mantra and prayer.

This is how things would be if you had been born into a traditional Buddhist Himalayan family. And there would probably be a statue of the Buddha that had been handed down in the family for generations.

Let's dance at the thought of that!

If you get involved with Tibetan Buddhism you may want to run out and buy a lot of pictures, statues, and prayer flags. If you are like that I would say restrain yourself a little. In a few years, you'll have more knowledge of what to look for in Tibetan art, both in terms of quality and in terms of the imagery matching the lineage you will land in.

Also, your money, if you have any, might be better budgeted toward residential retreats with your spiritual friend. These days, it is really expensive to stay at retreat centers. Yet, it is so helpful to spend time in person with authentic teachers and other people doing the same practices that you do. If you are practicing ngondro formally, your teacher or center can tell you what you need for your home shrine.

Cultural Considerations

There are two cultural things about shrines in the Tibetan tradition that you should be aware of. The first is that, unlike some other Buddhist traditions, Tibetans have their shrines above waist level. According to this system, up is good and down is bad. For sure, up is further from the floor, therefore less dusty.

Pointing the soles of your feet at a shrine (or people) is viewed as highly disrespectful in Tibetan culture. Position your shrine so you don't need to do that. While it may not be meaningful to you, if you ever have a traditionalist visit you, you will avoid offending them.

The obvious question is where to put your shrine. Attics are common in Himalayan societies, and the shrine is often found there. (Up is good!) I think a minority of us in the Americas and Europe have a comfortable finished attic. The choice is usually a bedroom, living room, or office.

What Goes on Your Shrine?

A Representation of Embodied Awakening

What goes on a traditional ngondro shrine? There are different traditions, so ask at your center if you attend one. If there are tiers (and tiers are nice) the upper level would have either the Buddha or, if you are in the Nyingma tradition, probably Guru Rinpoche. This would, ideally, be in the form of a statue. There are good Buddha statues for ten bucks USD online as I am writing this, and almost infinitely more expensive ones for wealthier people. Guru Rinpoche statues run about $50 and up.

If you have other statues of awakened ones, they could go on the top level as well. But, the main point is that you love them and feel inspired by them. If you don't have shelves or steps on your shrine or bookshelf, you can use a box or a piece of wood wrapped in pretty fabric or paper to elevate the statues.

Gosh, it just crossed my mind that people may think we are worshipping idols, a concept from the Bible. Also, I recall an awesome teacher of engaged Buddhism, Joan Halifax Roshi, complaining that all religions seem to boil down to making little statues.

Both the Bible and the Roshi have a good point. I have met people who worshipped Buddhist statues as the be-all-and-end-all of their practice, telling me that each statue created a different kind of good fortune if you made offerings to it. Buddhas are not gods who take bribes to help us out, favoring our team. If they were, they would be ordinary sentient beings who are not suitable sources of refuge.

The country of Nepal is unique in that there are families there who have specialized in making statues for generations. Statues with traditional shapes, proportions, and hand implements. A good statue maker is a knowledgeable fine artist. The metal Buddha statues they make, or the less refined knockoffs from Chinese factories, are hollow. You, as the purchaser, sponsor a lama or monastic to fill them with sacred substances, a central pillar, mandalas, mantras, and even relics, according to the old ways. They may do a consecration ceremony, or you can take it to a monastery or center for that.

If an expert lama fills, consecrates, and blesses a statue for you, you should be financially generous with them to the degree that you can. They will probably spend a lot of time on the project, and they are just as skilled in this area as your doctor or therapist is in theirs. You are essentially a sponsor of the creation of a great blessed heirloom that may be passed down in your family or dharma community for generations.

It brings to mind photographer Peter Menzel, whose book, *A Material World: A Global Family Portrait*, documented all the material possessions of thirty families around the world in photographs. They would bring every item they owned outside and the family would sit down for a portrait with their things. I remember a Bhutanese family, headed by a couple named Namgay and Nalim, whose statue of the Buddha was elevated on a table. I imagine it had been nicely taken care of for generations. To me, this spoke of dignity and devotion, like the heart of the family was love, wisdom, and compassion, no matter how hard things got.

Less expensive modern statues are made of solid resin (plastic). You can discuss with your spiritual friend or center how to bring these new plastic embodiments to life.

A Representation of Awakened Speech

Now we move on from the representation of awakened embodiment on your shrine, your statue, to the symbol of enlightened speech. For that, an authentic dharma text is placed on or above the shrine.

A Representation of Awakened Mind

The symbol of awakened mind is a stupa, a miniature version of Buddhist monuments that dot the Asian landscape and contain physical relics of sages of the past. Like statues, there is a procedure for filling a traditional metal stupa for the shrine. Nowadays, there are also lovely clear plastic holders that resemble stupas that you can use as a simpler holder for any relics you may be given. I have several on the top of my shrine, including one holding a few of Lama Tharchin's hairs. I wasn't his closest, best, or most important student, but I asked his wife if I could have hair from his brush. She said yes!

Offerings

On a ngondro shrine, the lowest level is for offerings. There are seven offering bowls on a traditional Nyingma shrine. In the Kagyu tradition, there are eight bowls, the eighth representing an offering of sound. I am not familiar with Sakya or Gelug shrine protocols. You can find traditional metal offering bowls, typically made in Nepal, of various sizes, online. Some people prefer to use clear glass ramekins or custard cups instead because they do not require polishing and are easily available at the hardware store, online, or at a housewares store.

You will need a pitcher with a pointed spout. A measuring cup will do. Ideally, at night, while the shrine is closed, the bowls are kept upside down, or leaning one against the next to dry out completely after cleaning, in a line or a semi-circle. In the morning, upturn them, and fill them with pure water, mindfully, from left to right, opening the field of merit for the day.

While you do this, you say an offering verse and visualize all the buddhas and bodhisattvas in front. The first bowl represents water for washing, the next is water for drinking, then flowers, incense, light, perfumed water, and food. The story goes that the order reflects the sequence of what was offered for welcoming guests arriving at an ancient Indian home. As I said before, some traditions add a final bowl symbolizing the offering of sound. For ngondro practice, we don't need literal objects representing each of these offerings. Clean water is fine.

If you are doing ngondro accumulations, you may want to purchase a tiered mandala offering set for your shrine. No hurry. The rings create a beautiful wedding cake shape, filled with dry saffron rice or semi-precious stones, that resides on the shrine, called the Accomplishment Mandala. If you have three levels on your shrine, this would go on the middle shelf. But, there is also a simpler version of this same mandala that does not require this specialized ritual equipment. I will go through that in detail in Chapter 14.

Incense

Incense is a common offering that is lit after the water bowls are poured. Tibetan households offer incense sticks horizontally in a tailor-made burner box. However, it is fine to offer incense sticks in a bowl, stuck upright into a clean non-flammable material such as clay or sand.

Sometimes, the recipes for making incense come from the revelations of great teachers of the past, or the Tibetan medicine system. They often include sandalwood, agarwood, pine or cedar; myrrh, amber, frankincense, snow lotus herb, hibiscus, saffron, red orpine, clove, borneol, and cordyceps. If you want genuine incense, you should buy it from a monastery or Tibetan medical institution. An exception is Nado Poizokhang incense from the

Buddhist kingdom of Bhutan, which is universally highly regarded. In contrast to them, some commercial manufacturers may reduce the amount of higher quality materials to increase their profit. If you are allergic to Tibetan incense, you should know that many a practitioner has switched to Japanese incense, which is usually more delicate.

Our sense of smell bypasses the processing that our other senses such as vision and hearing undergo. It leaves a direct impression on the brain. Smells become associated with feelings and activities. The amygdala, the part of the brain that performs the smell function is directly connected to the hippocampus (a brain area that is responsible for memory and learning). So you can use the smell of your lit incense to invoke the recollection that you are there to practice, as well as to enjoy the calming qualities of the airborne molecules.

What if You Don't Like Shrines?

If you're not drawn to the art of the shrine, and you've decided to do the ngondro practice for a few years, my advice would be to use one deep elevated bookshelf, or two shallow bookshelves, one above the other, perhaps covered with glass doors (if you want to be fancy), or a retractable curtain or blind—to reduce the need to dust. There is no size specification for the symbolic objects, so you can print out small versions of most of the traditional items. Buddhas on the top shelf, offerings on the lower, or all arrayed together on one shelf that you can reach to refresh the offerings from time to time.

If that is too much, you can forego the evocative imagery of the shrine and practice in an empty place, free of reminders of your worldly concerns.

Other People in Your Home

Years ago, when I was looking for a spouse, I filled out a long digital questionnaire for a dating site. One of the questions was whether or not you would date someone who had a large religious shrine in their living room. The answer for the vast majority, albeit in the San Francisco Bay Area where no religion is hugely popular, was a hard no. Another question was, "Would you date someone who placed their spirituality at the center of their lives?" Again, most people noped out.

You probably share a home with someone. That person; your spouse, roommate, or parent, may not think highly of shrines, or Buddha. It's not good to force your spirituality on anyone. If the shrine is going to cause negative feelings, it is working against the Buddhist value of loving-kindness. It creates a bad feeling about Buddhism for the person. We want that person to like Buddha in their future lives, not have feelings of resentment spill over.

So, we are usually looking at small shrines tucked away in bedrooms and offices. A layperson's bedroom may not be considered ideal for a shrine in some traditions, because of the desire-related activities that happen there. But you can also look at it another way. You can imagine that the sensual pleasures and delight you experience there are offered to the buddhas and bodhisattvas.

Because of the custom of not aiming your feet at images of enlightenment, and the high-is-better-than-low idea, it follows that you should place your shrine to the side or head of your bed, and higher, rather than at the foot.

Do you have room for a shrine with a comfortable cushion or chair in front of it, and a little table between them to support your text? Practitioners typically use a bed tray or TV table for that.

Do you feel a "yes" inside when you think of opening the shrine in the morning, acknowledging the beauty of symbols of awakening in front, and arranging fresh offerings? If so, sit down and have a conversation with the people you share your home with, both about having this unfamiliar thing in the space and your growing commitment to daily practice. Listen to their concerns, and try not to be defensive.

If you are living in your parent's house, or have a spouse who can't abide by this, you may need to forgo a shrine. Through the merit of being patient, things may open up as time unfolds.

CHAPTER 10

Interconnection

Practicing with your Body, Speech and Mind Simultaneously

Why Practice Prostrations, Verbal Recitations, and Visualizations?

This chapter focuses on three aspects of practice that may be new to you; the psycho-physical practice known as prostrations; the voice practice of verbal recitation; and the mental practice of enthralling visualizations. These three—along with other practices that combine aspects focused on your mind with those focused mainly on your body or speech—foster complete immersion.

This way of explicitly working with the body, speech, and mind triad in practice permeates Tibetan Buddhism. Every practice works with these, including sitting meditation, with its focus on mental meditation, silent speech, and still body. Tibetan Buddhism focuses explicitly on the transformative power of each of these three. In the ngondro, we consciously work with the body, speech, and mind either one at a time, or simultaneously, to swiftly clear away our samsaric imprints.

We normally think of Vajrayana practice as working our entrenched mental and emotional patterns. But our bodies and our subtle channels also have karmic imprints. Not only that, but our voices and subtle energies *(vayu)* are also entrained in samsaric ways. The subtle energies of unawakened people flow through channels related to afflictive emotions; in awakened ones they enter a central channel.

Clearing the Way with the Body

Prostrations

Entertaining Korean detective shows have made their way onto our Western streaming services. Have you watched any Korean shows yet? If so, you will notice that Korean people bow to each other when meeting and parting, even in the workplace. Mobsters bow, corrupt politicians bow, and good people bow. If you put your palms together at heart level and bend your head a bit you can feel how it could show respect and humility. On Korean TV, you can see actors communicate every human emotion in the way they bow their heads and shoulders.

We Buddhists, whether heritage Buddhists from Asian families or converts, bow. Except for a few unusual traditions (such as the Jodo Shinshu, known in the U.S. as the Buddhist Churches of America) we take off our shoes when we enter a shrine room and bow toward the buddha statues in front. We show respect and humility with our bodies and enter a different head space when we bow at the threshold of a sacred space.

Several Buddhist traditions go a bit further and integrate bowing with practice. In ngondro, the physical practice of bowing to the ground many times accompanies the recitation of certain parts of the text. Tibetan bowing involves bending from the hip socket instead of bowing the shoulders only.

There are three reasons practitioners do this.

The first is for the purification of the karma connected with the physical body. In ngondro, we bow all the way to the ground in a practice known as prostrations. While you are doing prostrations, you are not engaged with your usual way of moving. This prostration motion has respect and admiration for the Dharma baked-in. Can we say that about anything else we are regularly doing with our bodies in our daily lives?

Running is associated with fleeing or chasing. Weight training is associated with looking and feeling strong and sexy. Getting into the driver's seat of a car connotates traveling toward what we want and going away from what we don't. Prostrations are... pretty much useless for accomplishing anything else but the path of Dharma.

The second reason to do prostrations is to boost genuine humility and a receptive, non-judgmental, mind. In a teaching about the *Seven Branch Offering Prayer*, Lama Tharchin once said,

> Prostration means appreciating the qualities of others. When you are open—when your mind is pure, gentle, soft, and genuine—you can appreciate the amazing qualities of everything. When you shut down that openness, everyone and everything you come in contact with can become some kind of enemy. 'Oh, I don't like that!' or, 'I hate them!' Your mind is chewing on and getting the taste of that experience, but no one is getting hurt besides you.

The third reason to do prostrations is simply for physical exercise. A practitioner who sits and practices a lot can become unfit.

Most lamas encourage you to do prostrations while reciting the words of a refuge verse. We'll get to that in the next chapter. A less common style is to prostate with the Seven Branch Offering prayer that's often included in ngondro texts. The teacher who gives you transmission of a ngondro will tell you how it is done in their lineage.

What is a Prostration?

Instead of describing this exercise in detail, I recommend you find videos of Tibetan Buddhist prostrations on YouTube or Vimeo. I specifically recommend one called *Prostration demo, plus the best prostration mat set-up ever!* by Paloma Lopez Landry on YouTube. You'll quickly get that prostrations are a vigorous whole-body exercise that is somewhat similar to what a gym teacher would call a burpee. There different ways of doing them, according to your lineage. If you are doing the ngondro accumulations, it's best to have someone show you exactly how you should do them. In any style, there is a sense of humble heroism about it. Notice that your hands are cupped together at your heart like a lotus bud at the starting position.

Try it out. Put your hands together at your heart, then move them to your head, throat, and back to your heart. These simple gestures represent the awakening of your body, speech, and mind into their pure aspects. Then put your hands on the ground and slide out to the floor with your arms out in front of you. Touch your joined hands to the back of your head. Push yourself back up gracefully to standing with your hands returning to their starting position.

The most important thing to remember is not to go down onto your knees as your first point of contact. You can injure them by doing that repetitively. Again: place your palms down on the surface in front of you. Then you push your whole body in that direction.

In my day, we used a smooth two-by-eight board to slide out on, protecting our hands with fingerless gardening gloves to swoosh our body forward. Since furniture sliders have been invented, though, some people have been using them to slide their torso out with their hands on them on top of a folded blanket over a yoga mat on the floor.

If you plan to do the 100,000 or more prostrations of formal ngondro practice, it would be best to talk about it with a spiritual friend. Get guidance about the recommended landing surface, how you count, and protective gear.

Many people love prostrations. If you go to India and look at the designated prostration places at the Dalai Lama's palace in Dharamsala, or the Memorial Stupa in Thimphu Bhutan, you will see people (mostly women) doing this practice outdoors. It is slightly easier for short, light people.

You can read in the autobiographical writings of Sera Khandro, the great twentieth-century female lama from northeastern Tibet that, "she continually prostrated, persevering through snow and icy wind to complete some 6,000 prostrations per day. By the seventeenth day, she had completed the required 100,000 prostrations." Dr. Sarah Jacoby translated some of her writings about her life in *Love and Liberation: Autobiographical Writings of the Tibetan Buddhist Visionary Sera Khandro*.

As regular modern people, we are impressed with ourselves if we do 108 prostrations per practice session. Sera Khandro, on the other hand, was probably doing 1,500, four times a day. Bullies threw clumps of rotten grass on her back or head. When she was down flat on the ground, they pressed down on her with the soles of their shoes. This isn't some myth from the distant past. She lived in the early twentieth century. When that level of cruelty didn't deter her, her abusers put both human and dog feces on her landing spot or dumped it on her head. She never stopped. She was that determined.

So, if you decide to embark on this path of practice on your nice clean floor, or a board, or a blanket, think of how easy you have it compared to Sera Khandro!

Tibetan people commonly make pilgrimages to holy places hundreds of miles away. But some don't drive there and they don't walk there. They prostrate all the way there, one body length at a time. Lama Tharchin Rinpoche's father prostrated from eastern Tibet to central Tibet.

Typically, we are only encouraged to do 100,000 prostrations, fewer than the greats of the past. If you think that is still a lot... it is! It is supposed to be a heroic amount.

Obstacles to Prostrations

Prostrations, as you can imagine, were the most frequently mentioned obstacle amongst people surveyed about their ngondro experience. Some Western practitioners said that they did not want to do prostrations. Some said that they were too difficult and they took too long to complete. They found it hard to find a place in other people's homes to do them when they traveled.

Some injured their knees (what did I tell you about going down first on your knees? Don't do it!). Some people gave up doing any part of the ngondro because they got discouraged about, or simply did not like, prostrations.

Others love doing prostrations. Mark, an American practitioner living in Mexico, told me, "The whole thing just looked so daunting, so many numbers and so much work. But I found just chipping away at it worked."

A Vietnamese ngondro practitioner living in Seattle named Rachel, told me:

> For me the hardest is prostration, and the obstacle is laziness and prioritizing other things over practice. But I'm working on prostrations now, already one-third done. When I feel tired physically, I keep doing it and pray in my mind to be blessed so I can finish my daily commitment of prostrations. And it usually works. The tiredness goes away. Unsure why but prayer works. Probably because it has to do with my mind overcoming the physical fatigue.

I adored doing prostrations. I had fantasies of prostrating to our center in remote mountains seventy miles from San Francisco. I bought a trail map and highlighted a way to do it! Sadly, I only got to 50,000 prostrations and hurt my back, even though I was relatively thin back then. Every time I tried to resume I would re-injure myself. I had to give up that dream and do alternative practices. Weirdly, that map vanished into thin air!

Alternatives to Prostrations

Circumambulations

Each center or teacher will have options available for people who truly can't do large numbers of prostrations. One option, admittedly my favorite, is to do circumambulations instead. If you have a temple or a stupa in your town, you can walk around it while you recite and visualize. Or you can put a properly consecrated statue of a Buddha, such as Guru Rinpoche or Vajradhara, and a Buddhist text on a small table and walk around it clockwise while reciting your verse. Do you count the number of times you recite or the number of full loops you complete? That's another thing that you would discuss with your spiritual friend.

Circumambulations are also a beautiful and powerful practice. It is the practice of the best Himalayan grandfathers and grandmothers, who reverently walk the circular path around a stupa or temple. They refrain from talking about the worries and wishes of ordinary people. Instead, they recite the name mantras of Chenrezig, the Buddha of compassion, or Guru Rinpoche, and imagine them out beyond their right shoulder. As they go, circling clockwise, their whole being is attuning to awakening.

Additional Vajrasattva Mantra Recitations

Another way some lamas prefer is for their students to stay on the cushion and recite twice as many of the purification mantra in Chapter 13, called the Hundred Syllable Mantra, as they would ordinarily do. The logic of this is that it, too, purifies everything, including your body.

Shared Accumulations

One Kagyu dharma center in my area lets their students count the prostrations of everyone in the room when they practice together in the same physical space. If ten people each do a hundred, each person counts a thousand.

Reduced Accumulations

Another lama, Nyingma, requires his students to do only twenty-one prostrations a day. Lama Pema Dorje Rinpoche, one of my dear root lamas, allowed people over fifty to recite ten million of the Vajra Guru mantra of Guru Rinpoche as an alternative to the ngondro.

There are lots of potential options out there for how this might work if you need an alternative. This is a subject to discuss with your spiritual friend.

How We Are Different

Before the communist takeover of Tibet in the 1950s, apart from a few merchants or fat cats in the capital city of Lhasa, people practiced either in the context of monastic life or in farming/herding life. There were also a small number of centers for serious lay practitioners, called mantrins or yogis. Like you, they had plenty of work and responsibilities and lived immersed in family life.

The life of everyday people in the Himalayas was more physically demanding than most of us can imagine unless you have been a farmworker or laborer. One of my Tibetan language teachers in Dharamshala, in 2016, was from a remote roadless part of India that was at one time viewed as part of Tibet, called Pema Köd. She attended years of residential school and worked as a tutor, both far away from home. One day, while tutoring me, she told me about a time she went home to her family farm to help with the harvest when her farming family was short-handed.

She arrived home at night and started work the following morning. She worked and worked until every muscle felt like it was on fire. Her soft hands bled. She felt like she was going to die from exhaustion. At the end of each day, she had harvested a pittance compared to her relatives. Her brother laughed at her. The way she told it, her family didn't find her to be much help.

Similarly, people like her brothers and sisters could probably knock out 300 prostrations in one session before sunrise and easily be done with 100,000 in a year without missing a day of work. Only athletic people can do that here in the West. I knew an American woman who was both a personal trainer and a yoga teacher. She did thousands every day while she was in retreat.

My Advice About Prostrations

If you are under fifty and fit, it is not a big deal to do 108 prostrations a day. I know a few people who have done them in their mid-sixties. Sure, you have to build yourself up to it. It takes twenty minutes more or less when done at an average pace. Ten minutes is not uncommon. I've met people who never did prostrations with other people and didn't know that you should do them fast like that if you can. The idea of the practice is to put some energy and speed into it. Older or obese people do them more slowly.

I've sometimes seen people get bogged down with prostrations and stop practicing the ngondro altogether. Prostrations are a beautiful practice. As I said, I loved it. I think circumambulations are more appropriate for many Western people. We rarely start practice in our teens or twenties. We are often sedentary and overweight. If you are drawn to this system of practice, please keep practicing the nine steps of your ngondro consistently, whether or not you can do prostrations. Don't give up on the whole practice because one piece does not work for you!

Clearing the Way with Your Speech

Vocalization and Repetition

In Tibetan Buddhism, the practices have words that are said out loud. Or sung. A verse of metered poetry evokes what you are visualizing. By singing, chanting, or saying it aloud, your understanding of the Dharma will deepen.

It is like you are committing yourself, proclaiming your resolve. Your old habits are always pulling on your sleeve and whispering in your ear, encouraging you to revert to polarized, egocentric thinking. By speaking your noble intentions out loud, your wandering mind returns to them. By verbalizing, you are also putting more energy into your commitment, using the power of your breath. We'll come back to that later when we talk about mantras.

The lines of these verses in your booklet will appear in three styles. One style is the original Tibetan script. Below that is the Tibetan, sounded out for you in your country's alphabet. Below that is a translation into your language.

The art of translating Tibetan Buddhist texts into English has advanced since I started in the early nineties. Well, duh, of course it has. So, look around for the most recent translation of your text available. In general, it will be more accurate and well-written.

Clearing the Way with Your Mind: Visualization

Joel Pearson, from the University of New South Wales, is a researcher on the effects of visualization. In an August 2019 article in the scientific journal *Nature Reviews Neuroscience*, he wrote that studies have shown that imagined imagery has effects on the brain much like real sensory perception, but not as strong. In other words, if you can vividly imagine yourself in a cage with an angry tiger, you can taste a bit of what that experience might be like.

We use several areas of our brain when visualizing. They work together as a network involving the frontal cortex (the gray matter right behind your forehead) and sensory areas. This network overlaps with the default mode network.

The default mode network is a hot topic in psychology and medicine. This network of far-flung areas of the brain could be called the seat of what you and I call our "self." Why? Because it reflects on past events, and our past interactions with others, and anticipates the future. This neural network allows us to think about others and understand stories. It is also known for being active when the mind is passively resting, and when we are appreciating beauty.

Wouldn't it be interesting if the visualization part of these time-tested Buddhist practices affect how our default mode network works? Our practices shed light on the underlying lie that creates our suffering, the lie of "I" and "me." Of course, we don't want to reduce the grand scope of Dharma down to a biological function. Interesting, though, isn't it?

The Power of Visualization

Vajrayana Buddhism uses visualization of Buddhas as a practice. They may look male or female, normal or fantastical, and can be of any color. In the ngondro, the primary visualizations are imagined in front of you or above your head. Representing your hidden enlightenment, they gaze at you with unconditional love. The visualization may include only one or two figures, or hundreds, depending on the specifics in the text you use.

The question is why do these practices represent awakening as deities with bodies? Lama Tharchin Rinpoche told us that this is because we strongly believe in our karmic material flesh and blood body. When we engage with immaterial deity bodies, they appear to have forms but are insubstantial. Their bodies are translucent, pure, and made of light, like a rainbow in the sky. They are not made out of anything you can catch; they are naturally pure. Meditating on this familiarizes us with immaterial wisdom. As a result, we gradually change our belief systems and reduce our obsession with the temporary bodies, our own and others.

In ngondro texts, deities represent the guiding principle; the Buddha Jewel. They are usually arrayed like a three-dimensional tree—with a trunk and branches—referred to as a Refuge Tree. The tree is a powerful symbol in Indo-Tibetan lore. It harkens back to three tree legends. First, there is the Wish-Fulfilling tree, a tree that can give you anything you want. That's a symbol that comes from ancient pre-Buddhist Indian legend. Second, the Buddha's mother, Maya Devi, supported herself by holding on to a tree when she gave birth to him at Lumbini in about 563 BCE. And, finally, there is the famed Bodhi tree in Bodhgaya, India, under which the Buddha attained enlightenment.

In this visualization, the central figure is usually Guru Rinpoche, Vajradhara, or Je Tsongkhapa. Less commonly there may be a different figure, such as Vimalamitra or the female Buddhas Troma Nakmo or Yeshe Tsogyal.

Guru Rinpoche

Om Ah Hum Vajra Guru Padma Siddhi Hum
or
Om Ah Hung Benza Guru Pema Siddhi Hung

In Nyingma Buddhism, the tantric deity Guru Rinpoche (which means "precious spiritual guide") represents the perfect teacher who has mastered all aspects of Buddhist knowledge and practice and achieved total buddhahood. According to Tibetan religious history, the historical Guru Rinpoche, who this visualized symbolic figure is based on, was an astounding teacher who came to Tibet from greater India. He is portrayed in art in various forms that relate to his prodigious study, practice, and deeds, accomplished during a mind-bogglingly long life.

Guru Rinpoche received every teaching of the sutras and the tantras, and countless empowerments, and transmissions from all the most realized teachers of the vast area now known as India, Nepal, and Pakistan. He mastered them all, becoming a second Buddha. At different times in his life, he looked like a great scholar, a pure monk, a yogi, a bejeweled and flexible perfected light form, an intimidating subduer of demons with a fiery aura, or whatever form was most beneficial for beings of the time and place.

Guru Rinpoche arrived in central Tibet in the ninth century based on the pleading of messengers who summoned him from India to help subdue the demons who were preventing the first monastery from being completed. As the story goes, each night they tore down what had been built during the day at Samye Monastery.

After accomplishing that mission, he took up residency in Tibet and found an ally in the powerful king who had invited him and later became his student. This sparked the transformation of Tibet, then a regional superpower, into a mainly Buddhist country.

Guru Rinpoche can, and perhaps should, be looked at as the personification of perfect mastery, the accomplishment of complete buddhahood, and the perfection of the ability to be a spiritual leader. However, the practice of the mantras and prayers of Guru Rinpoche can make him very real in our personal experience.

In the most common representation of him in Nyingma Buddhism he looks human, but is white with a reddish hue, and wrapped in layers of robes representing his accomplishment of all levels of practice. He holds objects laden with meaning.

Some ngondro practices depict Guru Rinpoche in seated sexual union with his most well-known consort, Yeshe Tsogyal. In Vajrayana Buddhism, the masculine represents compassion and skillfulness, and the feminine represents wisdom. These two principles are inseparable.

Vajradhara

Vajradhara, or "Vajra Holder," is a symbol of perfect awakening. He doesn't have a back story like Guru Rinpoche. He is the essence of all Buddhas. He is dark blue and holds implements that represent wisdom and compassion.

Color

These colors I'm talking about are symbolic codes that reference the Five Buddha Families and have nothing to do with the skin colors of human beings. The visualized deities are made of translucent light, not flesh and blood. A reddish hue represents desire transformed into Discriminating Wisdom. The blue color symbolizes ignorance transformed into Wisdom of Ultimate Truth. Green symbolizes envy transformed into All-Accomplishing Wisdom. White is anger transformed into Mirror-like Wisdom. Yellow is pride transformed into Equanimity Wisdom. This keys into a fascinating area of Buddhist study that you can go on to explore in Vajrayana Buddhism. The point for now, though, is that the visualized colored light is a positive catalyst toward awakening.

If you have already decided on your fully qualified personal guide, then you can imagine they are your Guru Rinpoche or your Vajradhara, etc. Also, the deity represents your ability to see the non-dual nature of reality, known as *rigpa* in Tibetan, and *vidya* in Sanskrit. That probably sounds like a lot, but as you mature as a practitioner your mind will become more relaxed and flexible and you will know how to unify these effortlessly.

The Process of Visualizing

We practice with our eyes open, blinking normally. There are two reasons. It reinforces that we're part of the world, practicing to benefit the beings here. We are not aiming to cut ourselves off or bliss out. Likewise, it's not necessary to create a super quiet place to practice.

So, it's not like smoking weed and watching the colors and lights inside your eyelids while blocking out the world. We aren't tuning out, we are tuning in. Closing our eyes while practicing tends to foster ever-shifting visualizations, a passive process of looking at auto-generated images, like being stoned. That's not what we're going for.

However, if you are having a hard time creating the image you want, you can close your eyes for a short time when you need to. Then open them and do the practice with your eyes open. There is no need to bug out your eyes or anything else weird.

The visualization instructions are usually right in the words of your practice text. Some great Tibetan teachers recommend studying painted images of your exact visualization before practicing. These days, images like these are easy to find on the internet (although, buyer beware, many are inaccurate). Other great lamas prefer their students conjure them up in their minds based on the words in the text and the body of literature that has grown up around it without relying on painted or drawn images.

Because these archetypes are unfamiliar to us culturally, I suggest starting out using a traditionally drawn image, and then abandoning it when you've got the picture.

Practice texts have become shorter in recent years because of the limited time modern people have. These pithy ngondro texts may not have the visualization fully described within them. If this is the case, you will need to consult an additional book or oral teachings to get all the details.

Take good notes at oral teachings! You don't need to be staring at the teacher to absorb their vibes. When details are being given, write them down. The lama then sees you are serious about practice and learning. Many times in my life, I've needed to consult notes I took decades before, for example, after Lama Tharchin or Lama Pema Dorje passed away. I also have had the devastating experience of having one of my lamas not be able to leave his home country or communicate with me for more than fifteen years. And counting. I would have been mortified if I hadn't done my best to take notes and file them, back then when we were together.

Difficulty Visualizing

Is it easy for you to hold an image of something in your mind? Most people would say it is somewhere between easy and hard.

Right now, bring your mother or father to mind. You can probably get a pretty good picture going. If you are Tibetan, the common Tibetan images of buddhas and bodhisattvas, such as Green Tara, Amitabha, and Chenrezig may be as familiar as seeing your parents in your mind's eye. You may notice, though, that even when picturing your mother, there are parts of her face and body that are a bit fuzzy. If you sat down on a stool, with her posing like a model, and studied her face to paint a portrait, that would likely increase the detail of your visualization.

Some people are not able to create an image in their minds, a condition called aphantasia. A little less than one percent of people in a 2022 study couldn't do mental imagery at all. Almost four percent could never get it very clear.

I have friends like that. They've told me that they adapt their practice in several ways.

Sometimes they may focus on the sound aspect, singing or chanting resonantly and feeling it reverberate in their body. At other times, they may focus on the definitions of the words, going more into the subtle meanings. There are also times that they focus on tuning into the physical sensation of devotion in their bodies. Where is it located? What does it feel like?

Classically, your mind is supposed to be absorbed in a detailed visualization during your practice session. What else do people with aphantasia do, considering they don't have that going for them?

I called up a friend who I know has this issue. He asked me if we could FaceTime so he could show me something. There, in front of him, was his practice text, along with a stack of multiple five-by-seven cards with deity images on them. He had printed them out to gaze at while he was doing his formal practice.

A beautiful thing about these practices is that they combine many methods simultaneously. If one part doesn't work for you, another will.

Perfectionism

A lama named Choying from Switzerland shared with me on Facebook that, when he was a teenager doing ngondro, he "feared to not visualize correctly all the details, like to have in mind all the 100 syllables perfectly, or to miss such an important lama on the tree." He felt as though he should start all over again from the very beginning. Looking back at that now he ascribed this anxiety to "a lack of understanding and maturity about the mechanics of visualisation."

Paralyzing perfectionism is not an uncommon problem. We count the number of reps of five different practices. Something about recording a number triggers a feeling in some practitioners that their practice is not good enough to warrant counting. I have a vague memory of people who told me that, years into their ngondro, they threw out the numbers they had written down and started over. Who were they? Their names have faded from my memory because they dropped out of Tibetan Buddhism entirely and I haven't seen them in twenty years.

So don't let a tendency towards perfectionism hinder you. Just keep going!

Peace and Focus

I have a really important point to share with you that some people miss.

If you have ever taken a meditation class, the teacher has likely taught you to use your breath as an object of calm abiding (*shamata*) or mindfulness meditation. They told you to gently bring your attention back to the breath when it wanders, without scolding yourself for having been distracted.

These visualization practices have that aspect to them as well. When your mind wanders from the mental imagery (because you are a human being, not a failure), do the same. Gently bring your attention back to the picture again. If you are bored, you can focus on another aspect of the visualization, the sounds you are making, or the sensations of your body as they connect with practice.

One aspect of ngondro is like that. The peace that comes from mindfulness and focus. When you are first starting ngondro, this will probably be a lot of what you are accomplishing. Just like garden-variety meditation, apply some light effort toward showing up for the practice, being mentally present on the chair or cushion. Don't go at it with a sledgehammer. You are fundamentally okay the way you are, my friend. You aren't trying to force yourself into becoming someone else.

With those principles in mind, let's move on to the first of the five accumulations: Refuge.

CHAPTER 11

Protection

Step Five—Going for Refuge

Why Do We Go for Refuge?

Once you have deeply internalized the four thoughts, you will feel a profound shift inside. Although you look the same on the outside, the things you care about the most have changed. A yearning to make a radical mental shift toward spiritual transformation in this life wells up from inside.

Looking out through new eyes at the people on the street and the people at work, you may think to yourself that many of them are living according to the role expectations that others have of them, like following a script. Tedious routine thoughts repeat perpetually. How can I get what I want? How can I avoid trouble? How can I zone out with my cell phone, or weed, or the next drink?

How terribly sad.

You may ask yourself... was I like that before? Is this the first time in a series of countless lifetimes that I've paused to consider leaving this nauseating carousel? Birth, old age, sickness, and death... over and over. Am I walking on the bone dust of trillions of my previous bodies?

Like an actor appearing from stage right, drawn into the scene by your growing weariness-with samsara, the Buddha suddenly enters your life. Going for refuge means you have arrived at a decision to take a vow to seek spiritual refuge only in the Buddha, Dharma, and Sangha and not in gods and goddesses.

All around this planet, from the blue oceans to the green and brown lands, millions of people have gone for refuge in the Three Jewels. Many think about it this way: their main teacher is the Buddha. His words are the path toward the end of suffering, the Dharma. Their friends and support on the path are the Sangha.

The historical Buddha passed away over 2400 years ago, and we may not have a teacher who represents him in our lives yet. We use pictures or statues of the Buddha, books of Buddhist teachings, and friends who are also doing their best to follow the Three Jewels, to remind and inspire us day by day.

When you are ready, you can ask at a dharma center for a refuge ceremony to mark the occasion that your refuge vow becomes active and you become a Buddhist. A refuge vow is a prerequisite for bodhisattva and Vajrayana vows.

That refuge vow is the entry point into actual Buddhism, and it is one of the nine steps of the ngondro practice. It is called refuge because you are deciding to enter the path to awakening and leave the repetitive suffering of cyclic existence. Buddha, Dharma, and Sangha become your protectors. Let's go through some of the reasons you would want to choose that direction in life.

Your North Star

Sailors have been navigating ships at night based on the relative distance of stars and planets from the horizon for over a thousand years. Of these stars and planets, the most important is the North Star, Polaris. It is positioned one degree away from true north as we look at nighttime heavens above.

If there were no celestial bodies before the era of compasses, sailors would have easily perished, lost at sea. The North Star has saved more lives than any single human being could.

Without a spiritual North Star, we too will perish without realizing our highest purpose in life. The Three Jewels are like that for us. In that sense, they are our protection, our refuge. Our teachers, male or female, however they look, whatever language they speak, are like living representatives of Buddha.

So, here we are at a watershed moment. Do we want to shift to making these three our guide stars, like those ancient mariners?

More About Guru Rinpoche

Since Guru Rinpoche is viewed as a second Buddha by the Tibetan people, and the one who first brought Vajrayana Buddhism to Tibet, he symbolizes the Three Jewels in most Nyingma ngondro texts. His body is Sangha, his speech is Dharma and his wisdom mind is Buddha.

It's said that Guru Rinpoche sleeps right on the doorstep of those with faith. That no one is shut out from his compassion, even if they have never heard of him. If our practice text is focused on Guru Rinpoche, we see him seated in a magnificent tree in front of us or above our heads. All the buddhas and bodhisattvas are there, all the practice deities, the lineage lamas, and so on. Some Nyingma ngondro texts will have dozens of figures in a complex visualization of a refuge tree, occupying branches in the cardinal directions and the sky above.

To Develop Your Receptivity

Lama Tharchin Rinpoche used to point out that if we can develop intelligent trust and admiration—he liked to use the word faith—that is unshakable, our minds can become receptive and open. Then the Buddha's wisdom flows into us like blessing nectar.

Gathering the Two Accumulations: Merit and Wisdom

"Gathering the two accumulations" means generating tremendous positive karmic force and discovering non-dual wisdom. The refuge practice can do exactly that. If we do it sincerely, karmic tendencies in our minds that obscure our awakening are purified and we can no longer go into hellish states, nor become a ghost or a non-human animal after the end of this life. This is a faith-based belief that I buy into.

The great gurus of the tradition will also go as far as to say that by sincerely going for refuge we are guaranteed to attain complete awakening someday because it will cause a cascade of effects that inevitably lead to that result. The fuel for that process is what is called the "two accumulations."

Personal Healing

If you have experienced personal, or particularly intergenerational, trauma, healing must occur right at the get-go. The author Rima Vesely-Flad noticed an interesting pattern. In her book *Black Buddhists and the Black Radical Tradition,* she wrote that more than half of the forty Black Buddhist teachers and long-term practitioners she surveyed for a study said that they engaged seriously with Buddhist practice, at least in part, to heal racially induced trauma. Buddhist meditations, art, and rituals can be soothing, peaceful, and restorative. Some people think of the Three Jewels as beloved companions through life.

I am all for this prescription of meditation as medicine. I haven't seen it work out well when people try to jump over personal healing and into more intensive practices from the get-go.

For example, I know Americans who have leaped into serious Vajrayana practice while struggling with moderate to severe PTSD, schizophrenia, and active alcoholism. It hasn't gone well for them. As I said, Buddhist practice is not about trying to become someone else. It happens within your mind and body. You can't fly out of your existing body and brain. You need to work with reality as it is.

Jetsunma Tenzin Palmo, a well-known nun who founded a thriving nunnery in India, told me she's met a lot of senior Western practitioners who felt blocked in their spiritual development until they went back and focused on establishing a foundation of unconditional love for themselves. They retraced their steps and spotlighted again the practice of loving-kindness, this time strongly including themselves. After doing that work, which I will describe in the next chapter, they were able to do advanced practices more effectively.

There are no higher or lower practices when we look honestly and lovingly at our actual condition. The highest practice for a person at a given time is the one that works. It may be that you will need years of basic meditation, bodywork, and therapy before doing the ngondro accumulations. Or, ngondro may never be helpful for you. That's okay... something to talk over with your spiritual friend.

If we can summon a genuine wish to be free from cyclic existence, have faith in the Three Jewels, and, on top of that, make our main motivation compassion for others, we have reached the gold level. If we can develop the confidence to aim for fully awakened buddhahood in order to be of maximum benefit to all beings, we've reached platinum.

What is Involved with the Practice of Refuge?

In ngondro, the practice of refuge is imagining a vivid refuge tree in front of you, then reciting a refuge vow whole-heartedly while prostrating. You count both the prostrations and the recitations, which are done together in most ngondro systems.

The Outer Refuge

Some refuge tree visualizations are complex. The practitioner holds a vast visualization that includes all the important lamas of the lineage, the lineage holders of Shakyamuni Buddha (known as arhats and bodhisattvas), all the specific symbolic tantric deities, the Dharma Protectors, and the female embodiments of wisdom. There are piles and piles of Dharma texts. Dozens of figures are there, on the vast blooms of lotus flowers emerging from a central trunk and four directional branches. Collectively, these are called the "objects of refuge."

Sometimes, you will become enraptured by your visualization. Your usual unpredictable emotional world will change into stable feelings of awe and wonder. You prostrate with that palpable devotion in your heart. If you are circumambulating, imagine that the refuge tree is out by your right shoulder while you walk. Recite the refuge vow verse and count with a Tibetan-style rosary (mala) or an electronic counter.

In these visualizations, you are standing on the ground. All sentient beings are with you, stretching out almost infinitely. All your female relatives are on your left, all your male relatives are on your right. You lead all sentient beings in prostrating to the objects of refuge. As they all bow down, the countless bodies extending to infinity look like a field of grain blown by the wind.

Does this feel foreign to you or familiar? For some people, it seems foreign. I remember one American woman told me that doing a prostration seemed like something out of a melodramatic old movie to her. She dramatized it for me with her hands as she said that. On the other hand, a sixty-three-year-old disabled Dharma student wrote to me that this refuge practice, "felt like going home." I felt that way too. I never felt like I was appropriating someone else's culture, or being too demonstrative. Perhaps that was because I was coming to know wonderful Tibetan and Bhutanese lamas, traditional Tibetan art, and Dharma texts in real life. My teachers felt these gestures and images transcended culture, but I can understand if it doesn't seem that way to you.

Each lama or center belongs to a specific tradition with its own ngondro. They will explain to you how unique and special it is, to motivate you. They will introduce you to lineage-specific books that will fill in all the special details. If you aren't comfortable reading books in translation, they can teach you orally. Many of my Dharma sisters and brothers who started ngondro practice at the same time as me weren't big readers.

Whatever wonderful ngondro practice you may decide to do, the meaning is ultimately the same. The refuge deities represent our awakening, currently shrouded by obscuring clouds. When you immerse yourself in practice, you will feel the love, protection, and guidance of the long lineage of teachers going back to ancient times.

Reciting a refuge vow a great number of times reaffirms our intention for awakening.

Leslie Rinchen-Wongmo is a master artist of traditional appliqué fabric scrolls depicting images of buddhas and bodhisattvas. In her book, *Threads of Awakening,* she wrote,

> We use refuge again and again to pull ourselves back into line, to point our bow in the intended direction. It may take a long time, but if we keep returning our nose toward our destination, everything we encounter in life will become fuel for the journey.

There's that North Star idea again.

You and I may not be talented artists, like Leslie, but most of us can create a visualized world where we are present with all sentient beings, gazing with devotion at the refuge tree. You can stay on track for the rest of your life if you go for refuge daily.

After bringing forth a feeling of love and trust for the objects of refuge, you begin prostrations. With each prostration, you recite the refuge vow from your booklet.

In the Nyingma tradition, our view of the Three Jewels deepens over time. Some practices follow after ngondro, if you decide to continue. These are called creation and completion stage practices, Mahamudra, and Dzogchen. The Nyingma ngondro makes this deepening explicit, by calling going for refuge to the Buddha, Dharma, and Sangha, the "outer refuge." There are also inner, secret, and innermost secret refuges. The word "secret" here means profound and precious.

The Inner Refuge

One important aspect of Vajrayana practice, traditionally undertaken after ngondro practice, is meditation on oneself as a fully awakened buddha. In all the schools of Tibetan Buddhism, we eventually come to rely on a guru as our source of transformative power. The deity we affirm ourselves as is the *yidam* (meditational deity), the source of spiritual accomplishments. Visualizing ourselves as a meditational deity and reciting the mantras of that deity helps wake up our wisdom. There are also Dharma Protectors you will come to know, who enact enlightened activities.

The Nyingma tradition goes a step further and parses out three different kinds of yidam: guru, yidam, and dakini. (Yes, there are yidam yidams!) Going through our formula again: Guru practices, such as meditating on oneself as Guru Rinpoche, are the source of transformative power, yidam practices such as Vajrakilaya or Hayagriva, are the source of spiritual accomplishments; Dakini practices, like Yeshe Tsogyal, Troma Nakmo, or Tara, are the source of enlightened activities. These correspond to Buddha, Dharma, and Sangha jewels, respectively.

The Secret Refuge

Some people, having completed at least one of these deity practices, can go on to what is known as the completion stage of the practice, working with the latent awakening that is present in the subtle body as channels, winds, and vital essences. These three become equivalent to the Three Jewels for them. They are three secret objects of refuge. Physically capable people can learn vigorous yogas in a secluded setting from a skilled guide if they have completed the prerequisites before they are too old. The practices involve postures, exercise, and Buddhist breathwork.

Innermost Secret Refuge

The Great Perfection, Dzogchen, is more openly taught these days than it used to be. On that exalted level of practice, we go for refuge in the awakening always present in our bodies and minds. As Dudjom Rinpoche wrote in his book about ngondro, *A Torch Lighting the Way to Freedom*, "The mind free of anything to be purified and anything to be attained is the Buddha; its unchanging nature, free from stains, is the Dharma; and its qualities, spontaneously complete and perfect, are the Sangha."

Dudjom Rinpoche here was referencing the innermost secret counterparts of the Three Jewels, *ngowo, rangzhin,* and *tukje* in Tibetan. Some Nyingma ngondro texts, such as the *Heart Essence of the Vast Expanse*, introduce practitioners to a few words associated with Dzogchen right here in the refuge practice. As I understand it, Dzogchen terminology is a technical language that most Tibetans don't know. We don't know the lingo of other people's trades or professions in our own country. It's like that.

When Dudjom Rinpoche said, "The mind free of anything to be purified and anything to be attained," he was referencing *ngowo*, a word for the empty essence of our mind. "Its unchanging nature, free from stains," refers to *rangzhin*, our minds' nature of unobstructed clarity or lucidity. "Qualities, spontaneously complete and perfect," refers to *tukje*, resonant compassion. *Tukje* is our hidden potential to spontaneously benefit beings in the most profound way possible without conceptual forethought. Basically, to manifest as a buddha in the world.

That's some pretty heady stuff, eh? We have no visceral experience of essence, nature, and resonant compassion as things stand right now. But eventually, we will find our deepest refuge, right inside our consciousness (once it has been freed from schmutz) and it is clear, bright, and without concepts of one, two, (or more), this or that. This is the wisdom that I talked about in Chapter 1, which has the same nature as the Three Jewels. It's always been with us.

A Guided Meditation on Refuge

Imagine you are standing in a vast pure land, utterly peaceful and joyful.

In front of you is an enormous tree. It's more beautiful and perfect than any other tree you've ever seen. It's not like an ordinary tree. For one thing, it has perfect fruits and flowers and leaves on it, all at the same time. It's strung with gold chains, silks, and jewels all over, like a Christmas tree. Delightful bells that would tinkle if a wind blew, their chiming perfectly communicating the essence of Dharma.

You sense that there are others nearby. When you look to your left, you see that your mother, your grandmothers, any sisters you may have, aunts, and female cousins are standing next to you. Turning to your right, you see your father, your grandfathers, brothers, uncles, and male cousins.

Along with you and your relatives, every living being is arrayed on the infinite plain around the base of the tree. All the humans, all the animals, reptiles, amphibians, birds, fish, and insects. You can imagine that there are invisible entities there, too, if you like the idea.

Down in front, closest to the tree, are your enemies.

It is breathtaking. In this state of awe, you feel your heart open. As you gaze at the tree in wonder, you notice something else. It's translucent! It's as though it is made of colored light.

Now, you see something else amazing that completely arrests your normal rational mind. Elevated, in the center of the tree, is a square platform. On the platform are eight regal, yet fantastical, white lions. Their manes and tail puffs are turquoise blue. Each stands on its powerful rear legs, its magnificent paws pressing down on the platform. Their heroic front legs support another square, like a dais, above their heads. Two lions are on the left side, two on the right, two in the back, two in front. All four sides are supported, holding the platform even and rock steady.

Each of the lions symbolizes one of the eight hallmarks of those who are far along on the path of awakening; wisdom, compassion, power, activity, merit, aspirations, qualities, and blessings.

On top of the dais is a large lotus flower with a thousand petals in every imaginable color. Two luminous discs are stacked on the yellow flower filaments at its center. The lower one is a flattened red sun, and the upper is a white moon. The lotus symbolizes a perfect womb. The sun and moon symbolize the refined male and female essences uniting in sublime conception.

On top of the sun-moon stack is a luminous couple seated in a loving embrace. We call the male, who represents compassion, "Precious Teacher." The female, who represents our wisdom, is named "Oceanic Wisdom Queen."

The legs of the supple translucent white female embrace the blue male around his waist. Her arms encircle his neck. They're in sexual union, symbolizing the way wisdom and compassion arise together on the path of awakening, inseparably. Both are smiling, beautiful, perfect, and thoroughly ornamented with the loveliest silks and jewels you can imagine. They each have silk headbands, an upper garment, a scarf, a belt, and a skirt. They both wear crowns with five jewels, symbolizing the five aspects of wisdom.

There's more! Gold hoop earrings dangle from each of their ears, denoting perfect insight into absolute and relative truth. They each wear three jeweled necklaces of different lengths, short, medium, and long. They have bracelets on their wrists and ankles, and above their elbows, too. Elegant rings adorn their fingers. Brilliant, shimmering rainbow-colored light rays emanate from them in every direction.

You can imagine them facing you, thinking of you and all beings with a loving, joyful heart. Their minds are the same as the wisdom mind of the Buddha. Their sacred speech transmits all the Buddhist teachings. Their utterly pure bodies are resplendent with all the qualities of awakened form.

With respect, think: no matter what happens in the future. I will stick with the Three Jewels as my source of refuge and protection. Say this out loud, three times:

> Homage
> Until awakening, all beings and I
> go for refuge with utter devotion
> in the guide as Vajra Holder,
> essence of the Three Jewels.

Naturally, you put your hands together at your heart, palm to palm, in love and wonder. You lead everyone in bowing down deep to the wish-fulfilling tree and the central couple it supports. As you do, all the infinite beings around the tree, overcome with admiration and devotion, follow your cue and also bow, like wind blowing across a ripe field of wheat.

The five-colored light rays touch everyone with liberating potency. The karma of the harmful actions of all sentient beings toward one another is cleared away instantaneously. Each one flies off as they are touched by the light rays to a pure land, a perfect place of practice—like a flock of birds scared off by a loud sound.

The central couple melts into light and dissolves into you. You rest in a state of evenness for a while.

Now, bring to mind any positive effect that may have come from this meditation and give it away to all living beings equally.

The Refuge Ceremony

If you have decided you're ready to take the plunge and formally go for refuge, you can request a ceremony to do that. You can go for refuge in any tradition, but if you want to do so in a Tibetan tradition you will need a preceptor such as a monk or nun, or a teacher (usually with a title such as Lama, Loppon, Geshe, Khenpo, etc.) It must be someone you respect. It is an exciting and joyful occasion for both the preceptor and the student.

The ceremony requires a shrine with symbolic representations of Buddha's wisdom body, speech, and mind. You, and probably others, will sit in front of the preceptor. The officiant will recite a text that will guide you through the process. You request refuge, they agree; you go for refuge and they then grant refuge. You will be taught about the vows you will hold. The ceremony will end with auspicious prayers. They'll tell you exactly what you need to say and do at each step. It's normal to be a little nervous.

During part of the ceremony, they will ask you to get down on one knee, if you can, and recite verses making the Buddha, then the Dharma, then the Sangha as your refuge until death.

You will ask your preceptor to accept you as a lay follower. This person may or may not be your personal ongoing spiritual friend, but they serve as one on this special occasion. Your preceptor may clip a little hair from the top of your head, symbolizing the shaving of the head hair by people who become monks or nuns. They may give you a new name called a refuge name, that you can use publicly or not, as you wish. Mine is Yudron Wangmo.

There are many vows and pledges on the Buddhist path, and every single one is built on the foundation of the refuge vow, meaning that you are a Buddhist and are committed to waking up.

All the levels of Buddhist vows are designed to keep you on target toward awakening. So, it makes sense that the first one would be about establishing your guiding star to begin with. This vow is held until we die.

The essence of all the specific points of maintaining the refuge vow is to do our best to not harm any sentient being. If we truly become a non-harmer, negative karma is prevented. On top of that, a strong positive force, merit, is generated. This is something life-changing that you can do!

What We Abandon to Hold the Refuge Vow

After we've gone for refuge, we are then Buddhists. We no longer go for refuge in others, for example, worldly gods and other spiritual paths. It is not that we think they are bad. We may admire them, but we have chosen to leave samsara and head out under the guidance and protection of the Three Jewels toward bodhi—awakening.

As I've said, we should no longer harm any sentient being.

The renowned twentieth-century female lama, Khandro Tare Lhamo, never deviated from her refuge vows, even during the horrifying Chinese communist cultural revolution. In her area, a state policy required Tibetans to kill rodents and dogs.

"I would rather die myself than kill those creatures," she declared. You can read more about her in the book *Inseparable Across Lifetimes* by Holly Gayley. You'll be happy to hear that she tricked a Communist Party official into thinking that she had killed a dog when she hadn't. She went on to live into old age, a major force in the restoration of Buddhism in Eastern Tibet after the failure of the cultural revolution.

In addition, after taking the refuge vow, we no longer hang out with people with negative views, or ethics at odds with Dharma.

What We Take Up

Here's what you would need to adopt in order to keep your refuge vow.

If you have symbolic representations of a buddha around the house, treat them respectfully. Even a chipped buddha from the dollar store is kept in a thoughtful place. If you have Dharma texts, even one letter, don't put them on the floor and step over them. Take good care of pictures and statues of buddhas and teachers if you have any. Treat monks or nuns (whether pure or merely presenting the superficial signs of ordination) with respect. Generally, we don't find fault in others.

Supplementary Precepts

Additionally, you can imagine your special spiritual friend as a Buddha, and think that everything he or she teaches is the Dharma, and all our fellow students are the Sangha. Make a firm commitment that under no circumstances will you forsake the Three Jewels. Don't even joke around about it.

That completes the list of commitments we make in a refuge ceremony.

Optional Vows of Conduct for Lay People

After you have received the refuge vow, you may be given the opportunity to take five more vows, if you wish. The first, abstaining from killing, is implicit in the main ceremony. You can also commit to optional vows not to lie, not to take what is not given, not to engage in sexual misconduct or get intoxicated. In the Tibetan tradition, these are not flexible. Once they are broken they are broken, so think long and hard before you take them. Another option is to do what Tibetan lay people do and take virtuous vows temporarily for a day or two.

How to do the Ngondro Practice of Refuge, in a Nutshell

1. Refresh the offerings on your shrine each morning. Make sure everything is clean, organized, and well cared for.

2. Sit in front of your shrine.

3. Recite your text up to the beginning of the refuge section,

4. Take a moment to get your visualization as clear as possible.

5. Feel the refuge tree is actually present in front of you. Let awe and faith arise in you.

6. Recite the refuge verse three times while sitting with your hands together at your heart.

7. Imagine that you are leading all the infinite beings around you in prostrating to the refuge tree.

8. Now rise and prostrate toward your shrine with good form, reciting one refuge verse with each prostration.

9. Count the number of prostrations on a sturdy 27-bead mala. Over time, increase the number you do from twen-

ty-seven to fifty-four to eighty-one to a hundred and eight. If you decide to do more in each session, you can then increase from there using your mala.

10. If your teacher has told you to also recite the bodhicitta verse while prostrating, or even include the mandala offering (as in the Gelugpa ngondro), seek clarification about how they like you to do it.

11. When you have recited your refuge vow as much as you like, rays of light emanate from the refuge sources and permeate all sentient beings, including yourself. The beams of light purify all your veils and karmic pollutants. All sentient beings merge into that purity.

12. Rest in equipoise, feeling that the refuge deities are completely inseparable from yourself.

CHAPTER 12

Motivation

Step Six—Generating Bodhicitta

Why Do We Cultivate Bodhicitta (The Mind of Awakening)?

What supercharged my passion for Buddhist practice wasn't the idea of sitting around and meditating forever, like a flower pot. I wanted a practice with purpose, a practice plugged into the valiant aim to help others. When I discovered that Buddhism has such a purpose, it was a game-changer for me. To think of the goal of your practice as ultimately being for the benefit of others is called *bodhicitta*, the expansive heart-centered mindset of special practitioners on the path to awakening, known as bodhisattvas.

People who arouse bodhicitta are extraordinary because of the depth of their spiritual goals and the vast scope of their concern for other beings. *Bodhi* means awakening, *citta* (sounds like "chitta") means heart-mind. *Sattva* here means a living being. A bodhisattva takes on a great vow to awaken into complete buddhahood in order to free all beings from samsara. They are suffused with immense compassion *(karuna)*. They always act benevolently, putting others' welfare before their own.

Accomplishing the ngondro includes reciting a concise bodhisattva vow over 100,000 times while generating bodhicitta. This chapter will explore the reasoning behind it, the broader

Why is it Necessary?

All the guiding lights of the Tibetan Buddhist tradition have insisted that establishing bodhicitta in our minds is indispensable for every practice and for every breakthrough that occurs in our practice lives, culminating in the perfection of bodhi. If this is true, it means—frankly—that no one who strives toward personal peace without embracing bodhicitta can reach the goal of becoming a freshly-minted buddha. Whether they are a software engineer meditating in their Silicon Valley home or a saffron-robed monk with lifelong perfect conduct and a genuine realization of egolessness, without bodhicitta the qualities of a buddha will elude them.

But don't all other spiritual and religious paths lead to the same awakening? Since I myself am not omniscient, I can't answer that question from personal experience. But the wisdom books of the bodhisattva way insist that our intention powerfully influences the quality of our realization and our future capabilities. Practitioners who are only interested in their personal liberation cannot actualize their full spiritual potential to the same degree as those who have roused the vast intention of gaining full awakening for the sake of all beings. All universally respected teachers have taught this, including modern ones such as Patrul Rinpoche and Dudjom Rinpoche (Yes, I am saying just do it because they say so.)

In case you are skeptical of authority, and bridle at being told what to do, I will reason through it.

Love and compassion are qualities that are obvious in people who have awakened. It is inseparable from their jnana wisdom. Do you feel that you have an untapped well of compassion and wisdom inside you? Whether you do practices related to discovering wisdom or practices connected to intentionally developing universal love and compassion, you are constructing a facsimile of that abundant well and its water, your buddha within. The deeper elements of this ngondro practice foster an affinity for that. They will help you shift your attachment from the temporary meaningless things of cyclic existence to deathless wisdom. That's a big deal.

It's said that people who seriously apply themselves to developing bodhicitta will not lose it in their future lives. The positive imprint of their holding the bodhisattva intention in the present life will continue into the next life. This understanding comes from a movement called Mahayana Buddhism that initially gained popularity in the first and second centuries CE. The written works of this big-hearted style of practice say that, in the course of cultivating bodhicitta lifetime after lifetime for four immeasurable eons, you will gradually traverse the five paths and the ten bodhisattva stages and attain buddhahood.

If you would like to learn more about these paths and stages, which are landmarks in the development of a bodhisattva, read Gampopa's famous *Jewel Ornament of Liberation*, written by a twelfth-century great of the Kagyu school. All Kagyu students pay special attention to this text, because it reliably conveys the continuity underlying all Mahayana teachings and practices, from basic Buddhist meditation all the way up to Mahamudra, drawing from the sutras and commentaries about buddha-nature.

To give a simple summary, the *paths* describe the unfolding of the qualities needed for spiritual progress, and the *stages* describe the hallmarks of each phase of a bodhisattva's development. These consist of progressive realizations, spiritual virtues, and meditative accomplishments, along with the corresponding powers to benefit living beings, which gradually increase along the way.

Many working practitioners of Nyingma ngondros, unlike our friends in the Kagyu, Sakya, and Gelug traditions, don't spend as much time on the detailed study of Mahayana doctrine. Instead, they simply retake the vow of a bodhisattva at least once a day, contemplate the "four boundless qualities," and engage in the practice of "sending and taking" (*tonglen* in Tibetan) described below. Every practice text reminds them, at the start of a session, to generate bodhicitta. If using a practice text instead of simply sitting down and meditating is new to you, you will quickly discover that reading aloud helps remind you of the key points of practice in every session.

Arguments Against Training in Bodhicitta

The idea of arousing bodhicitta has few nay-sayers. For example, I think most people would commend the value of extending love and compassion to all. That being said, some may fear that cultivating the Buddhist idea of altruism will divert men's energy and make them soft. Many societies see the role of a father as being a strong protector of their family, both their safety and their financial interests and this altruism might render them unable to protect and provide.

Does it, though? I don't see the male lay practitioners in Himalayan Buddhist communities failing to fulfill their expected roles. Instead, bodhicitta is an additive, additionally valorizing the six perfections: generosity, morality, patience, courageous zeal, and realization. All of these qualities will make one a better father, protector, and provider.

The second reservation people have about cultivating bodhicitta is connected to the stereotypically feminine role; of a woman as a kind, supportive, loving, and compassionate wife and mother. Many women have been burned by setting aside their own welfare to nurture children and support a husband and felt trod upon by an ungrateful or abusive spouse. Will cultivating bodhicitta make the situation worse?

I don't think so, and here's why. In looking out for what is best for everyone over the long term, a Mahayana practitioner also considers the welfare of the people who are trying to harm them. Harmful thoughts, words, and acts will have inevitable long-term negative consequences. The karma of harming a bodhisattva is heavier than harming a regular person or animal. Therefore, we cannot ethically participate in relationships with people who harm us.

Thirdly, there are some Buddhists who are attracted to claims of a more "direct" approach to practice and prefer to try their hand at nakedly accessing the awakened nature of their minds from the get-go. These styles of practice are related to certain interpretations of the Great Perfection (*Dzogchen*) and Great Seal (*Mahamudra*) approaches. People focused on these approaches may see the gradual path of cultivating the qualities of a bodhisattva as unnecessary, contrived, outdated, or cultural.

If you have profound confidence that you have found the true nature of your mind, for example from a mentor introducing it to you, anything other than simply resting in that nature may seem artificial. And, in theory, you can go straight to that direct approach and the qualities of a bodhisattva will naturally blossom. But I can't say I've met anyone who did things solely that way and stuck with it. Maybe some have… I don't know.

What I do know is that we humans tend to subconsciously protect our unenlightened karmic habits from change, like my rescued greyhound I mentioned before, still running in circles. Could it be that we have samsaric habits hidden in our bodies and minds like a pus-filled abscess, ready to burst forth when conditions are right? Someday, when we are hungry, sick, oppressed, or exhausted, will it open up and spew forth on the people around us?

I'd like to say this hasn't happened to me, but it has. I remember a time when I was in prolonged physical pain at a dharma event and then lost it in an organizational meeting, ruining what was supposed to be a positive group experience. These incidents are embarrassing, but they are also instructive. They have taught me about the remaining places where my love light is obscured, my compassion narrow, self-centered anger and judgment hiding beneath the surface. Persevering the cultivation of bodhicitta daily can really ferret that out. I believe it will change you, too, if you let it.

Pitfalls of the Practice

There are no downsides to doing these bodhicitta practices, but there are some mistakes we can make that prevent the practices from working properly. We want to let them transform us, right? If that's true, then our practice needs to go beyond simply listening to lectures about love, compassion, or other soothing and uplifting subjects as a way of easing our psychic pain and feeling better about ourselves.

Of course, there's nothing wrong with soothing our pains and feeling good. But if we're serious about awakening, what we are signing up for is going to be a lot more intense and challenging, more "metal." The goal is not to loll around in an ocean of love forever. We must gradually peel away our defenses and meet the world as it is, not wrap ourselves in cotton batting. In the process, we will find a greater strength in ourselves than we knew we had.

The practice calls on us to let our bodhisattva vow permeate our time off the cushion as well. In my case, that has meant questioning my thoughts and actions frequently, with a high degree of honesty. When I have that strong urge to repost a political meme on social media, is it done with genuine bodhicitta? Or will it incite anger and sow division, instead? Am I looking out for the welfare of all living beings equally, including the repercussions decades or centuries from now? Or, in my relationships with others, am I thinking transactionally, trying to get something from them by doing something kind for them? At the end of each day, we should evaluate ourselves.

We can take the vow 100,000 times in our ngondro practice, but if we aren't displaying the qualities of bodhisattva, there is no point.

The practices of a bodhisattva may make you feel happier, but they may also make you feel sadder at times. Whether personally happy or sad, we persevere. But while we're all about being as courageous as we can be, bodhicitta practice should not run roughshod over the threshold that marks the limit of what we are capable of at any given point in time.

In chapter six I mentioned passive-aggression, where we present a false front of being nice while sending out disguised aggressive messages at the same time. For example, we might organize a big fundraiser for a charity and seem to overlook it when volunteers don't show up or promised donations are never made. And then every time their names come up we bark out belittling or sarcastic zingers about them. That is because we were doing bodhisattva activities before we were capable. As Lama Tharchin once said, you can't give away a thousand dollars if you don't have a thousand dollars. Building inner riches is a process. In the meantime, we start with "aspiring bodhicitta" before engaging in "active bodhicitta."

More About Mahayana Buddhism

Buddha-nature

Becoming a bodhisattva with realization, or even a complete buddha, is not about adding qualities that we lack. It may, however, feel like a gain when we discover, for example, that we are newly able to refrain from reacting with anger when we've been wronged. Such fruitions of practice might tempt us into thinking that enlightened qualities have been somehow "zapped" into us by an exalted Tibetan teacher from his high, ornate, throne. But it is not like that. These newly discovered qualities are inherent within us. The philosophy of the bodhisattva path introduces the new idea that we all have buddha-nature.

The buddha-nature idea was based on the experience of embodied in-depth practitioners called *yogis* (male) or *yoginis* (female). It is the potential for complete awakening that each of us has, which, like a seed, can grow and grow from one lifetime to the next. While each of us has this seed within us, it may be hidden.

Like the makings of a majestic tree that are already present in its seed, the potential for awakening is present in all life forms. Looking at our situation in this way, we see that ascending toward buddhahood is not really ascending *to* anything. It's an unveiling of the Buddha within. Sometimes the literary masterworks on the topic of buddha-nature describe it like it is an element that is present in our body, right alongside the material that makes up our regular samsaric body.

Starting with aspirational bodhicitta, we fertilize this buddha seed by cultivating unconditional love, compassion, and empathetic joy for all living beings equally, right down to the smallest flea or ant. Everything we do is for everyone, not only ourselves.

Insight into the absence of a true self is sought by all Buddhists. The Mahayana Dharma goes further, proclaiming the absence of a fundamental realness of anything in the world, in the universe. It is this absence of solid reality itself that guarantees our ever-present potential for awakening. This holy brew of bodhicitta, egolessless, and confidence in the illusory nature of the cosmos, fosters genuine awakening.

In a 2018 talk, Chagdud Khadro, the leader of a large Buddhist center in Brazil named Khadro Ling, said:

> The Buddha taught that all beings have buddha-nature. So, there is an equality in the buddha-nature of animals, humans, ghosts, hell beings, and worldly gods... all of them have buddha-nature. It is essential to understand that on the Mahayana and Vajrayana path. Without that understanding, you don't know what you are doing. It becomes more and more essential as you go higher. The essence of all of us, sugatagarbha, is the same.

Translated literally, *sugatagarbha* means "the heart of the bliss-gone ones." It is another name for our buddha-nature.

Although the seed of the bodhisattva ideal existed in early Buddhism, the Mahayana movement took the bodhisattva idea as its central model of spiritual development and gradually amassed a vast literature of philosophies and practices. These incredible works include primary texts called *sutra*, commentaries called *shastra*, and memory-aiding or magical formulas called *dharani*.

Mahayana Buddhism eventually became a large religious movement in India until gradually dying out there by the twelfth century. While Buddhism underwent a slow decline in India due to large-scale political and cultural changes, by the time of its disappearance there it had spread throughout Asia, and the Mahayana movement took root in China, Japan, Korea, Vietnam, Southeast Asia, the Himalayan regions, and Mongolia.

The Buddhafield

In the Mahayana sutras, transcendent higher-level bodhisattvas and buddhas live in abodes called "pure lands." Though they are outside of ordinary time or space, bodhisattvas manifest as emanations from these pure lands into our realm in whatever way is necessary to help all of us ruffians eventually arrive at that same state. We ordinary beings can't see the pure lands, but it is said that higher-level bodhisattvas can.

Practices focused on those great bodhisattvas have specific functions. As you are reading this, people are reciting the mantra of Manjushri, or praying to him, to increase their wisdom, memory, and intelligence. People are invoking Sarvanivaranavishkambhin to remove obstacles and disturbances and Vajrapani to protect them from harm. They are praying to Maitreya, who will arise as the next Buddha when Shakyamuni's teachings disappear from the world, that they will join him in his pureland, Tushita. The bodhisattva Kshitigarbha rescues people from hell and protects beings from natural disasters. And saves babies. Somewhere in China right now, a parent is placing a pebble next to a statue of him to request that he save their baby from serious illness or protect it in the afterlife. Akashagarbha improves wisdom and creativity… mystical experiences can be induced by reciting his dharani (like a mantra): *namo akasagarbhaya om arya kamari mauli svaha*. Practitioners take vows connected with the bodhisattva Samantabhadra committing them to revere the Three Jewels, practice generosity, study the Dharma, and the like.

The bodhisattva Tara is known for helping right away. She has at least twenty-one forms. You can petition any or all of them for assistance with various specific problems, particularly scary things.

The late Lama Wangdor once taught about Tara in my garage shrine room in Oakland, California. He recounted a time when he was riding in a horse-pulled cart on a narrow mountain-side road. At a particularly treacherous part, the passengers got out of the cart, then stood and watched as the horse, the driver, and the cart traversed the crumbling dirt road, sending rocks and dirt clods down the cliff-like mountainside to the valley below. Then, the worst happened. The road collapsed, sending man, horse, and cart tumbling into the chasm.

Based on sheer instinct and his devotion to Tara, Rinpoche shouted, "Arya Tara chag tsal lo!" (Noble Tara, I prostrate to you!). There was a loud cracking sound as the cart smashed onto the ground. People were afraid to look down to see if man and horse had survived. At first, there was no sign of life. Then, the horse stood up and shook off the dirt, uninjured. Finally, up came the head and then the intact body of the driver, waving and shouting that he was okay.

Many Buddhists think of these top-tier bodhisattvas as historical humans who became deathless transcendent beings over the course of millennia, invisible except to very accomplished practitioners in our present day. Others think of them as symbols of the qualities that need to be cultivated by practitioners on the path. But not all bodhisattvas are from ancient times or other worlds.

There was, for example, an august Buddhist scholar and practitioner named Mipham Rinpoche who lived until the early twentieth century. When he was nearing the end of his life, he said to his lama assistant,

> If you speak truth nowadays, there is nobody to listen; if you speak falsely everyone thinks it's true. I have never said this before: I am not an ordinary person; I am a bodhisattva who has taken rebirth through as-

piration. The suffering I have experienced here in this body is the residue of karma, but from now on, I will never again have to experience karmic obscuration.

This was reported by Khenpo Kunzang Palchen in his spiritual biography of Mipham, translated by John Pettit for the introduction of his translation of Mipham's *Beacon of Certainty*.

As this quote shows, a bodhisattva can consciously choose their parents and the place and circumstances they are reborn into. They position themselves to bring the greatest benefit to sentient beings of a certain time and place. It is comforting to think that in this world right now there must be beings like Mipham, who are—in a way—not human, but look like someone you might see on a bus on your way to work.

As an ordinary person, you may have stumbled into situations where you felt you needed to set everything aside to try to help someone. Yet, instead of a positive outcome, everything went to hell. That's certainly happened to me. Things have sometimes turned out worse than before I tried to help. These messes happen because we haven't developed the ability to see deeply into the situation the way someone who is more spiritually advanced could.

Emptiness and the Middle Way

Deeper and deeper we go, from simply doing practices to ignite love and compassion and invoke the blessings of external Buddhas in their heaven-like pure lands, to the radical discovery of our own hidden potential, our buddha-nature. But there is still more. If we delve into Mahayana practice, we will eventually run right smack into the mind-bending chasm of middle-way philosophy, the sphere of sober monks and nuns debating in the courtyard of their monasteries.

Up until now, through infinite rebirths, we have been projecting inherent and separated existence onto everything we encounter, assigning rigid designations. But there is an alternative to that way of operating that is more true to the nature of things. As soon as we commit to becoming a real bodhisattva, we start heading in a different direction, toward a clear and unobstructed vision of things as they are. We can train, both through meditation and study, in experiencing everything—ourselves, others, the inanimate world—utterly directly. We can familiarize ourselves with relating to reality, without filtering through conceptual interpretation, even the concepts of "this exists," or "this does not exist."

Another way of expressing this experience of the world is, rather than as solid "things," taking appearances as merely temporarily arising based on causes and conditions and then passing away. Insubstantial, temporary, and illusory.

When our minds, as aspiring bodhisattvas, permanently shift from taking everything as solid and real to seeing this essencelessness, called emptiness (*shunyata*), we will become Noble (Arya) Bodhisattvas. At that time, we will also "get" the suffering of each and every being on a gut level. Our compassion and loving-kindness will naturally well up without our needing to contrive anything.

Because of the era that I came up in as a Buddhist, when many teachings were not yet widely available, I had some wrong ideas about "emptiness" for a long time. There was a semi-conscious assumption on my part that emptiness was another dimension of reality, almost like a parallel universe, that bodhisattvas access. It was an enchanting idea to me, but that is not what the Buddhist philosophers are driving at. That view would mistake emptiness for a permanent, eternal, "thing."

Likewise, some people may go to another extreme that nothing exists at all. A reckless life could follow from that perspective, without a care in the world about karma, cause, and effect. This extreme view also lacks a basic sense of practical realism. After all, the keyboard I am typing on right now is indeed *functioning* as a keyboard. It can't be said to be mere nothing.

All things, that are impermanent and compounded, lack a true independent identity. They neither exist nor don't exist. Many a mind has been blown by continuing the analysis further: things neither exist nor don't exist, nor *both* exist and not exist, nor *neither* exist nor not exist. They also are neither both existent and non-existent, nor do they lack both existence and non-existence. This four-fold approach, negating our ideas and assumptions about things, helps to undercut habitual patterns of mind and reveal the non-conceptual Middle Way.

This analytical insight may seem far removed from simply sitting on your cushion and doing practices related to love and compassion, but it is inseparable from these practices. We need to bring the middle way into our practice by being free of rigid notions of the self who is offering compassion, compassion as a "thing" offered, and the recipient of our compassion. When we stop reifying these three and rest naturally in the wide-open state that is present for a few moments in the afterglow, then we are truly following the path of a bodhisattva.

I'm doubling down on this point because in the ngondro we are clearing away obstacles to awakening. Our goal is not only to become nicer. We must marry compassion with insight into emptiness.

What is Emptiness?

If you hear a Tibetan Buddhist teacher refer to *shunyata* or "emptiness," the above summary is one way you can understand what they are driving at. The word existed in Buddhist teachings before the emergence of the Mahayana tradition, but its meaning was expanded in Mahayana sutras to refer to the emptiness of all things, not only one's personal identity.

As humans, we perceive the material things around us as very, very real. We learn their names—tree, house, kumquat—and then take those labels very seriously. But a label is just a word. Where do you find "orange"? Is the skin an orange? Is the pulp an orange? Are the seeds an orange? Orange is only a label for a fleeting collection of parts, each of which you can break down ad infinitum without ever finding "orange." But once we realize that there's no "orange," we can see that what we originally called its components aren't parts of anything. The orange is "empty" of being an orange, and its apparent parts are "empty" of truly being parts.

Many causes and conditions temporarily came together to make this thing we call "orange." A so-called orange is found through our limited human senses at a point in time in which these components (which are themselves compounded) come together from various causes and conditions into a round object of a certain texture and color. Then "orange" ends in your stomach. Its name changes to "pee" and "poop." But in truth, there is no underlying thing that changes names. There are only different combinations of factors that are labeled according to evolving conditions and shifting norms.

In the buddha-nature section above, I said that the process of awakening doesn't involve adding anything. Words like emptiness, and the process of reversing negative habits, karma, hatred, unfeelingness, stinginess, impatience, laziness, and distraction might sound as though we are subtracting something. But purging our unfortunate qualities does not truly subtract anything, because those qualities were never solid and real to begin with.

The Perfection of Wisdom

There is an extensive collection of sacred literature, the *Prajnaparamita*, (Perfection of Wisdom) that is very close to the hearts of practitioners of several Mahayana traditions. Those works develop the same arguments we have been examining here, and they bring them home to us by using metaphors for how things appear without truly existing. Our selves and the things we encounter are like a dream, an illusion, a bubble, a shadow, dew, or a flash of lightning.

Until the direct realization of emptiness occurs, turning us into actualized bodhisattvas, we should practice applying these metaphors to everything we encounter in our lives. Practicing like this gradually reduces the grip that our mistaken convictions about reality have on us. This is how we unify absolute and relative bodhicitta.

Relative and Absolute Bodhicitta

In the ngondro, you cultivate the four boundless qualities of boundless love, compassion, joy, and equanimity while reciting the bodhisattva vow. Lama Tharchin Rinpoche taught that the first three of these are trainings in relative bodhicitta and the fourth is a training in ultimate bodhicitta. I think Rinpoche was simplifying the approach of the Nyingma sage, Longchen Rabjam, for us. You'd be surprised how differently the practice is described and engaged with in the various schools of Buddhism. If you want to explore this more deeply, I recommend Alexander Berzin's article, The *Four Immeasurable in Hinayana, Mahayana, and Bon*. Frankly, it makes my 65-year-old head spin!

Some traditions have their students pair prostrations with both refuge and bodhicitta recitations, especially in a concise ngondro practice. In that case, you would say the refuge verse on the way down and the bodhisattva vow on the way up. As your body rises, your bodhisattva motivation is elevated. I've read that in the Gelugpa ngondro, refuge, bodhicitta, and mandala offerings can all be practiced together.

But, in a full-length ngondro practice, you are usually asked to do the bodhicitta practice while seated, paying special attention to developing each of the four boundless qualities. After completing all the recitations you want to do in a session, you stop speaking and do tonglen, sending and taking practice, with the breath for a while.

Let's go through all of this.

How to Do a Ngondro Bodhicitta Practice

The Visualization

Visualize the refuge tree from your specific text. Take time to make it feel real. Feel the presence of the refuge deities in front of you or above your head. Now, tune into all the sentient beings in the universe arrayed around you. At this stage, your meditation becomes more horizontal than vertical. The deities in front serve as respected witnesses to your practice of bodhicitta.

The Bodhisattva Vow

Next, you make a vow to heroically arouse bodhicitta, as the Buddha did in his previous lives. You could take the vow formally, in a ceremony with a lama officiating. But in this case, you do it on your own, by reciting the short verse in a ngondro text, with feeling.

Aspiring bodhisattvas gradually shift from striving for personal peace into a shepherd-like role. We put others' enlightenment before our own. A bodhisattva may persist relentlessly, lifetime after lifetime, over eons, toward the eventual goal of perfect buddhahood, a state of full awakening (*annutara samyak sambodhi*).

As I said, in this practice you double down on your vow. If you decide to do a formal ngondro practice, you recite it out loud at least 100,000 times. You recommit yourself, again and again, by stating your intention. By relentlessly proclaiming developing bodhicitta as essentially the purpose of your life, eventual enlightenment is inevitable.

Here is an example verse from the *Dakini Heart Essence* text:

> Ho! To free all beings, infinite as space,
> from the ocean of existence,
> I will fully rouse the supreme
> Mind of Awakening beyond compare.

Counting with a Mala

In each session, you count the number of times you recite the verse using an electronic counter, a mala, or a clock, depending on which method your mentor or center favors.

A mala is like a Buddhist rosary. It is traditionally used for counting and usually has 108 or 110 beads. There is abundant symbolism and lore about the materials the beads are made from, exactly how you pull them through your fingers, and how they are tied. For the purposes of ngondro, bodhi seed malas are highly praised. Lotus seeds are always positive (the beads will turn amber as you use them.) Stone beads are not practical because they will cut your mala string. Bone beads are never used in this practice.

In old Tibet, there were no clocks. What was timekeeping like back then? While you might set an alarm to get up in the morning at a certain hour, sit down to practice, and turn on the Insight Timer app to to alert you when your available time is up, there was nothing like that. You would have woken up according to your internal clock, or someone in your family shaking you. You measured the extent of your practice experience by the number of repetitions, counted with a mala.

You hold the mala in your left hand and move one bead at a time by pulling it with your thumb over the side of your pointer finger. The two ends of the mala strings unite at a single larger bead, called the guru bead. When you have pulled all those beads through your hand and gotten to the guru bead, you flip the mala around and go back the other way.

That's 108 repetitions. How do you record it? Usually, people use two small contraptions known as "counters." A counter is a thick cord hugged by ten small metal rings that are tied to the mala. Two are hung on the mala symmetrically, the same distance from the guru bead in opposite directions. You use the first counter to record each time you have completed 108 repetitions, by pulling one ring apart from the other nine. When you have moved all ten rings, you've completed 1,080 repetitions.

At that point, you move one bead on the other counter and push all the rings on your first counter back to zero. Before you know it, you will have ten beads pulled on your second counter. That means you made it to 10,000 recitations!

Can you count more than 10,000 with a mala? Yes! There is a little clasp you can buy for that purpose. When you have completed 10,000 you fasten it between the first and second beads on your mala. You then move it from bead to bead with each 10,000 that follows. Because you will mispronounce or miscount something every now and then, you recite an additional ten percent over your goal number.

There are electronic counters and phone apps for recording, too. But any of these systems can fail, so it is best to write down your totals as well.

Ups and Downs

There will be ups and downs in your bodhicitta accumulation. Sometimes you may be all cleaned up and crisp and practicing on a nice meditation cushion on a polished wood floor, chanting a practice text like a monk straight out of a monastery. At other times, who knows? You might wake up in the drunk tank in the county jail. Either way, your refuge source will always be there to return to.

Eventually, you will internalize the verse you are repeating so deeply that you can fruitfully work with mental exercises related to the four boundless qualities while you're reciting it. In the meantime, sincerely reciting your vow while rousing good heart is plenty. When you are ready, you can work with any of these four in any order and to whatever degree you like.

The Four Boundless Qualities

Boundless Equanimity

Have you ever had someone who was once your enemy, someone you had long dismissed as a jerk, who later turned out to be your best helper? I have. If not that, you probably have had a bestie—maybe someone you had put a lot of energy into helping—who turned into a foe. Perhaps you stretched yourself beyond your comfort zone, doing things you wouldn't do for anyone else for that person because you loved them so much... and it totally backfired.

The practice of resting in equanimity toward others is vital to our bodhicitta. It has been crucial for me. One aspect of equanimity is bringing your clinging to friends and family down a notch. We can loosen the emotional tendrils we have wrapped around them. I realize that this may be a deal breaker for you. So, let me explain.

I remember, long ago, I was married to a woman who had to have a hysterectomy. I have a vivid picture of myself in the waiting room, fretting and tortured, as though she had gone through the gate to hell instead of through the door into the surgical suite for a routine procedure. I may have been more upset about it than she was! It's been twenty years now since our divorce. We're not in contact with each other at all. What appeared to be eternal love was not. Was my over-enmeshment with one person's welfare truly pure love? Did it benefit anyone?

As an older woman, looking back on life, I have formed the opinion that Buddhist practitioners should dial back our obsessive attachment and enmeshment with others. The Buddha didn't comment on cell phones, but I don't think he would have recommended, for example, texting one another multiple times a day, every single day. (If you have children, of course, that is another story.)

And what about those enemies? I had to laugh at a recent graphic by a right-wing YouTuber, a cartoonish drawing of a human brain. It represented the self-preservation instinct center of the liberal brain (I guess that is my brain) as being the size of a pea. Usually, brain scientists who compare liberal versus conservative brain structures conclude that conservative brains are characterized by larger centers associated with fear and disgust. The cartoonist turned the tables!

We need to protect ourselves from harm by others. We need to have boundaries, and not be a sucker or a doormat. On the other hand, we don't need to frame reality as an existential war between the black hats and the white hats. Buddhist practitioners need to equalize our concern toward all living beings.

Coyotes are not beloved here in rural California. They eat pets and chickens. This practice radically proposes that your concern for the coyote, your chickens, and your pets should become equal. In the world of humans, your equal concern can include both politicians who upset you and people who agree with you about everything.

The formal practice on the meditation cushion is to start with concern about the welfare of one person or animal who you love and then gradually extend it to those you feel neutral to. All of them! When you have a handle on that, extend that equalness or evenness to those you think you dislike or despise.

All the practices that you will do in Tibetan Buddhism presuppose that you have done this process of expanding your empathy. This is the time that you do that inner work. Of course, if someone has abused you or someone you love, this will be a very challenging, long-term process.

Remember though, that Lama Tharchin said this practice of boundless equanimity can be an ultimate bodhicitta practice. Practicing in the way I have described so far doesn't quite take us there.

Rinpoche was a master of the Dzogchen, Great Perfection teachings. From that perspective, the boundless qualities can also be practiced without a rigid reference point by starting with equanimity first and letting the view of the Great Perfection imbue the other three. Here you begin by resting in an expansive pure awareness, free of concepts of friend or enemy, near or far, unstained by afflictive emotions.

Boundless Love: Two Ways of Sparking It

Traditional Buddhist teachers often use our mothers as the prime example of someone we love, someone we only want happiness for. If you don't feel that way about your mother, use someone else in your life whom you feel nothing but love for as the starting point for your practice of boundless love. Or you can use yourself as your loved one. If even that is too difficult, you can start with a pet that you have loved.

Using your mother as an example, this is how the practice might go: reflect on the fact that your mother wanted to be happy, but chances are that she did things that led to unhappiness. You can probably think of an example of that, such as an ill-advised relationship or a move that did not work out. On a more subtle level, she may have gleefully killed insects or mice—imprinting a habit of enjoying the suffering and death of others onto her consciousness. She may have been stingy or lost her temper and scolded you or others. I'm sure you can think of many things about your Mom or your other beloved person that illustrate that she did not know the true causes of happiness.

You might say, "She's only human," and that is true. We are all only humans until we get free from our human habits of looking for happiness in all the wrong ways.

We may think we only have one mother. But over an infinite number of lives, we would have had an infinite number of mothers. They, in turn, have been reborn. If you think about it that way, as a training exercise for your mind, anyone you encounter; friend, foe, or stranger, could be your mother. Maybe all of them are.

The practice here is to train your mind to have the same love toward every living entity you encounter that you would have for your dear old mother. To feel that love for her and spread it out to include everyone. Based on this empathy, you can rejoice when they do something purely positive or when the positive karma of their past virtue has yielded comfortable life situations.

In a fascinating anthology called *Radical Dharma: Talking Race, Love, and Liberation,* Rev. Angel Kyodo Williams wrote, "One of the things that we really have to do that is completely radical is utterly invest ourselves in love and to continue to practice that." She's right. It's a critical part of Buddhist practice that is completely radical. I treasure the process of training to attain the ability to love indiscriminately.

There is a second way of thinking about this practice that does the trick for me. In this style of loving-kindness meditation, I am the mother. A mother bird, making a nest for my babies, softening the inside with straw. I may pluck my own feathers to make the nest softer for my eggs and chicks.

Contemporary experts, such as Jetsunma Tenzin Palmo, will tell you that an inability to extend loving kindness to oneself fully is a major obstacle for Western practitioners in particular.

But, how do we do that without clinging to a sense of self? I do that by looking for the buddha-nature inside of me, instead of this "Yudron" built from fleeting memories and entrenched patterns of self-concept. I relax in simple presence and transparency without trying to catch the thoughts and feelings streaming up like bubbles in a glass of fizzy water before they burst. I just let it all go. Then I find that the loving-kindness practice can permeate inward and outward without blockage.

Boundless Compassion

If love is wanting each and every sentient being to be happy, compassion is wanting them all to be free of suffering, sorrow, and pain. In your ngondro session, you could bring to mind a sentient being who is suffering, perhaps one you have encountered recently. Whole-heartedly show up for that and witness their pain without shying away.

Next, move on to others, gradually extending compassion to everyone who is suffering, a country or continent at a time. Stretch yourself to imagine the suffering of perpetrators of harm, not only the victims. Wish from the bottom of your heart that you could help them. If you are a highly sensitive person, you can flash only briefly on each state of suffering. We will return to training in compassion and work with it further in the sending and taking practice, below.

Our compassion doesn't start and end on the meditation cushion. We do our best to prevent others from being harmed every chance we get.

Boundless Joy

When we see someone who is happy, the practice is to be happy that they are happy. We try not to not go to a place of longing to have their situation and happiness ourselves or resenting their joy. Maybe they are rich and live in a large house on a hill with beautiful landscaping. In your ngondro practice, you can imagine them there, a happy family with a good life. Instead of thinking envious thoughts, you can reflect on the great acts of generosity they must have done in past lives for this to have been the karmic result.

If you can be truly happy for others, then you will be happy wherever you go. I find Boundless Joy to be the most subtle practice of the four, and one worth delving into.

Sending and Taking: Courageous Compassion

When you have repeated the bodhisattva vow verse enough in your session, you end your practice with a short period of silence. This is where you insert the practice of tonglen, sending and taking, on the breath. Breathing normally, and remembering the bodhisattva spirit, bring to mind specific people or groups who are suffering. Imagine that your out-breath is sending them everything that they want or need. With your in-breath bring in their suffering. It may look and feel like dark, dense, smoke, or soot.

Again, on the out-breath, send relief to them; peace or comfort, health or wealth, for example, or a sense of sky-like spacious openness.

Eventually, extend out your compassion to include everyone, equally, the hallmark of the bodhisattva way. When practicing in your ngondro session, you can refresh your visualization of all sentient beings arrayed around your refuge deities and use them as a reference point. Practice tonglen for as little as one breath, or for as long as you like, depending on your time and inclination.

Recently, after all these years, I learned something new about tonglen. The practice emerged from the great intention of realized bodhisattvas to exchange themselves for others who are suffering.

You can imagine an American crime drama where innocent customers are being held hostage by cornered bank robbers. The hero volunteers to exchange himself for one of the hostages. Now, in the movie version we know that the hero will save the day and all the hostages will be freed without harm. But what of someone who simply exchanged themselves with someone frightened and in danger in that bank when the situation was entirely hopeless? That kind of mindset that literally puts a stranger's welfare before their own is incredibly rare.

I hope and pray that someday I will be capable of a great act of compassion like that. But, since I am not, I work with the practice of tonglen to build that heart muscle.

A friend wrote me, asking me to address, "...what to do with their suffering when you bring it in? I know this was a real obstacle to me when I first started tonglen because I felt I already had enough suffering in me, thank you very much, and couldn't take on more."

Tonglen is a practice that turns out better when you do it than when you think about doing it. This practice is about blossoming your own compassion and allowing it to encompass not only people and animals you are partial to, but also wishing that no being should suffer, whether I like them or not. Tonglen is not intended to be a form of remote healing for the other person.

All adults know what grief feels like, or what anxiety, depression, or fear feel like. We certainly know what it is like to suffer during illness. By breathing in that sympathetic feeling of dense pain into your chest cavity, you experience it as a bodily sensation. You can feel the sensation, but it is no longer attached to the thoughts that turned loss, sickness, threat (and the like) into true suffering. Metaphorically, all the oxygen is taken out of it.

What is left when we exhale is that indescribable state that all writers about dharma none-the-less try to express. Spaciousness, brightness, openness, freedom. Do the practice and see for yourself. I think you will very quickly find that the ideas of sending happiness, wealth, and health expand out and dissolve into something even better.

Absolute Bodhicitta

After completing our practices of relative bodhicitta, we should again briefly touch base with the bodhicitta of the absolute meaning, which means the same thing as emptiness. Here we relax our concepts of being a sender or a receiver, or compassion being exchanged. In that brief moment before thoughts and opinions start to arise, there is no subject, no object, no self or other. Our perception of the world around us softens. We may get a sense of what the Prajnaparaita texts are talking about when they use words like "illusory" and "dream-like."

Emptiness itself is not a thing, remember? It is more like a breakthrough in our gut-level understanding that is difficult to express in words. Sometimes we will have brief experiences of emptiness...aha moments. Mahayana practice promises that we will eventually experience that radical, permanent shift, called realization. This will be when we move from being an aspiring bodhisattva to being an arya bodhisattva on the Path of Seeing. That is a momentous occasion; Rinpoche told me that it will be obvious when it happens.

Relative and absolute bodhicitta are like the two wings of a bird. We must have both to fly into total awakening.

Please rouse your courage to grow your bodhicitta. Be heroic! Think, "I am going to persist on the path to awakening until I am a pure and perfect Buddha. May I become a perfect Buddha and free all living beings from suffering!"

A Short Guided Meditation on Bodhicitta

Imagine Guru Rinpoche and Yeshe Tsoyal as the embodiments of all sources of refuge, in the abundant refuge tree. They gaze at you with love, as the witnesses and support for your profound process of blossoming your bodhicitta.

Look around you at the vast array of sentient beings. Every conceivable species is there. The inconceivable species are present, too. These are the objects of this practice. If you like, you can pick up a Mary Poppins' magic umbrella, or a jet pack, and fly out over the multitudes. Herds of wildebeests, mountains of termites, oceans of every kind of fish. A flapping sound brings your attention to a flock of geese to your left. To your right, you hear the buzz of bees swarming. The entire population of humans of every sort look up at you, with a "who's that" expression as you fly by. They are vastly outnumbered by birds and insects.

Out of the corner of your eye, you catch a shimmer on the ground in the shape of a snake, but when you try to focus on it, it vanishes. In other places, you hear desperate cries for help that seem to come from the ground or boulders or trees. You can't pinpoint them, but you feel pain in your marrow from their wailing.

You eventually return to your spot before the refuge tree and sit there amongst the multitudes, knowing that you only saw a tiny fraction of all sentient beings on your journey. Whisper your vow to yourself with them in mind. "Ho! To free all beings, infinite as space…" They truly are like that. Each and every one in this seeming ocean of life forms is subject to pain, stress, and dissatisfaction. "…from the ocean of existence," Can I find the courage inside to center bodhicitta in my life, and strive for awakening so that I can free all of them from cyclic suffering? Yes, I can. I will! "...I will fully rouse the supreme mind of awakening beyond compare."

Counting with your mala, resolutely recite your vow 108 times. When you stop, sit silently in the afterglow of your intensity. Thoughts will slowly pull on you, like children vying for your attention. Say hello to the emotion they are infused with, to learn what your dominant affliction is. Is it a fear that bad things will happen if you don't do x, or hope that good things will happen if you do? Think of someone you know who is suffering from that feeling. Breathe it in, removing it from them. Flash on its pain as a bodily experience, and relax. As you breathe out, feel their suffering dissolve and send them back the experience of release from their stress; comfort, relaxation, and space.

Your refuge source in the tree in front of you, perhaps Guru Rinpoche and Yeshe Tsogyal, smile approvingly. Job well done.

How to do the Practice

1. Sit still on a cushion or chair.

2. Refresh your visualization.

3. Arouse bodhicitta, reciting the verse from a ngondro text softly, while arousing good heart.

4. If you have memorized the verse and become adept at that practice, you can add in the practices of the Four Boundless Qualities, in any way you like. Bound-

less equanimity, boundless love, boundless compassion, boundless joy

5. Rouse your courage

6. Light rays emerge from the refuge deities and purify all sentient beings' karma.

7. All sentient beings depart for pure lands.

8. Practice tonglen, sending and taking.

9. Relax the concepts of subject, object, and the compassion offered, and rest in ultimate bodhicitta.

Chapter 13

Purification

Step Seven—Purification with Vajrasattva

Why Do Vajrasattva Practice?

What if it were possible to intervene at the point after we have created negative karma and before its bad effects ripened? I'm not aware of any teaching in early Buddhism that indicates this possibility. Good conduct is strongly emphasized. When we have committed negative deeds or broken our vows, the Buddha encourages us to reflect on them, feel remorse, and make amends. Then we bolster our determination to do only positive deeds going forward. If you are always doing that, your present virtue influences how you experience the consequences of past actions.

Mahayana and Vajrayana Buddhism build on that understanding by teaching us purification practices. Chief among them is the Hundred-Syllable Mantra of Vajrasattva, which can purify the worst deeds that would normally lead to rebirth in a hellish realm. But, only if it is practiced well.

Our consciousness has never been freed into awakening up to this point. Instead, it has been conditioned, lifetime after lifetime, by our dualistic thoughts and feelings, and the negative acts that result from them. We've harmed others and we've harmed ourselves.

It's like we've been drunk for so long that it seems normal. Completely confused, with no idea how to live a sober life, we stagger around embarrassing ourselves, blurting out our anger, pride, and jealousy. We recklessly chase after every desire, laughing one minute, crying the next.

From the point of view of traditional Buddhist teachings on karma, most of us would seem crazy. We want to be happy but we regularly create the causes of misery.

Vajrasattva is the main practice to purify all of that. With this one cleanser, we can launder a thousand kinds of stains that hide our buddha-nature. It reduces the aftermath of every wrong, by pacifying the potential of our karma to ripen. This includes preventing future karmic diseases. Because of that, Vajrasattva can foster a longer lifespan.

The catch is that part of the process is sincerely committing to never doing any non-virtuous things again, nor breaking any of our vows.

What is Vajrasattva Practice?

The Vajrasattva practice in the ngondro is a meditation on a beautiful white buddha, seated above our head, the essence of utter purity. If you are in a committed teacher-student relationship, he can also symbolize your chosen mentor. Sometimes Vajrasattva is imagined in a singular male form and sometimes in loving embrace with the female buddha Vajratopa. As I said before, this frequently seen imagery of male and female buddhas in union is symbolic. Whether singular or coupled, the deity becomes utterly captivating in your mind's eye.

After you have got the visualization down and developed a sense of Vajrasattva really being there, the next step is to look your past and present misdeeds straight in the eye. You have to be fearless in acknowledging whatever harm you may have caused to others—whether of body, speech, or mind and not fall into the trap of excusing or minimizing the impact you may have had. White nectar then descends and cleanses you before continuing on to flow into a chasm below, carrying all of that dark stuff with it. While visualizing, recite the long purification mantra with a deep sense of remorse. Promise yourself that you will never commit harmful deeds or break your vows again.

The word *vajra* is from pre-Buddhist India. It was a uniquely shaped club wielded by the god Indra. The vajra is associated with the thunderbolt. Its Tibetan equivalent, *dorje*, is more associated with the hardest stone, the diamond. Both are indestructible. The empty yet appearing nature of yourself and other sentient beings, and the impermanent illusory nature of the inanimate universe are also indestructible. In Buddhism, vajra refers to emptiness; like space, you cannot cut it. Like a diamond, you cannot crush it. It is unimpeded because it pervades everything.

Sattva means a being. Practitioners on the path make aspirations to help beings in specific ways in the future when they become high-level bodhisattvas and, eventually, perfect Buddhas. According to the Mahayana Buddhist mythos, long ago the bodhisattva who later became Vajrasattva aspired to become a buddha who would help people purify their most intense negative karma, the karma that comes from especially heinous deeds and vow breakages, preventing the hellish consequences.

Broken Pledges

The traditional ngondro texts also refer to pledges that are both implicitly and explicitly given to Vajrayana practitioners at the ceremony known as an empowerment. The karma of breaking those pledges is considered particularly grievous, but even they can be purified by Vajrasattva practice. Not all lamas require empowerment as a prerequisite for the practice of ngondro. Some do.

When you behold the bejeweled beauty of Vajrasatta and Vajratropa's light bodies you resonate with them because they have eyes, ears, arms, and legs like you do. Sure, you could use a ball of white light instead. But, drinking in their perfection with your inner eye will gradually relax your sense that your body must be grasped at as solid, dense, and real.

Here is an example of how a ngondro text will describe Vajrasattva visually, from the Dakini Heart Essence:

> Above, on a lotus and moon seat,
> from HUNG, the guide as Vajrasattva,
> conch shell white, one face, two hands;
> he embraces the consort holding vajra and bell.
> They're adorned with silks and jewels.
> On a moon in the hub of a vajra, at the heart
> one hundred syllables surround a HUNG,
> from that, nectar of awakening flows.
> By descending, bad deeds, darkness, faults and failings
> become cleansed and purified.

While holding the visualization and bringing remorse about your misconduct to mind, you allow the pure nectar of Vajrasattva's total awakening to wash your stains away while reciting the purifying mantra, known as the Hundred-Syllable Mantra. It is practiced in all schools of Tibetan Buddhism and in Chinese Buddhism. There are only a handful of Buddhist mantras that are widely practiced by large numbers of Buddhist practitioners; this is one of them. If it weren't effective, why would it be so widely practiced, up to this day?

The Four Remedial Powers in Detail

Let's go into the nitty-gritty of the practice. There are four key aspects to it, that are known as the "four remedial powers." They all work together.

The First Power: The Power of the Basis

Usually, as I have said, the first thing that you do in this practice is to imagine the Buddha Vajrasattva four inches or so above your head. But, in some practice texts, you start by imagining a white HUNG syllable in that spot. The five distinct parts of the syllable symbolize the Five Wisdoms (suchness wisdom, mirror-like wisdom, sameness wisdom, discriminating wisdom, and all-accomplishing wisdom.). From that HUNG, light rays radiate out, making offerings to all the awakened ones. The buddhas then send blessing lights back to the syllable. The HUNG then transforms into this bright white form of Vajrasattva.

The sound of HUNG is important. You will sometimes see it written as *hum*, which is based on how it is pronounced in the Sanskrit language. But that is misleading. The *m* is sounded nasally, in the cavity behind your nose. Try it out. You will discover that it is very similar to the *ng* sound, which involves touching your palate with the base of your tongue. Houng!

All the ornaments on the deity's body reflect a sambhogakaya buddha form. We will be getting into the three kayas of buddhahood; dharmakaya, sambhogakaya, and nirmanakaya, in Chapter 15. For now, it's enough to say that these sambhogokayas represent apparitions of total awakening that can arise for extremely advanced practitioners. Since we are still ordinary people, we contrive them to use as training wheels; training in the beauty and bliss of being free from our heavy and limited range of experience. Vajrasattva appeared in several Mahayana sutras as a bodhisattva, but in Vajrayana Buddhism, he is thought of as the essence of all the buddhas in one.

His body is white and translucent, like a crystal vase filled with white nectar. He shines as bright as 100,000 suns on a snow-covered mountaintop. He is serene and smiling. There is a tiara on his head with five jewels of five colors mounted across the front. Half of his long blue-black hair is tied up in an elegant knot on the crown of his head and the other half flows down around his back and shoulders. His lithe body is bejeweled with necklaces, earrings, bracelets, anklets, and so on, and further adorned with silk scarves. He holds a bell in his left hand, upturned by his left hip, and a vajra at his heart level in the right. When both vajra and bell are present it means that the masculine and feminine principles, compassion and wisdom, are in inseparable unity.

Vajrasattva sits on a horizontal flat moon disc upon a thousand-petaled lotus flower. His legs are intertwined, with the tops of both his feet resting on the opposite thigh. If Vajratropa is present in his lap, she is also white like the moon. Her right arm loops around his neck and she wields a flaying knife, symbolizing cutting through ego. Her left hand holds a skull cup of alchemical blood representing the transmutation of desire into wisdom.

Study a beautiful Tibetan painting of Vajrasattva. What is he wearing? What is his facial expression? What is inside his body?

Is there a consort? Get enthralled with the beauty. Merge your teacher in there, thinking that he or she is inseparably blended into the image.

As pictured above, Vajrasattva has a small white HUNG syllable in his heart center, on a moon disc with the white letters of the hundred-syllable mantra encircling it.

The spiraling mantra revolves, circling the HUNG clockwise, causing the outpouring of bounteous light rays. When I say clockwise, I mean that if you were looking down on Vajrasattva's heart center from above him, you would see the standing syllables of the mantra facing in and turning to the right.

If you cannot forge a mental image, have a sense that there is a source of utter purity and wisdom above your head.

The Second Power: The Power of Remedial Action

Once you have that all going, you begin to recite the mantra.

> OM VAJRASATTVA SAMAYA
> MANUPALAYA
> VAJRASATTVA TENOPA
> TISHTHA DRIDHO ME BHAWA
> SUTOKHAYO ME BHAWA
> SUPOKHAYO ME BHAWA
> ANURAKTO ME BHAWA
> SARWA SIDDHI ME PRAYACCHA
> SARWA KARMA SU TSA ME
> TSITTAM SHREYANG KURU HUNG
> HA HA HA HA HO BHAGAWAN
> SARWA TATHAGATA
> VAJRA MA ME MUNCA

VAJRI BHAWA MAHA SAMAYASATTVA
AH

As you do, the mantra starts to circle, and mercury-colored nectar (or white if you prefer) begins to flow. It fills the deity and pours down through the stem of the lotus which enters your head at the soft spot where your fontanelle was when you were a baby. This has become known in translator-speak as your "crown aperture." The wisdom nectar descends through that opening and down into your central channel, a straight immaterial tube that runs from that opening, down through your body in front of your spine. It powerfully washes the three poisons, the three kinds of diseases, and the three negative forces (masculine, feminine, and neutral) out through your anus and urethra and all the pores of your skin.

This visualization is expanded upon at length in the classical Tibetan texts. But that is the basic idea.

Lama Tharchin taught us that the three poisons wash out as ink, smoky liquid, coal, or dirt. The three categories of diseases (according to Tibetan medical texts) wash out as blood, phlegm, and pus. The three evil forces wash out as poisonous insects, scorpions, snakes, spiders, frogs, and tiny insects. These details always appealed to me. I tried to visualize all of that leaving my body.

Where does it go? It flows into a great chasm that opens up in the earth in front of you. All the beings you owe a karmic debt to stand below with their mouths open. They reach up for it with their grasping hands. They take it all in. Then, at the end of your session their hands come down, their mouths close, and they are completely satisfied. The chasm shuts and your body is filled to the brim with white nectar. Make sure to pause for a moment and feel this deeply.

The Third Power: The Power of Rejection

The third thing you'll do in this practice is to bring to mind past misconduct with a feeling of regret; lay it bare.

This can be a little tricky in some cultures. This practice is not at all about regarding yourself as inherently flawed. It's also not about thinking of your body as fundamentally polluted, repulsive, or foul. At the risk of sounding like a broken record, we're going all-in on buddha-nature. Our karma can be cleansed, because there is nothing fundamentally wrong with us.

On the other hand, we might go to another extreme and think we were once enlightened at some point in the past and we have fallen away from that pure state. That is also not true. According to the Buddha's insights, we have been led from one birth to the next, like dogs with tight leather collars around our necks. Karma is the dog walker. We haven't had a clue up to this point that we can take off that collar. Through learning how to recognize the cause of our suffering, and how to end that suffering, we can transform or free our thoughts and emotions.

We are not the kind of people who are doing this solely to heal our personal illness or have a better life in the future. Since we are dedicated bodhisattvas, we have a higher goal.

The Fourth Power: The Power of Not Reverting to Bad Conduct

The fourth power builds on the foundation you may have already set by embracing the idea of karma and, especially, accepting that pain, stress, and dissatisfaction are inevitable in cyclic existence.

You know that tightness in your throat that comes right before throwing up? It may get to the point that, when you flash on the possibility of making more negative karma, you feel that tightness. You think, "Why would I do that to myself? I won't. I absolutely will not."

After the end of the practice, you express your gratitude to Vajrasattva:

> Protector, from ignorance and misconceptions,
> I've gone against and damaged my pledges
> Teacher, protector, please grant me refuge!
> Foremost Vajra Holder,
> you embody compassion and love.
> Leader of beings, I go for refuge.
> I openly acknowledge and let go of all impairments
> of the root and branch pledges of body, speech, and mind. Please purify and cleanse all misdeeds, obscurations, faults, downfalls, and taints.

At that point, some ngondro texts have the deities dissolve into you. You become Vajrasattva for a short while and recite a mala of his short mantra, OM VAJRA SATTVA HUNG in the bliss of inseparability. This symbolizes a shift to recognizing your own utter purity, your own divinity. Vajrasattva and Vajratopa then smile in appreciation of your job well done:

> Vajrasattva smiles with delight and says:
> "Noble child, all your misdeeds, obscurations, faults,
> and downfalls are purified."
> Melting into light, Vajrasattva dissolves into me.

You then rest in meditation. That concludes the practice.

Do You Have Doubts?

There are several things you might be skeptical of about in this practice. First of all, you may still have a bookmark in the karma idea. Still not sure. Or you may come from a Western religious context that made you feel inherently dirty and sinful, making the idea of purification loaded for you. Also, you have probably never deeply immersed yourself in mantra recitation before, and have questions. I feel it is better not to suppress our doubts, but to bring them out in the open.

There is something else we should not bury, too. At root, Vajrasattva practice requires you to spend some time reflecting on both the negative things you have done, and who you want to become. I bet you have never thought to yourself; "Gee, I want to be someone who ignores the feelings of others when I get worked up about something." Nonetheless, if you are like me, you have done exactly that. What better way could there be to transform yourself than to brave the pain of remembering times when you have behaved shamefully?

Vajrasattva has no sense of an "I" to protect. No sense of the world as unchanging and solid. He is naturally loving and naturally joyful. Vajrasattva would have no reason to have a meltdown and lose it.

The Power of Buddhist Mantra

Mantras, as you probably know, are specific combinations of words and syllables recited repeatedly by meditators or religious practitioners. In Buddhism, there are many standard mantras. They're based on the ancient Indian languages of both Sanskrit and Pali historically, even when they have been subsequently interpreted into other Asian languages. Snippets of Tibetan have been incorporated into some mantras used by practitioners of Tibetan Buddhism, for example.

People who are not interested in awakening are sometimes most fascinated by ancient mantras that have magical lore around them. There is a large collection of Buddhist magical mantras, which, like western magical incantations, are aimed at creating advantageous circumstances for a person or group and protecting them from bad things happening. For example, there are traditional mantras for healing, bewitching potential lovers, and protection from black magic.

As we develop into genuine Buddhist practitioners our wants should diminish. It follows that our interest in magic to manipulate the circumstances of others and our own lives decreases. At the same time, our interest in methods that can help us become great awakened beings who can altruistically help everyone, increases.

It follows, then that the most commonly used mantras in Vajrayana Buddhism invoke the names of, or allude to, specific buddhas and bodhisattvas who represent awakening, such as Amitabha, Avalokiteshvara, Arya Tara, and Padmasambhava. All mantras help us focus our peaceful concentration (*shamatha*) and help us develop insight (*vipassana*.) Each specific deity mantra is associated with awakening particular qualities that are dormant in us, such as knowledge, wisdom, compassion, or purity.

Mantras are so central in Vajrayana practice that the word Mantrayana—the mantra vehicle—is seen as a synonym for it. While all mantras have words with meanings; for example invoking the name of a deity, most also have mystical syllables, like OM, AH, or HUNG. They aren't exactly words, but they are definitely sounds that penetrate beyond our conceptual mind.

The Hundred Syllable Mantra

Will this be the first time you have recited a lot of mantras? Well, *mazel tov*! This one is a doozy. Below is the Hundred Syllable Mantra again, with a translation from the Rigpa Wiki website that they are graciously letting me use. You'll notice that seed syllables OM, AH, HUNG, HA, and HO are given a traditional explanation as though it is a translation, but they aren't words. As I understand it, these interpretations are from the esteemed nineteenth-century lama, Jamyang Khyentse Wangpo. You will also see the word *samaya*. That refers to the Vajrayana pledges we have made if we have received empowerment.

> OM
> The most excellent exclamation of praise
> VAJRASATTVA SAMAYA
> Vajrasattva's Samaya:
> MANUPALAYA VAJRASATTVA
> Vajrasattva, protect the Samaya
> TENOPA TISHTHA DRIDHO ME BHAWA
> May you remain firm in me
> SUTOKHAYO ME BHAWA
> Grant me complete satisfaction
> SUPOKHAYO ME BHAWA
> Grow within me (increase the positive within me)
> ANURAKTO ME BHAWA
> Be loving towards me
> SARWA SIDDHI ME PRAYACCHA
> Grant me all the siddhis
> SARWA KARMA SU TSA ME
> Show me all the karmas (activities)

TSITTAM SHREYANG KURU
Make my mind good, virtuous and auspicious!
HUNG
The heart essence, seed syllable of Vajrasattva
HA HA HA HA
Symbolizes the four immeasurables, the four empowerments, the four joys, and the four kayas
HO
The exclamation of joy at this accomplishment
BHAGAWAN SARWA TATHAGATA
O blessed one, who embodies all the Vajra Tathagatas
VAJRA MA ME MUNCA
Do not abandon me
VAJRI BHAWA
Grant me the realization of the Vajra Nature
MAHA SAMAYASATTVA
O great Samayasattva
AH

As you begin quietly reciting the mantra, it will probably feel clunky, awkward, and slow. You will stop at the end of one out-breath and restart on the next, always feeling a bit oxygen-deprived. You may wonder; how could this be flowing, pleasant, or swift? Is this supposed to be relaxing? Here's the answer: learning to recite mantras properly is a process.

Let's start with pronunciation. The kind of basic mantra pronunciation we do is (in some ways) easy for us. The "Indo" part of the Indo-European languages we speak, such as English, French, Russian, Spanish, Dutch, and Portuguese means we have a common ancestor language with Sanskrit. It's not as foreign to us as Tibetan. Generally, we follow our teacher's pronunciation. Listen to them carefully. They may have a strong Tibetan accent and that is okay. The Sakya tradition emphasizes learning Sanskrit pronunciation on its own terms. The rest of us, not so much.

I have intentionally omitted the phonetic helper marks above letters (known as diacritical marks) in this book. English-speaking Americans, like myself, aren't used to them. To us, they are like another foreign language within themselves. If I write my Tibetan name, Yudron, as Yudrön, it may seem helpful or it may seem pretentious to you.

The first thing you want to do is to memorize the mantra by repeating it a lot. Enunciate clearly, so that you get the hang of not mumbling, not pretending you are saying the mantra when you aren't. Develop good habits early. Once you have memorized it, gradually increase your speed. Check yourself periodically to make sure you haven't dropped syllables in the process. (Spoiler alert: you will.)

Breath

The next level of training is becoming accustomed to breathing normally while reciting. You will need to train yourself to recite on the in-breath as well as the out-breath. After that, you bring it all together by normalizing your breathing pattern while reciting continuously. This is essential, says nurse Yudron, because your whole physiology is regulated by your breathing. For example, exhaling more than you inhale (hyperventilation) can cause scary symptoms like lightheadedness, numbness, and chest pain. Learn to breathe at a normal pace and rhythm while reciting.

Speed

I remember practicing ngondro with others the first few times. We were quietly reciting the Vajra Guru Mantra, *Om Ah Hung Vajra Guru Padma Siddhi Hung*, in a group. I bet my eyes were bugging out as I watched the practice leader clicking away with his mala about ten times faster than I could. I questioned myself. Am I in the right section of the ngondro? He couldn't possibly go that fast, right?

Yes, he could. Gradually, month by month, I, too, became able to recite very fast without omitting syllables. Like an athlete training for the Olympics, it is a physical skill. You will develop rapid fine motor control over your tongue. Promise.

Mantra and Brain Science

Since this may be the first in-depth practice of mantra recitation you have done in this life, I would like to chat about it from my POV as a modern person with a health sciences background. You might think that mantras are so tied to faith-based beliefs that there would be no way to connect them to science. But, some ingenious researchers have begun to look into what the practice of mantra recitation does in our body, here at the convergence of sound, prayer, and meditation.

There hasn't been any research done on the Hundred-Syllable Mantra yet, but there has been some on a mantra associated with Buddha Amitabha, the Buddha of Infinite Light. The practice of Amitabha mantras is widespread in both East Asia and the Himalayas. The subjective experience of practitioners reciting an Amitabha mantra, while visualizing that Buddha in his pure land, is of bliss accompanied by fewer thoughts of self.

In 2019, a study was published in the peer-reviewed journal *Scientific Reports* (part of the group that includes the famed journal *Nature*) by researchers at the Buddhist Practices and Counseling Sciences Lab at the University of Hong Kong. The team, headed by neuroscientist Dr. Junling Gao, compared the effect of the recitation of a Chinese version of the name mantra of the Buddha

Amitabha to a sham mantra, and to a control group not reciting a mantra.

Their article, "The Neurophysiological Correlates for Religious Chanting," concluded that the two mantras stimulated different brain waves. Nowadays, scientists can determine not only the kind of EEG waves that are happening in our brains but also the brain structures they are centered in. During mantra recitation, the researchers found that delta waves are specifically increased in the posterior cingulate cortex (PCC), an area that may be connected with introspection. They theorize that these daytime delta waves—the same waves that dominate our brain in deep sleep—reduce brain oscillations (rhythmic waves that come about when the neurons in our central nervous system get stimulated). The researchers hypothesize that distraction is reduced by inhibiting these brain oscillations, allowing for a more continuous interior focus in meditation. In other words, fewer random thoughts are popping up in our meditation.

Located deep in the central and rear parts of the brain, the PCC is thought to help us get out of our intense preoccupation with self, reducing both our thoughts about ourselves and our monitoring of input from our senses.

Delta wave activity in the PCC desynchronizes that region with the rest of the brain, causing a decentralization that shows up on fMRI scans. This decentralization is greater in experienced meditators, who describe feelings of bliss and a reduction of thoughts about themselves. They also noted that the Amitabha mantra had additional positive effects on the heart and circulatory system.

For all the above reasons, meditation that includes chanting mantras has specific effects that are different than the general effects of mindfulness meditation, qigong, or Zen.

Dr. Deepika Chamoli headed up an unrelated study on the effect of the Manjushri mantra on children. A hundred and eighty children, aged eight to thirteen, in Dehradun, India, took part in a fifteen-minute daily group Manjushri mantra recitation for one month. They were tested on their performance IQ and speech ability before and after. Performance IQ measures attentiveness to details, the ability to use visual cues to guide movement, the ability to use reason and logic in new situations, and the ability to register where objects are in space. There was a highly significant improvement in performance IQ after the month of Manjushri recitation. They also noted that the children in the study enjoyed the group practice. Their article "The Effect of Mantra Chanting on the Performance IQ of Children" was published in the *Indian Journal of Positive Psychology* in August 2017.

These two studies say to me that the effects of chanting mantras probably varies depending on the specific mantra. In traditional Buddhism, Buddha Amitabha is associated with great bliss and Manjushri is associated with intelligence, and the effects noted in these two studies corresponded to that.

I'm bringing this up to help us work with our skeptical modern minds. To open the door a crack to the possibility that the Hundred-Syllable Mantra may indeed have specific effects related to purification, as promised.

Signs of Success

When you are practicing Vajrasattva intensively, you may have signs of progress. You may have a vision or dream related to your purification, such as dirt, blood, insects, etc coming out of your body. You may dream about throwing up, washing your body, wearing white clothes, flying, swimming across a river, or the sun or moon rising in the sky. In waking life your body may feel lighter, your mind more clear. Your confidence about karma may increase. These are traditional examples of good signs that Dudjom Rinpoche mentions in his ngondro commentary. He said, "If you practice sincerely and in a focused way, you will have more and more good experiences, and your realization will increase."

Vajrasattva Practice in a Nutshell

1. Imagine a very bright white Vajrasattva on a lotus and moon disc four inches above your head.

2. Dwell on the visualization until it feels like the deity is truly there and think strongly "I must purify my negative karma!"

3. Bring to mind the harmful things you have done in this life and your broken vows and promises. All the unremembered deeds from previous incarnations and the risk of accumulating negative karma in the future. Feel remorse.

4. Recite the Hundred-Syllable Mantra in a very soft whisper, continuously, without interjecting any other words, eating, or drinking, for as long as you can.

5. As you recite, see the white mantra turn clockwise around the HUNG in Vajrasattva's heart, swirling the purifying nectar down and into the lotus stem and into the opening on the top of your head, filling your body.

6. See all your defilements leave you through the lower openings of your body in all the forms mentioned above.

7. See the Ruler of Death and your Karmic creditors being satisfied by drinking the cleansing nectar.

8. Thank the deities and see that they are pleased with you.

9. The deities dissolve into light and dissolve into you

10. Rest in meditation.

Chapter 14

Multiplication

Why Make Mandala Offerings?

Mandala offering, an integral part of the foundation practice of Tibetan Vajrayana Buddhism, allows us to harness positive karmic forces through relentless generosity. This practice has mental, verbal, and physical aspects, that work together to efficiently foster the conditions for your awakening by using positive karmic force.

Mandala offering practice injects more and more merit (*punya* in Sanskrit) into your practice through this generosity, which builds positive momentum for your present life and future lives. According to the Indian sage Nagarjuna, merit is necessary for two of the three aspects of the total buddhahood you are preparing for; your nirmanakaya and sambogakaya forms that appear to others. The material body (nirmanakaya) manifests to all sentient beings and the enjoyment body (sambhogakaya) appears only to high-level bodhisattvas.

This process also reduces your personal feelings of attachment, helping you find a place within yourself of open-handed nobility. On top of that, it also can be an amazing practice for breaking down dualistic thinking. It "expands your consciousness," as we used to say in the hippie era, getting you in touch with a purity that has never been stained by conceptual thought.

The first offering is mental. You bring to mind images of everything you love and desire, multiply them to infinity, and present them to your refuge sources as a gift.

While you are doing that, the second aspect comes into play. Your voice is used to recite a beautiful offering verse. The words help you dig deep to identify everything you hold dearest and offer it up.

The third aspect of the practice is pairing the mental offering, and your voicing of superabundant generosity, with physical gestures of giving. You place piles of small, clean offering substances, such as grains or semi-precious stones on a polished surface to create an imagined world of everything wonderful, and let it go.

It's like building a big beautiful sandcastle, with turrets and horses and banquet halls, at low tide, all the while loving that it will be offered to the sea at high tide.

Your Hands

If you are able, would you please stick your hands out in front of you? Stick them out and take a look.

What do they mean to you?

To me, my hands represent several things. The things that come to mind relate to my activity in the world. Building, writing, grabbing, cooking, gardening. My hands interact with my iPhone. They give and take money, and count it. I'm not a big fighter, but some people use their fists for brawling!

These everyday movements we make don't come from nowhere. Common sense would say that we think before we act. As I said in Chapter 1, these days some scientists are thinking that we overestimate the role of conscious intention in taking action. Instinct and subconscious drives may initiate more of our physical movements than we can imagine. Subliminal drives are as powerful as conscious intention.

Before we start making things happen, we imagine the outcome we want. If we feel hungry, an image flashes in our minds of us enjoying a sandwich. So, we start putting meat or cheese on bread. Or, we feel a little tingle sparked when we imagine the caress of a body we desire. By far, most of our actions are driven by wanting, conscious or unconscious. Our hands are instruments of our mind, enacting our wish for physical and economic survival, and pleasing sensations.

While it's obvious that gestures can be generated by our minds, it's less obvious that the reverse is true; gestures can affect our thinking. Psychologists Sotaro Kita, Martha Alibali, and Mingyuan Chu proposed that they can in their 2017 article in *Psychological Review*, "How Do Gestures Influence Thinking and Speaking?" They noted many examples from previous research where that is the case. When young kids used their hands to represent abstract metaphors, such as what it means to "spill the beans," while puzzling through it verbally, they understood and internalized it better than kids who did not. Also, if they gestured they were more likely to include multiple perspectives in their problem-solving process.

Gestures can enhance recall. For example, when study participants practiced a route on a street map by gesturing with their hands, they remembered it better than if their hands were voluntarily restricted.

In other words, I am not going out on a limb here to say that we can learn new things, broaden our minds, reason better, and retain new information more easily when we pair gestures with speech. In other words, if you don't yet know what the expression "go out on a limb" means, you can extend your arms out like the branches of a tree and say, "Take a risk or hazard a guess." You will, then, remember it better.

I feel passionate about this mandala offering practice because it uses our human drives, symbolized by our hands, as a way to support our spiritual transformation. In my opinion, it will be especially powerful for you if you are in the stage of life during which you have a strong drive to be productive and industrious… say about age twenty to age fifty. You're making things happen then! That very point in life when our body is often taut, poised to make our mark on the world, is exactly the time when this practice is most potent (That's just me talking, no Tibetan lama ever said that).

Merit

According to the bodhisattva approach, it is impossible to awaken without having generated merit and wisdom on a vast scale. Mandala offerings are Vajrayana Buddhism's method to address this need in a concentrated way, honed to get the job done more quickly. Particularly the merit part.

Merit builds from positive things we do in our lives in general. If they are done in the spirit of bodhicitta, and mentally dedicated to all living beings, then they are part of the path to awakening. In that case, merit builds and builds. On the other hand, if good deeds are done with ulterior motives, the positive karmic outcomes will be temporary.

Merit is essential for clearing obstacles to awakening and creating the good circumstances needed for spiritual practice. According to the Mahayana view, if positive actions are done altruistically and the virtue of doing so is dedicated to all living beings, then our actions become part of the path to awakening. On the other hand, if our positive actions are tinged with transactional ideas, their positive effects (such as a higher rebirth, wealth, and access to dharma teachings) decay over time.

The goal of ngöndro practice is to clear away any obstacles to awakening our latent buddhahood. Once we have attained buddhahood, we will be of benefit to beings everywhere. However, unless you initiate ever-increasing positive momentum through constructive altruistic deeds done with pure bodhicitta, that will be impossible. The good circumstances we need to be able to practice in this and future lives require vast merit. Without merit, we will not meet with great teachers and receive the ripening empowerments and liberating instructions that we need to practice Vajrayana, Mahamudra, or Dzogchen. Even if the Buddha or Guru Rinpoche (Padmasambhava) were to appear to us in person, we would not have the pure and positive mind necessary to see their qualities.

The formal mandala offering practice in the ngöndro provides a structure that allows us to generate merit by harnessing the benefits of making offerings while undermining subtle or overt thoughts of personal benefit and our judgmental minds.

People raised in good Buddhist families know the importance of creating pure merit. Most homes keep a shrine in the common area of the house with a statue of a buddha or bodhisattva on it, such as Shakyamuni or Kwan Yin. They clean the shrine frequently. Every morning yesterday's offerings are taken away, and fresh offerings are placed out. Flowers, candles, fruit, and bowls of water, are beautifully arranged—like a fresh work of art—while mentally offering them to the sources of refuge. Finally, they light an incense stick, offering a pleasing scent. Uplifted, they bow to the shrine and start their day.

On the other hand, some people raised in a Buddhist culture have a completely transactional attitude toward making offerings to buddhas. For example, there was an outdoor Buddhist shrine in the city where I used to live, maintained by some Southeast Asian people in the neighborhood. The matriarch of the project told me that offerings made to one buddha statue would create personal wealth; she called that statue, "the money buddha." Offerings to another buddha had helped a relative pass her hairdresser's licensing exam.

The formal mandala offering practice in the ngondro structures your merit-making so that it is much more difficult to lapse back into self-centeredness. To me, the purity of the practice is almost palpable. It holistically harnesses the good feeling of making offerings—or donating to charity—while undermining subtle or overt thoughts of personal benefit. The whole thing snowballs into a lofty practice.

Tara As an Example

Perhaps the most famous tale of a bodhisattva's gradual awakening, over millions of years, is the legend of Tara. Have you met her? She is depicted in art as beautiful, supple, and lithe. Seated on a moon cushion, she is ready to leap up and help anyone instantly, at any time.

Tara's legend unfolds over, not only one lifetime but countless lifetimes. Eons. Of course, she did various meditation practices as part of her spiritual training. We would expect that. Yet, the first ten million one hundred thousand years of her development as a bodhisattva couldn't truly be called a meditation, as we usually think of it. Instead, as the human Princess Wisdom Moon, she made bounteous offerings every day to the buddha of that timeless time, and his realized attendant.

The mound was enormous… something like twelve miles high and wide by today's measurements. Well into the stratosphere! It also extended twelve miles deep into the ground, most of the way through the Earth's crust. Every inch of that area was filled with offerings of various sorts. Her daily offerings might be likened to a stuffed Christmas stocking or a piñata… but the size of Lake Tahoe.

Tara's process of offering elevated her to the first level of realization, where you truly see the empty nature of yourself and the universe. She became an Arya Bodhisattva who can work miracles. Not satisfied with that, she meditated for ten billion years.

This view of how enlightenment takes time highlights the heroism of the achingly slow path of mastering the six perfections of bodhisattvas; generosity, morality, patience, zeal, meditation, and wisdom. Of these, generosity comes first.

Here in the U.S., we have the legend of Paul Bunyan, who cut down entire forests in a single day, demonstrating strength and acquisition. Tara's tale is about generosity, patience, and giving. Who is the real hero?

What is Mandala Offering Practice?

You've probably heard the word mandala, right? We use it in English now to refer to a beautiful, radially symmetric design, whether a drawing or a painting. In Buddhism, the meaning can be similar, a center point and its periphery. But in the mandala offering practice, it symbolizes the material universe as the container and all sentient beings as its contents. When looked at purely, meaning without opinions and ever-multiplying thoughts, the universe is experienced as complete and perfect, like a pure land occupied only by buddhas.

There are two physical mandalas in this practice, the accomplishment mandala and the offering mandala, reflecting our inner visualization in physical form.

Let's dig into both of these.

The Accomplishment Mandala

To set up for this practice, many traditions have you clean and arrange a three-dimensional tiered mandala on your shrine, almost like a miniature wedding cake. The gear for that, called a mandala offering set, is sold in Buddhist shops. The largest pan—it looks a little like an upside-down cake pan—is used as a base. There are three layers above that are shaped by bottomless rings and filled with saffron rice or semi-precious stones. A simpler version is recommended by Dudjom Rinpoche in his ngondro book, and in the Karma Kagyu tradition. It goes like this: You clean a mandala pan and purify it with a mantra. Then you make five cone-like heaps of dry saffron rice on it. Since I don't know every tradition in detail, you should check.

This is called the "mandala which is the support for accomplishment" or the "accomplishment mandala" for short. It is the domain of the deities of your refuge tree, such as Guru Rinpoche, Yeshe Tsogyal, Vajradhara, or Troma Nakmo. The piles you make represent the main deity and their entourage. If your refuge visualization is complex, with many figures, you would gradually fill the three layers, while imagining that each handful represents deities. In another style, the practitioner makes a 37-point mandala offering and this transforms into your refuge deities. (There's a text for that).

If you are making only five piles, with one in the center and four in the cardinal directions, they represent the Buddhas of the five wisdoms. Each of these male buddhas symbolizes a painful emotion that can be transformed into an aspect of your underlying pristine consciousness. There are also five female buddhas that represent the elements; Dhatvishvari, Mamaki, Buddhalochana, Pandaravasini, and Samayatara.

Male Buddha	Family	Affliction	Wisdom	Color	Direction
Vajrasattva/Akshobhya	Vajra	Anger	Mirror-like	White	East
Ratnasambhava	Ratna	Pride	Equanimity	Yellow/Gold	South
Amitabha	Padma	Desire	Discriminating	Red	West
Amoghasiddhi	Karma	Envy	All-Accomplishing	Green	North
Vairochana	Buddha	Ignorance	Dharmadhatu	Blue	Center

Whether you have filled the layered array, or made the five piles, it is then set on the shrine.

In front of the accomplishment mandala, closer to you, are placed the traditional seven to eight offering bowls containing water, that we discussed earlier in the section on how to set up shrines. They represent water for washing, water for bathing, flowers, incense, light, perfumed water, and food. In some traditions, there is an eighth bowl for an offering of sound.

If you don't like shrines and rituals—or you can't afford one—you can simply imagine your refuge visualization in front of you without this placeholder on your shrine.

The Offering Mandala

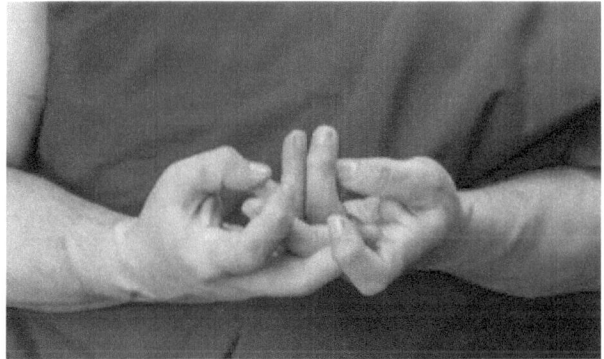

Now, imagine the refuge tree in front of you. Dial up the knob on feelings of faith and devotion toward them. Feel that the refuge deities are right there in front of you. Begin the practice by uniting your hands in front of your heart in a mudra—a gesture—that represents the universe, as it was known in ancient India. Recite the mandala offering verse in your booklet, followed by a Sanskrit offering mantra, one to three times. In our example text, the mandala offering verse goes like this:

Three realms, worlds, beings,
what appears and exists
along with body, wealth, merit, all are offered

as vast Samantabhadra offering clouds.
Accepting them, please grant your blessings.
RATNA MANDALA PUJA HO

This verse refers to another bodhisattva named Samantabhadra. Like Tara, his main practice was making offerings and multiplying them out infinitely.

Lay a towel or cloth (I am partial to the thin silk fabrics from Indian fabric stores) across your lap, covering both your thighs and the dip between them. Pick up a mandala offering pan (not the one on your shrine). It, too, looks like a shallow cake pan, that is slightly bowed out on top. It's usually made of brass or copper and is about the size of a dessert plate. It's highly polished. You hold it with the open side down at your heart level in the fingers of your left hand. Your mala is draped between your left thumb and forefinger. The smooth surface of the pan symbolically encompasses the entire universe.

Continuing to hold the pan horizontally, start by ceremonially cleansing it. Your right hand should be in the "vajra fist" mudra. The fingers are slightly bent with the middle two more so. The thumb of your right hand presses a few grains or stones into the base of the ring finger of the same hand. That blocks a negative subtle channel. Recite the Hundred-Syllable Mantra while you wipe the pan clockwise with your right wrist, polishing the surface three times. In Khenpo Ngawang Palzang's tradition, you then continue three more times while polishing counterclockwise. Think to yourself; I am cleaning away the obscurations that are veiling my awakening.

There is a subtle channel in the wrist called either "the bodhicitta channel" or the "channel which gives rise to wisdom." The wiping motion stimulates it and helps clear your mental murk.

In some traditions, they like you to use a little saffron water on the pan as you make the polishing motion. Dzongsar Khyentse

Rinpoche, for example, mentions this. If you wish to do so, a small squirty bottle filled with dilute saffron water will come in handy. Only a few drops are needed.

You are now all geared up to start the actual practice.

We will get to the traditional visualization in a minute. But the main point, as you go through these steps, is to bring to mind everything you love and desire that doesn't belong to someone else, and offer it to the refuge sources. Next, expand the size and quantity in your imagination to encompass a whole world. Make it grow a billion times. The key point is to visualize as clearly and as much as you can and offer it to the refuge deities without clinging. This generates merit.

Pro tip one: This is a little contemporary trick I discovered. If you're used to controlling lights or music around your house with Google or Alexa, you can increase your visualization abilities verbally. For example, before starting I might say, "Yudron... multiply the offerings a thousand times!" Or, "turn up the clarity 50%!" Or, "turn up the luminosity 33%!" The visualization should be clear and plentiful. If you can't visualize, cultivate a strong sense of it.

Pro tip two: I asked a friend who practices ngondro whether it was difficult for her to hold a visualization in her mind's eye. She said, "It took a while because at first, I kept thinking I needed to see exactly the same way as I do with my eyes. Then someone told me to imagine, and all of a sudden I could 'see' perfectly well, and also hold the visualization."

This imagining is paired with the physical piling of your offering with the right hand onto the round surface of the metal pan supported by the left. Typically grains or semi-precious stones are piled in an ordered pattern that represents an ancient Indian schematic of the world, while the offering verse is simultaneously recited, and the huge offering is made mentally. You then tilt your pan inward and drop the grains or stones into your catchcloth below. You wipe the pan with your wrist and immediately place your piles again while reciting the verse, and so on.

It is a lot like trying to rub your belly and pat your head. The first few times you do it, it feels impossible. But, that's kind of the point. Your distraction is eliminated by keeping your body, voice, and mind busy. It is distracting you from being distracted.

I am passionate about this practice. It works for me. The repetitions of the movement of the hand, the sound of the rice or tiny tumbled gems, splooshing onto the pan is delightful. Sploosh, sploosh, sploosh. Sploosh, sploosh, sploosh, sploosh. A feeling of non-sexual bliss is aroused by my wrist brushing metal. The dark tarnish that collects on my wrist as the pan gets shined... the muttering sound of a familiar verse... it's awesome.

How to Make Dry Saffron Rice

Supplies:
Rimmed cookie sheet.
Spatula.
Fine mesh strainer.
Liquid measuring cup: 16 oz or 500 ml.
A bowl.
Saffron threads: 1 gram (In the U.S., Spanish saffron is commonly sold in one-gram containers in the Mexican spice section of grocery stores).
Clean water.
Gallon Ziplock bags: two Rice: 1/3 gallon zip lock bag or about 1.75 liters

Preparation:

Preheat the oven to 325 F or 160 C. Put all the Spanish saffron threads in the measuring cup. Fill one of the zip lock bags one-third full of long-grain white rice. Boil the water. Pour about 4 oz, or 120 ml, of boiling water over saffron.

Let steep for ten minutes or longer until the water is deep orange and no longer hot. Strain the liquid into the bowl. Pour the saffron water over the rice in the bag. Close the zip lock, roll the top over, and grasp it tightly closed with one hand. Supporting the bottom of the bag with the other. Shake until rice is coated evenly.

Spread the moist yellow rice evenly onto the cookie sheet with a spatula. Put the sheet in the oven and set the timer for twenty minutes. Remove from the oven when dry. Set the sheet on a drying rack or stovetop and let it cool and dry even more for an hour, as steam evaporates. Break up the clumps with a spatula or other clean tool.

A cup of the dry saffron rice can now be used for mandala offerings.

Set the remainder aside for later re-supplies: Scrape the rice you want to reserve into a large bowl and leave it uncovered in a clean dry place (no cats or rodents) overnight to make sure all the moisture has evaporated. Then, pour it into a ziplock bag, plastic container, or jar and store it (where mice can't get to it.) Many people keep the rice they are actively using for mandala offerings tied up with their lap cloth and placed inside their mandala pan between sessions. Others use a container such as a small plastic container, place it inside the pan, and wrap their pan with their cloth.

The Traditional Offerings

In the standard ngondro guidebooks, specific traditional offerings from ancient India are visualized.

Grab a cup of coffee. Let's get into it.

The Outer Offering

The experiential "world" of sentient beings in samsara was seen by the Buddha, with his divine eye, as a three-dimensional schematic of a flat disc with a tall central mountain (called Mount Sumeru), an ocean with four continents in the cardinal directions, and two sub-continents between each of them, surrounded by a ring of mountains and filled with sentient beings. There is a sun and moon and various heavens of gods (with and without form) higher up, and hells below.

I think a scholarly-minded person could study this schematic representation in all its complexity, along with its roots in the sutras and shastras, for years, and learn almost everything in the Buddhadharma from this diagram alone. Don't buy into the idea that this is simply the flat earth thinking of backward people.

For us working people, it is enough to look at a drawing of this "world" online and commence practicing with that image in mind. Then, you multiply that visualization. One thousand worlds is called a first-order universe. One thousand first-order universes is a second-order universe. One thousand second-order universes is a *trichiliocosm*. This is the traditional calculation of how big Buddha Shakyamuni's field of activity is! If you want to read more, you can start by looking up trichiliocosm and Buddhist Cosmology on Wikipedia and keep reading until you've had enough.

Wealth

Once you have mentally given away everything you own, you can look into how wealth is portrayed traditionally. Offer every conceivable quality of abundance.

Lama Tharchin Rinpoche, in his ngondro commentary, listed: "Mountains of Jewels, wish-fulfilling trees, wish-fulfilling cattle, unplanted grains, treasure vases, sixteen offering goddesses who offer the five desirable qualities (form, smell, sounds, tastes, and touch)."

I wanted to learn the names of the sixteen offering goddesses and found them on the website of Sakya Tsechen Thubten Ling in Richmond, British Columbia, Canada. Do you want to know? Of course you do!

1. The blue goddess of the lute is Vajra Vine.

2. The yellow goddess of the flute is Vajra Vamse.

3. The brown goddess of the round drum is Vajra Mridange.

4. The red goddess of the clay drum Vajra Muraje.

5. The red goddess of laughter is Vajra Hasye.

6. The sapphire-colored goddess of charm is Vajra Lasye.

7. The saffron goddess of melody is Vajra Giti.

8. The white goddess of flowers is Vajra Pushpe.

9. The apple-green goddess of dance is Vajra Nriti.

10. The smokey-colored goddess of incense is Vajra Dhupe.

11. The red goddess of lamps is Vajra Aloke.

12. The blue-green goddess of fragrance is Vajra Ghande.

13. The crystal-colored goddess of form is Vajra Rupa.

14. The deep red goddess of taste is Vajra Rasa.

15. The green goddess of touch is Vajra Sparsha.

16. The white goddess of undefiled bliss is Vajra Dharmadhatu.

In addition, traditional emblems are offered. These are known as the Eight Auspicious Emblems. There are varied explanations of their symbolism in Buddhism. Here are some common ones:

1. Umbrellas symbolize the protection of the Three Jewels.

2. Golden Fishes symbolize good fortune and freedom from the fear of samsara.

3. Treasure Vases symbolize the treasure of the teachings as well as long life, wealth, and prosperity.

4. Lotuses symbolize the compassion of the bodhisattvas or the purification of defilements of the body.

5. White Conch Shells symbolize the melodious sounds of the Dharma teachings, waking beings.

6. Endless Knots may symbolize the infinite wisdom of the Buddha, the interconnection of cause and effect, or the various levels of unity.

7. Banners of Victory symbolize the Buddha's victory over the four kinds of evil forces.

8. Dharma Wheels symbolize turning the wheel of Dharma teachings.

Next, the Seven Precious Aspects of Universal Benevolent Monarchy:

1. A Thousand-spoked Wheel which represents power that

extends in all directions.

2. An Eight-sided Sapphire Jewel that illuminates darkness and grants all wishes.

3. A Sublime Queen who embodies wisdom and kindness.

4. A Minister represents honor, intelligence, diplomacy, and discernment.

5. The Most Powerful and Fearless Elephant carries the monarch around the world.

6. A Miraculous Horse embodies power and swiftness.

7. Generals who defend the kingdom and foster truth and justice.

In my own practice, I was able to find ways to make these relatable in the modern world. I thought I was a bit outrageous thinking of a universal monarch of today needing an airplane to fly around the world instead of an elephant. Wouldn't you know it? The other day I stumbled on a quote of Lama Tharchin about that exact thing. He proposed a helicopter!

Offer every quality of abundance to the refuge sources, knowing that they don't desire or need it. This process is for you. You're doing this for your eventual awakening, which will allow you to be of astounding benefit to the world.

The Inner Offering

Now that we have discussed the outer offerings, let's discuss the next set of offerings: the inner offering. The inner offerings are what makes up your personhood. Your body, the sensations you experience, your perceptions, your mental imprints and conditioning, and your consciousness. You offer all the merit you have accumulated, are accumulating, and will accumulate in the future.

You can reflect on offering each part of your body, laid out directionally like the five directions and the sun and moon you will be offering on your mandala pan (diagram below). Instead of offering Sumaru, etc., offer the trunk of your body as the central mountain, your arms and legs as the four continents, and your eyes as the sun and moon.

This inner offering also includes your capacities to experience the world; your eyes and what you see, your ears and what you hear, your nose and what you smell, your tongue and what you taste, your touch senses and what you experience through touch, your mind and the objects of your thought.

What about the many bodies your consciousness has occupied in the past? Offer them, too! How about the next body and all the other future bodies? Give it all, wholeheartedly, along with all their future possessions.

This inner offering of the body is expanded upon in some ngondro texts in a section called the *Kusali's Accumulation*, which involves a more elaborate visualization. A kusali is a penniless beggar, like a homeless person living in the rough. Lacking any possessions, they mentally offer their body.

Consider all the positive karmic force from the actions of those past and future bodies and gift it to the sublime. It's said that you can also offer the great deeds of bodhisattvas, like Tara and Samantabhadra.

The Secret Offering

After the outer and inner offerings, we come to the next level of offerings. In the Nyingma tradition, we offer up our future visions, the kind we will experience as advanced practitioners of Dzogchen who can see things as they truly are. At this point, we can only imagine what it would be like to see luminosity, pure realms, infinite buddha shapes, spheres of light, and all manner of other things invisible to us now. These will arise if we are diligent in practices that progress to reveal ultimate reality. As we imagine that, we don't cling and hoard it for ourselves but offer it up.

To review: fully-enlightened buddhas have three aspects; the perfect peace of empty non-conceptuality known as dharmakaya, sublime and blissful manifestations called sambhogakayas who guide advanced bodhisattvas, and emanations of manifest bodies in every realm of sentient life (that we muggles can interact with) called nirmanakaya.

Counting

If you commit to the ngondro process, you will offer a mandala 100,000 times. As always, add ten percent, just in case you make mistakes in your words or attitude, or flub up the count.

Here's how that goes; while you recite the verse, you make seven piles on the pan, releasing the grains or stones from the bottom of your right fist onto the designated spot for each. When the seven are complete, it is counted as one offering. Pull one bead of your mala through your fingers with the thumb of your left hand to record your count. It takes practice to do that while still holding the pan with the same hand. Then wipe the pan with your right wrist. The grains or stones fall into your cloth. Grains that fall outside the cloth should be discarded. Stones can be washed and reused. (It'll happen. It's normal.)

Next, you then scoop up a fistful and do it again.

Take a look at the diagram. Holding the pan flat in front of you, its surface has directionality. The way we do this in Dudjom Rinpoche's Nyingma tradition, as an example, is designating the point farthest from you as east. South is right, west faces you, north is to your left. Other traditions may reverse east and west. The order and placement of the piles are as follows:

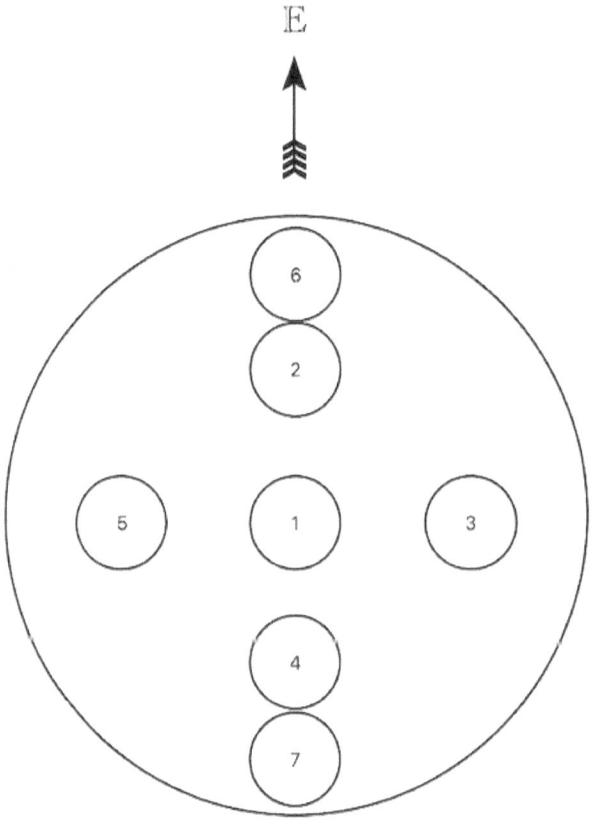

1. Center: Mount Meru
2. East: Purvavideha
3. South: Jambudvipa
4. West: Aparagodaniya
5. North: Uttarakuru
6. East: Sun
7. West: Moon

Merging the Traditional with the Contemporary

When I started doing this practice in-depth for the first time in the 1990s, I initially thought it was ridiculous. So complicated and archaic! For me, managing the pan, the mala, the piles, and the mental lists felt like trying to meditate in a New York City train station during rush hour. Nonetheless, I started doing it, because it was one of the assignments Lama Tharchin gave us all to do.

I still remember offering my past life children, my spouse, my mint chocolate chip ice cream, mountains, and oceans. I offered planets and stars, forests and bonfires, volcanoes, and aurora borealis displays. Plates of delicious snacks, trays of candles. All the cups of chai in India, and all the Frappuccinos in Starbucks.

I offered everything in my usual present life and I was very happy to replenish my supply with the traditional visualization list. What did the offering goddess for incense look like? Did the wish-fulfilling cows give chocolate milk? (Mine did for sure.)

Sitting there on my bedroom floor, grains of saffron rice incompetently scattered everywhere, I noticed a shift in my mind. All my usual thoughts were gone. That made me feel relieved, like I had been gifted a sense of internal freedom. Yes, I'd done sitting mindfulness practice—insight meditation—before, but this was so… lush. It became easy and uncomplicated once I got accustomed to it.

Turns out, offering everything I enjoyed with my imagination undermined that perpetual feeling of want. That takes us back to the Buddha's original insight, doesn't it? All our suffering comes, fundamentally, from desire. Once we give all the good stuff away, it's… freeing. What else is there to think on and on about?

Buddhists in almost every tradition make offerings to the Three Jewels, perhaps thinking of them as existing outside of our minds and bodies. As we approach Vajrayana practice, and regard the three kayas as present in our body, voice, and mind, it deepens the offering process. We see buddhas as awakening itself, and awakening as a hidden quality within our own body-mind. Is the process, then, buddhas making offerings to buddhas? Are the infinite worlds we are giving away with our hands, also the purelands of infinite buddhas?

I used to feel embarrassed that my thoughts were stopped by these questions... like there was something wrong with me. Now I know that the process of exhausting thought is what is transformational, not finding an iron-clad answer.

Returning to the practical aspects of the practice, I found that I wanted to do about 500 mandala offerings in each session. It took me less than an hour, back then. After an hour, my body would become too stiff and sore to continue. I wanted to offer as many mandalas as I could within my physical limit. Why? Because, to my shock, I loved it.

What if You Don't Make Mandala Offerings?

If you don't practice generosity extensively, you will always experience the side effects of grasping and clinging.

Imagine you're a stingy person. Ever since you were a child you wanted all the good things for yourself. You didn't share with anyone. Visualize yourself holding on to your most precious thing, a bit like Gollum, guarding the Ring in the *Lord of the Rings*. How do you feel in your body? How is your mood? How is your breathing?

Mandala offering practice releases that painful clinging. I can't measure my merit, but I trust that a powerful positive force was generated by the mandala offerings I have made, and that merit is helping me find the pure aspect of my consciousness.

Integrating Mandala Offering with Your Day

An acquaintance of mine, let's call her Yazmine, visited a Buddhist children's school in a rural area on a hot day. She was invited along as the kids went on a field trip to a local river to go for a swim. Everyone had their bathing suits on underneath their clothes. They filed into vans and headed off. When they got there, Yazmine popped out of the van, stripped off her outer clothing, and ran to the water. She jumped into the cool, refreshing, current.

Popping her head up, she glanced around for the children. There they were, standing beside the river making the mandala offering mudra and reciting a mandala offering verse. They were so well trained that, as they were anticipating the pleasure of the cool water on their bodies, they knew that it was a perfect chance to offer it up to awakening.

The children taught a grownup something that day.

How to Do the Practice

1. Seated in meditation posture, you refresh the same visualization of the refuge tree again. Use the accomplishment mandala on your shrine as an inspiration to imagine the refuge field in front of you.

2. Put your cloth across your lap. Make a small pile of rice or semi-precious gems on top of the cloth. The offering pan and mala are held up in your left hand.

3. Clean the pan by wiping it in clockwise circles with the wrist of your right vajra fist. Recite the Hundred Syllable Mantra three times.

4. Press a grain or pebble of your offering between your right thumb tip and the base of your right ring finger.

5. Scoop up the offering in your right fist.

6. Begin reciting a mandala offering verse

7. Drop small qualities of offerings on the pan from your fist in seven piles, as above, while imagining making offerings.

8. Clear the pan quickly with your right wrist again.

9. Repeat this as much as you can. Count with your mala.

10. At the end of your session, the dissolution of the refuge tree happens slowly from the outside into the center.

11. Rest in a natural state beyond anything that has ever been produced or accomplished, free of concepts of offerer, offering, and recipient.

Chapter 15

Unification

Step Nine—Guru Yoga

This final step of the ngondro comes with a great promise to us, made more than 1,500 years ago. The promise is that if we see ourselves as already awakened, a perfect and pure deity, with the most amazing and qualified human teacher we have ever met (also pictured as a pure deity) in front of us, by unifying the two, we will be catapulted up the levels of awakening.

Of all the questions that may come up for us about this, there is one that is central. If I am already a buddha, why do I need another buddha?

Without a doubt, since time immemorial people have attributed incredible qualities to immaterial deities. In this practice, called Guru Yoga in Sanskrit, and Lama'i Naljor in Tibetan, we use that very human habit to wake up hidden potentials in ourselves. We do it by imagining intermingling with the wisdom mind of a wondrous being. Lama'i Naljor literally means the yoga (practice) of the guru.

But, how could conjuring up an image in your mind's eye effect any real change?

Done in a dry and mechanical way, it can't. Done with great feeling, though, it is very powerful. To get that juice, we need to convince ourselves that the deity has every awakened quality and insight. A relationship with a real-world teacher, who really wows us, is the secret sauce. If we can come to see them—over the years—as something like an emanation of Buddha, here for our benefit, magic can happen.

The risks and benefits of going down that road with another person are pretty obvious, right? Serious benefits and serious risks. My job in this chapter is to help you minimize your risks, and increase your chances of experiencing the benefits of the practice. This is a responsibility I take seriously.

I know that you may have no interest in putting a human teacher at a central place in your world. Nonetheless, I will present my case here for doing just that.

Vajrayana: Taking the Result as the Path

Guru Yoga practice softens our resistance to making a big personal shift in how we see the world and our place in it. Up until now, we've been thinking of ourselves as ordinary. A regular human being with an undeveloped seed of awakening present in our hearts and minds. If we are doing the other eight steps nicely, we are gradually building up positive momentum and insight from the accumulation of merit and wisdom. We've begun purifying our karma. Through meditation, study, and our good deeds, our consciousness can elevate over billions of years, toward enlightenment.

Guru Yoga moves us into another approach, the world of Vajrayana Buddhism. Vajrayana modes of practice evolved in India. Between the eighth and the fifteenth century CE, extraordinary men who had studied and accomplished Vajrayana practices in India hiked over the Himalayas to Tibet carrying their books. The wide variety of illuminating practices they brought were translated into Tibetan and caught hold of the Tibetan imagination, sparking an explosion of interest in both lay and monastic practice, and fostering a relationship between Tibetan people and Buddhism that continues to this day.

Origins

Buddhist Tantras, the most important scriptures of Vajrayana Buddhism, were first recorded in seventh-century India, no doubt from earlier sources lost to time. Later, a whole body of tantric literature arose, filled with commentaries and rituals, in the different regions and tongues where this spiritual movement spread.

From a religious point of view, most of these original scriptures arose miraculously. These stories are told in various legends. For example, eighteen of the tantras central to the Nyingma School are said to have appeared on a king's palace roof, having previously been taught only from the dharmakaya to an audience of sambhogakaya bodhisattvas. The king, Indrabhuti, then brought the teachings to human beings. In this way, these texts can themselves be viewed as nirmanakaya: awakening in a material form.

This parallels the way fully-awakened buddhas are believed to appear in the world. They have a mother and father, yes. But, on a deeper level, they have arisen from the great peace of the formless dharmakaya into this world (and infinite worlds) as bodies with a form that we humans can meet. High-level bodhisattvas can see stunning blissful sambhogakaya bodies. But us? We need living guides who we can see, touch, and interact with. Because compassion naturally comes along with wisdom, buddhas are born in human bodies solely to help us.

Isn't that beautiful? Buddha emanations are always arising, not only in the human realm but in each of the six realms of samsara... even hell.

Mahamudra, a direct meditation on the nature of mind, on the other hand, sources its origins to non-monastic tantric adepts, called *mahasiddhas*, of medieval India.

Great Female Founders

Because of the prominence of remarkable men in Buddhist histories, let's take a moment to highlight female origin tales. The tantras say that all other factors being the same, women have an equal or superior capacity for awakening as men. As you can imagine, 1700 years ago this was a radical notion. Education was mainly available to men in religious institutes of learning, and to the nobility, in medieval India. And so it is that, while female adepts do appear in the origin stories of various Vajrayana transmission lineages, they are portrayed as teaching using symbols, actions, and spontaneous songs. Their male disciples, who had power over the written word initiated teacher-to-disciple lineages that continue to this day. These lineages became almost exclusively male in Tibet. Virtually all positions of religious power in Bhutan, Tibet, and the Tibetan diaspora today are held by men. The exceptions prove the rule.

The classic example of a female Indian guru is that of the Indian adept Saraha who attained realization while being shown the symbol of an arrow by his female guru. But many other female gurus were known, notably Sukhasiddhi and Niguma. For example, the Dzogchen tantras (written down later in Tibet) make mention of medieval Indian female teachers, such as Gomadevi, Kungamo, Bodhi the Yakshini and her disciple Sarati, and the courtesans Barani and Purasti.

While institutionalized Tibetan Vajrayana has always been a man's world, there have been female gurus in Tibet over the centuries, up until right now. The most famous are Yeshe Tsogyal, the mother of Tibetan Buddhism, and Machig Labdron, the founder of a tradition known as Mahamudra Chöd. The nuns at Larung Gar Monastery in Golok, a contemporary institution of higher learning for monastics, have compiled a huge collection of writings by or about female gurus throughout history.

You can read books on the subject in English, such as the classic *Women of Wisdom* by Lama Tsultrim Allione, and emerging works focusing on twentieth-century women like Do Dasel Wangmo, Tare Lhamo, Sera Khandro, the powerful women lamas from the family lineage of Mindrolling Monastery, and so on. Nowadays, a handful of women are filling roles of leadership and inspiration in Tibet, Bhutan, Nepal, and India, and have become educated, literate, and recognized.

Enlightened Perspective

Key elements of Vajrayana Buddhism are reflected in the guru yoga. The first is called the "view," the round-the-clock outlook a practitioner holds about themselves and the world they occupy.

As I said, starting in the guru yoga step of the ngondro, you make a conscious shift. You shift to practices in which you see yourself as already awakened. Instead of thinking of your body as tainted, or filled with microorganisms and maladies, you now think of it as pure and filled with deities. Your home is a palace of light. The world you inhabit is a vast pure mandala. Your speech is enlightenment in the form of sound, like a wisdom mantra. Instead of holding onto the belief that your mind is flawed, stupid, smart, or neurotic, you are invited to regard it as essentially pure wisdom. The same mind as the blissful awakened mind of a buddha.

Then what happens? Well, if you start your day as a buddha, it becomes obvious when you shift into solidifying things in your mind. When that dense web of concepts and feelings based on our karmic habits takes hold it feels dark and confining. The contrast with the spacious open place we discover in the guru yoga practice is obvious. Over time it gets easier to lean into that space beyond labeling and concepts, craving, numbing out, or disliking. This is an internal space, not a place you dissociate to.

It is in the guru yoga practice that we first encounter this amazing re-imagining. It is sometimes only present as a whisper in a ngondro, but this Vajrayana approach will be amplified in practices that follow.

In most ngondro guru yogas, you are a deity, usually female, but sometimes simply yourself in a translucent body made of light. The guru is seen in front or above your head in a pure form, such as Guru Rinpoche, Vajradhara, or Vajravarahi.

The Qualified Guide

This tantric style of practice requires choosing a qualified mentor who you can build trust with. You then decide to elevate them into a place of exceptional reverence and respect in your heart. To make them a guru. The word guru as an adjective means heavy. It entered the English language from Indian languages and arose from the same root as the Latin word *gravis* meaning heavy, grave, weighty, or serious.

The greats who emerged from Tibet in the last seventy years, such as the present Dalai Lama, the 16th Karmapa, Dudjom Rinpoche, and Dilgo Khyentse Rinpoche… would not have become what they were without a guru. The great twentieth-century meditation master Sera Khandro put it bluntly, "No discourse or tantra exists, of the attainment of enlightenment, without that individual having relied on a spiritual master." You can find her books on the Further Readings list.

But, we need to be careful, because when we choose a guru, we don't necessarily have experts to help us sort out the wheat from the chaff…. the qualified and honorable from the unqualified and narcissistic.

Wisdom and Compassion

Lama Tharchin Rinpoche said, "The point of guru yoga is to train in merging our mind with our lama's wisdom mind and to have those qualities of wisdom and compassion that we glimpse within our lama's mind inhabit our own minds."

Rinpoche had been a close disciple of Dudjom Rinpoche since he was nine years old, and later his eldest son, Thinley Norbu Rinpoche. He was a stellar example of the perfect Vajrayana student, who constantly practiced guru yoga, day after day, year after year.

One might fear that the process would produce a brainwashed zombie, a personality-less drone, like a cult member. But, no. He was lively, creative, joyful, frank, and real. His personality was actually very different than his lamas. At the same time, it was as though his body and mind were suffused with the nectar of the lineage. That's how it felt to me anyway. Almost tangible.

I think, too, of Lama Pema Dorje Rinpoche, who was another of my gurus, another disciple of Dudjom Rinpoche from a young age. Same indescribable essence. Lama Tharchin once told me, "his mind is always even." And that was true. We spent a lot of time together and experienced all kinds of wonderful and horrible events. In his later years, he lived in California, without institutional support, fame, or wealth. He and his family had an apartment as a home base for his travels all over the world to teach groups of students, large and small, who invited him. But the way you and I handled the ups and downs of life and the way he did was completely different.

For example, he had a wicked sense of humor. He'd joke about things that might make you or me burst into tears if they'd happened to us. He taught me to adopt a realistic perspective about impermanence. To become a practitioner who has deeply integrated the four thoughts of the outer ngondro.

Buddhism speaks of dharmakaya as total peace. It was like that. Lama Pema Dorje Rinpoche's mind seemed to me to always be resting in dharmakaya, while his subtle body was in the bliss of sambhogakaya. And all the while he looked like a normal human person that I could interact with. I know that may sound "over the top," but it was really like that.

When we practice guru yoga, we integrate with deep qualities of awakening in an intentional, undefended, way.

The Nature of Mind

Through guru yoga, we can access a natural oceanic state of blissful peace, infused with a sense of knowing everything at the same time.

When I was a kid, teachers wrote with white chalk on slate-colored blackboards at the front of the classroom. I am sure you've seen that in movies. I can still hear the sound of the squeaking and tapping of the chalk on the board, communicating... what? All kinds of things we'd need to know to thrive in the world when we grew up. Facts, numbers, letters, words, shapes. We piled these up in our noggins like cinder blocks and boards on a construction site. We used them to make big complicated psychological structures, built of thoughts and feelings.

Later, we discovered that those very structures never created any lasting happiness for us. The good stuff was fleeting, no matter how hard we tried to hold on to it or conjure it up again.

What if we had spent some time tuning into the blackboard itself, the uncomplicated wordless backdrop for everything? That's what my great lamas were attuned to, 24/7.

Transformative Power

Being open, receptive, and fully present with a great lama has a transformative power called *abhisthana*, usually translated as blessing. This is another aspect of guru yoga practice. Anam Thubten Rinpoche calls it, "liberating potency." When the guru with a mind abiding in that oceanic wisdom imbued with compassion, and a disciple who has pure perception and trust in him or her, connects there is something very special and freeing that can happen for the student.

Nurturing and Role-modeling

In practical terms, one's spiritual mentor should be a support for the disciple to stay on the path of practice. This relationship may, and should, look like kindness, non-sexual love, and gentle support. Later on, after years of trust building, the guide may be more firm with us when needed.

By viewing your lama as pure and realized, their way of being—their wakeful presence in the moment—will imprint onto your mind. They see you as fundamentally pure as well. In that matrix, you follow his or her guidance as best you can. When you experience deeply satisfying results, a heart-felt appreciation develops. It feels like you were cured of a life-threatening disease by an amazing doctor.

In his book *Love and Rage: The Path of Liberation Through Anger*, Lama Rod Owens expresses this as a homecoming:

> I invite all the manifestations of the guide into the space around me and cultivate the feeling of being held gently, warmly, and lovingly by them. This is

my sense of coming home. Like the rest of the homecomings, I can imagine receiving kindness from them while also offering things that I struggle with to them to help hold. I also pray to them for things that I need to be well and free from suffering.

The function of a Vajrayana guru is that sense of being held, coupled with spiritual advice, and also the formal aspects of the role: the bestowal of ripening empowerments, and provision of liberating instructions on how to do specific Vajrayana practices.

Choosing a Guru

Traditional Tibetan books outline the qualities and educational background of someone qualified to be a Vajrayana guide. The problem with using these as blueprints to find one is that it can read like a technical manual. What have they studied? What have they practiced? What lineage are they part of? The answers to these questions may sound like indecipherable jargon to you. You don't know the lingo yet… and neither do many lay Himalayan people who have busy lives with jobs and families like we do.

The truth is that in Tibet, Bhutan, Nepal, and the Buddhist northern borderlands of India, regular people choose their guide based on who is respected in their community and who their relatives follow. That lama could very well be a relative! In any event, the community knows pretty much everything about them. In that situation, the family would steer people away from teachers who have controversy surrounding them and toward a really good one.

So, there's the rub, right? We have neither the technical knowledge nor the word-on-the-street knowledge that indigenous Buddhist people do. We can end up choosing someone to guide us based on our own culture's idea of how fabulous a spiritual teacher is, their 'vibe', their charisma, the size and fanciness of their center, their social media presence, or even their physical attractiveness.

That way of choosing a guru is fraught with peril. There could be a perfect, truly awakened, lama who is famous, charismatic, and sexy, living in a center or monastery encrusted with gold and jewels on a glamorous hill. There really could be. Or there could also be the biggest narcissist cult leader in the world living up there. Likewise, there may be a simple lama living in a low-rent apartment with no followers who is perfect for you. You can't tell based on outer appearance or prestige.

Let's talk, then, about how to connect with someone really good who can go beyond merely coaching you on the how-to, to someone you can develop a deep love and respect for over the long term. Someone who can guide you in the highest practices when you are ready. Someone who also loves and respects you. But more than that, they can see the chains that bind you and call the dormant buddha from the deepest recesses of your heart.

Back in the day, when I was looking around, I went to meet teachers at dharma centers in the U.S. in person. I wanted a teacher who I could see regularly. I was lucky that several awesome Tibetan lamas settled here in Northern California.

These days, people look for gurus on the internet. That has an up-side and a down-side.

I've got to be straight with you. Seeing lamas online is great. But eventually, you need to go meet them. The best way is to attend a group retreat of a week or more with them. Then you can observe them. Overcome your shyness and go up and introduce yourself. Hang out with their students.

The majority of Vajrayana guides that I have met—who may have the title Lama (guru), Loppon (a respected Dharma leader), Rinpoche (precious one), Khenpo or Geshe (male scholar), Khenmo or Geshema (female scholar)—are the most kind, elevated, wise, and compassionate people I have ever met. They are a cut above people like me, not only in their knowledge but in the marrow of their bones. This usually comes from being raised in good Buddhist families and most likely receiving specialized training as potential spiritual leaders from their early childhoods. These designated kids had a personal relationship with a highly regarded mentor who directed their program of study and practice.

Ideal Qualifications

What then are the qualifications for the role?

Remember the requirements for a bodhisattva spiritual friend from chapter 7? They should be calm and disciplined, unconcerned about ordinary things, focused on future lives, sad about the suffering in samsara, skilled at caring for disciples, and full of compassion. A Vajrayana guide must have all those qualities and more.

They should have attended many empowerment ceremonies, received many reading transmissions, kept their vows well, accomplished the practices they will transmit, be a good educator, and have extensive ritual skills.

The empowerment ritual serves different functions. First, it is the necessary gateway into Vajrayana practice. Second, vows are conferred in the ceremony. A relationship between the officiant and the student is forged. Third, a complete empowerment ceremony, which may be hours or days long, can itself transform one's mind. This process is called ripening or maturing. All Vajrayana practice requires empowerment.

So, it goes without saying that a Vajrayana teacher needs to have undergone this subtle process repeatedly.

Likewise, whatever empowerments and transmissions the Vajrayana mentor will give to others, must have come from an authentic source to begin with. So, check the teacher's lineage out and make sure it is for real.

The next requirement is that they have not broken the vows given at the time of empowerment. The most egregious of these breakages would be to become enraged with their guru and smear their name in public.

Next, they must have accomplished the practices they teach themselves and be able to articulate the systems of Vajrayana spiritual development they hold. They also should have the ability to lead the rituals integral to Vajrayana practice.

Finally, they should have had signs of success in the stages of deity practice. The highest accomplishment is experiencing the state of Mahamudra, the actual nature of his or her mind, and being freed from samsara. The next highest is having a vision of the deity they are practicing. Below that is having dreams of the deity and the like.

However, after describing such a pure, learned, and accomplished person, Patrul Rinpoche, in Padmakara Translation Committee's translation of *The Words of My Perfect Teacher*, goes on to say, "Examining a teacher could be condensed into one question: does he or does he not have bodhicitta? If he does, he will do whatever is best for his disciples in this life and in lives to come, and their following him cannot be anything but beneficial."

Other Tibetan authors, such as Choying Topden Dorje and Jamgon Kongtrul, go on to clarify that. While the perfect teacher who is both consummately educated and realized is the best, other people are also qualified gurus. Some live in seclusion, have great discernment, and are modest, kind, patient, and articulate. Others have completely turned away from worldly life and embody renunciation. Others are scholars of Buddhist philosophy, whose conduct is exemplary, and teach from books according to what their students truly need. Finally, there are primarily upholders of a specific lineage, having received the instructions, practiced them thoroughly, and held a pure view of their lineage teachers.

How to Test

Say you have been listening to Dharma teachings from someone online, or going to their talks at a center or in a private home. If you are considering positioning them as one of your central guides, the first thing to do is to practice according to their instructions and see how it goes. Does your mind change?

Here are some good changes you might see, in my experience:

- You can let things go from the past, so you have less sadness.

- Your worries about the future are decreasing, so you plan and strategize less, and your anxiety decreases.

- The web of thoughts in your mind is becoming less dense, you can imagine being able to relax in your natural state.

- You are becoming more flexible, mentally, so you can see the perspective of others as well as your own.

- You can be physically still for longer periods, indicating that your focus is better.

- Your compassion arises naturally, so you can see the suffering of those you like, those you don't, and those you are neutral toward.

- The impulse to hurt others, both animals and human beings, is gradually fading.

- When things you did not want to happen, do happen, your emotional reaction is less intense and doesn't last as long as it used to.

- Your patience with people who turn on you, when you have been nothing but kind and generous to them, is increasing.

These are good signs that you have encountered a teacher who can lead you and others out of samsara. Also, they are knowledgeable, impartial, buoyant, and not envious of others. They see their student's development from a long-term, multi-lifetime perspective. They never lose hope for you. Even when you give up on yourself, they never give up on you. Their patience is infinite.

If you choose well and follow their advice as best you can for years, it will eventually lead you to realization and awakening. That could happen in this very lifetime. But even a bad connection with a sublime guru will eventually lead you out of samsara.

Four Different Kinds of Teachers Today

1. Tulkus

We have used the word nirmanakaya (*tulku* in Tibetan) many times in this book. Now we get to the specific use of the word in Tibetan religious culture. In the twelfth century, after the passing of the first Karmapa, a great figure, some disciples became certain that a particular baby was the rebirth of their beloved teacher. This kicked off a tradition of recognizing subsequent Karmapa incarnations that has continued up to the present day. When the system is working well, an amazing child inherits the leadership of the monastery and wealth of his predecessor and is trained extensively to fill his role.

The tulku idea then spread throughout Tibet and became an effective system for training young men from childhood to become great spiritual leaders of a specific monastery or lineage. They often become amazing hierarchs, with all the above qualities of a Vajrayana guru. Sitting on a high throne wrapped with the finest brocades imported from Varanasi, huge gilded statues of Buddha behind them, and rows and rows of monks and nuns filling almost every seat in the house, they project kind mastery and power. A few of them, like the Dalai Lama, inspire millions.

Sometimes tulkus do not turn out so well, even though they have been officially recognized as incarnations of highly respected lamas.

As Dzongsar Jamyang Khyentse Rinpoche said during the Pema Lingpa Tersar Wangs and Lungs at Bartsham, Bhutan in the winter of 2013-14:

> The buddhadharma can either be upheld or destroyed by tulkus. Identifying some people as 'tulkus' doesn't tell us their worth as teachers, because there are just so many different kinds of tulkus. There are those tulkus whose 'recognition' comes from their own parents, relatives, or friends. In China, there are supposed tulkus with titles and 'lineages' that have never existed anywhere before. And there are people who just seem to proclaim themselves as tulkus.

(Translated to English by Khenpo Sonam Phuntsho and posted on Facebook.)

Always spend time researching a Vajrayana master before you go to an empowerment ceremony with them, or ask them to be your teacher. Search for information online. Ask practitioners senior to you about their reputation. This is important so you don't end up taking vows with someone and later regret it.

2. Scholars—Khenpo/mo or Geshe/ma

Like Christianity and Judaism, Buddhism values scriptures and the learned writing about them. Today, there are special institutions of deep learning connected to big monasteries in India, Tibet, Nepal, and Bhutan. In these colleges, certain young people continue beyond basic dharma knowledge to become masters of the doctrine through in-depth study and contemplation of these texts. Some of the best of these scholars become the leaders of religious institutions, teaching the fine points of doctrinal studies, without deviation or decline, to the next generation.

These scholars are of critical importance. They also love the Dharma so much that, instead of merely being recruited, they intentionally embarked on the equivalent of doctoral degree level education. If they graduate, you are pretty much guaranteed to receive genuine Dharma without error from them. The majority teach Mahayana Buddhism. A minority will go on to fill the role of a religious expert on Vajrayana, or a guru.

There is a critique of dharma scholars, whispered by those who were trained mainly in practice-centered traditions. I think you can guess what it is. The concern is that scholars can make it all the way through their education without having practiced enough to gain any level of realization. A dry career path without heart.

To be honest, I have never met a dharma scholar I felt that way about. The ones I have have been absolutely sublime. But, it is something to suss out when you are examining a potential guru.

3. Yogi or Yogini

The term *yogi* (masculine) or *yogini* (feminine) as used in Buddhism isn't necessarily related to physical yogas. It means someone who has practiced a lot over the course of years. Generally, here we are talking about people who have done long-term retreats.

Some Tibetan traditions see yogis and yoginis as capable of serving the role of the guru. Lineage holders will authorize them to teach. Other traditions, on the other hand, value a proper education over extensive practice. Of course, everyone agrees that the greatest teachers are the ones who have done both study and practice for the entirety of their lives. People like that are rare these days, but they do exist.

4. Community-arisen Lamas

I've been told that in indigenous Himalayan communities, everyone knows the qualities of a good guru. Sometimes, especially in remote areas where there are no monasteries or yogin encampments, people see those qualities in a serious practitioner and naturally gravitate to them as a teacher. They rely on them for advice, divinations, simple practice instructions (like in this book), and that liberating potency we talked about, blessings. They are inspired merely by seeing them, being in their presence, hearing them, or receiving the touch of their open palm on the top of their head.

Just bringing someone like that to mind can give you goosebumps or bring tears to your eyes. Mostly, they don't do the formal ceremonies of a Vajrayana guru, but who's to say that their effect on their disciples isn't equally powerful?

From disgraced YouTube influencers to Kool-Aid cult leaders, the people in the culture that surrounds me generally lack the capacity to discern good from bad when it comes to spiritual teachers. Please be very careful before hitching your wagon to a community-arisen lama outside of a heritage Buddhist community.

How to Avoid Dangerous, Bad, Gurus

This Vajrayana system of practice calls upon one to build trust in a spiritual friend to the point that they are in some ways the most important person in your life.

From what I can tell, before Tibet fell under the control of the Chinese Communists in the 1950s, there were safeguards in place that reduced the chances of an evil manipulator rising into the lama role. Here are some red flags to look for:

- They don't have all the qualities that naturally emerge from studying, contemplating, and practicing, such as loving-kindness, equal concern for sentient beings, compassion, and emotional evenness.

- They have been appointed to teaching positions solely because of family or lineage expectations. They teach out of obligation, but their heart is not in it.

- They have narcissistic behavior from being praised and elevated to a leadership role in their insular community.

- They have little knowledge of Dharma and have never followed a learned teacher.

- They hold no lineage and don't talk about their guru.

- They haven't tamed their emotions. For example, everyone can see their anger and envy.

- They sexually harass their students.

- They don't keep whatever vows they have taken.

- They commit crimes or abuse people, implying that they are enacting the free and uninhibited conduct of a highly realized person. Yet, they resist facing the consequences for the harm they have done like an ordinary criminal. (Physically, sexually, or financially abusing their disciples then fleeing the country or paying off the victims.)

- They are hypocrites who teach one thing and do another. For example, they preach the importance of having equal concern for all sentient beings, but they treat people of different races, sexes, etc unequally.

- They are arrogant and talk down to people.

Carefully research potential teachers online. Ask around. Spend a few years examining them.

The Formal Practice of Guru Yoga

The on-the-cushion meditation on guru yoga begins with reading the text. It will spell out the details of your self-visualization and the front visualization. It will foster the sense that everything around you is pure.

As I've said, self-visualization is usually of oneself as the enlightened female principle, a dakini, standing and adorned with jewels or bone ornaments, often a magnetizing red or rosy color. These symbolic female buddhas are associated with enlightened activities. So, one foot is often raised... either slightly or high in a dancer's pose. She is made of translucent light, with no human muscles or organs.

In front or above the head is an image of the guru as another light deity. The exact form will, again, be specified in your text. Whether the image is male or female, we valorize the guru as totally pure, using words like sovereign, majestic, royal, supreme, heroic, powerful, or glorious. This beautiful language invokes a deep trust and receptiveness that charges up the transformative potential of the practice.

There are several sections in a longer guru yoga practice that we don't need to go through in detail here. Basically, after that sense of presence is there for you, you begin reciting a mantra. You keep track of your count with a mala or counter, as you did in your Vajrasattva practice. You will be given a goal number, which may be as small as 100,000 or well over a million mantras.

A common example is the Vajra Guru Mantra. This is the foremost mantra to invoke Guru Rinpoche, Padmasambhava: *om ah hum vajra guru padma siddhi hum*, (or *om ah hung benzra guru pema siddhi hung* in the Tibetan style.) The idea is that these penetrating Sanskrit syllables transcend conceptual thought. Of course, that has not stopped scholars from interpreting them.

Briefly, *Om Ah Hung* invokes the body, speech, and mind of awakening in general. Orgyen Chowang Rinpoche once said that these three sounds are like the area code, and the rest of the mantra is like the phone number.

The syllables *Vajra Guru Padma* connect with the three kayas; dharmakaya, sambhogakaya and nirmanakaya. *Padma*, being the nirmanakaya, refers to the specific teacher Padmasambhava—"Lotus Source." *Siddhi Hum* is your request to bestow all the spiritual accomplishments.

There are other guru yoga mantras. Because they are viewed as very special, they are only for people who are committed to doing the ngondro practice seriously.

While reciting the mantra, you enter into a state of relaxed focus on your visualization, the meaning, and the sound of the syllables, for as much time as you have available in a session. The practice resembles prayer, mindfulness meditation, and insight meditation, all in one.

Receiving the Four Lights

When the mantra recitation ends, you ask the guru to bestow the four empowerments. Based on compassion, white light rays emerge from a white Om syllable at their forehead and merge into you via a white Om syllable at your forehead. Red light rays emerge from a red Ah syllable at their throat and merge into you via a red Ah syllable at your throat. Blue light rays emerge from a blue Hung syllable at their heart and merge into you via a blue Hung syllable at your heart.

Following that, the fourth stage is symbolized in different ways in different texts, such as by a second hung syllable moving from heart to heart, or a green light ray beaming from a Hrih syllable from navel center to naval center, or five different colored lights beaming all at once.

OM, AH, HUNG and HRIH

The Corresponding Empowerments

Through this process of requesting and receiving lights, you are being purified and empowered by the guru. White light purifies your ordinary body and empowers it into nirmanakaya, red light purifies your ordinary speech and empowers it into sambhogakaya. Your ordinary mind is purified by blue light and empowered into dharmakaya. This is followed by light rays symbolizing the inseparable unity of dharmakaya, sambogakaya, and nirmanakaya, called the *svabhavikakaya*.

The guru then dissolves into light, either quickly or gradually, according to the specific text and tradition. The ball of light then dissolves into you and you dissolve into light. Or, you may dissolve into light and into the guru.

You then rest naturally in bright, wordless, freshness. You will gradually become habituated to this and able to experience yourself and the world you inhabit in their natural unity.

The war with the world is over, you have laid down your arms, and a simple undefended joy is present.

How to Try Out the Guru Yoga Practice

If you want to explore the guru yoga practice without commitment to a personal guide or lineage, here is what you can do:

1. Imagine you are in the highest pure land you can conjure up, populated only by buddhas and high-level bodhisattvas. You are a perfect female being of light, red, or rosy, beautified with necklaces and anklets.

2. Next, visualize the perfect wisdom teacher, a figure of light, out in front of you. Give rise to the idea that this is your personal guide, embodying every good quality.

3. Find a place of deep appreciation and gratitude in your heart for this face-to-face encounter. See if you can feel love and faith in this image of awakening. Make it real to the point that tears may even come to your eyes.

4. Imagine all sentient beings arrayed around you, including your family and your worst enemies.

5. Recite a guru yoga mantra for as long as you like. You can use the vajra guru mantra above.

6. When you stop reciting the mantra, receive the four empowerments, blessing you and purifying your obscurations.

7. The guru figure dissolves into you, or vice versa if you prefer. Imagine you are inseparable.

8. Dissolve everything into light.

9. Relax in that fresh and open state.

CHAPTER 16

Integration

Bringing the Ngondro into Your Life

Your Decision

Congratulations! Now you know how to clear away your obstacles to awakening. The rest is up to you. Would you like to go on trudging through the tedium of chasing after things that bring temporary enjoyment? Or would you prefer to aim, instead, for awakening; endless peace for yourself, and good for the many?

Geshe Ngawang Dhargyey (1921-1995), an esteemed Gelugpa scholar, in his *Commentary on the Root Texts for Mahamudra* wrote:

> In fact, among the masters of all the traditions of Buddhism in Tibet, there has been no disagreement that the way to lead disciples onto the path to enlightenment is through the preliminary practices of safe direction, bodhicitta, mandala offerings, Vajrasattva purification, and guru yoga.

Translated and published by Alexander Berzin on his huge *Study Buddhism* website, this Geshe confirms how indispensable these practices are.

Out of humility, most Rinpoches don't disclose how many times they have completed the five accumulations. It's a given that they have done plenty. We know that Dudjom Rinpoche (1904-1987) completed three. The mother of two important tulkus, Mayum Kunsang Dechen (Tulku Urgyen Rinpoche's spouse), completed thirteen. I've heard tell that Adzom Drukpa's early twentieth-century disciples from eastern Tibet completed ngondro up to one hundred times, with great hardship.

I knew Lama Pema Dorje Rinpoche very well. He was known for his accomplishment of Vajrayana practices other than ngondro. But when he was quite ill at the end of his life, I asked him what he was practicing. He smiled and told me he had let all formal practice go, except for the ngondro he had been doing since he was a kid. That says a lot about ngondro!

Your Call

If you've now given some steps of the ngondro a try, you've probably found that they touched something in you. Your encounter with these powerful trainings may have brought up feelings of joy and openness, or, occasionally, feelings of anxiety and resistance. Either way, you could tell that you'd suspended your usual way of thinking and being, whether it was for a minute or an hour.

Taking a mini-vacation from your usual pre-programmed obsessions and ruminations on personal gains is transformative. And you don't have to go anywhere.

Let's bring to mind, again, all the exceptional people we admire, watch, and listen to: great musicians, winning athletes, brilliant writers, round-the-world sailers, and elite mountain climbers. They have all devoted themselves to one thing in depth. Now that you've gotten a taste of ngondro, can you imagine yourself spending your mornings like that for a few years to do it?

The other day, I found myself saying to a friend, "Time is different now. What seemed like a short time when we were younger is now long." She nodded. We chatted about how we used to participate in Vajrayana group practices without watching the clock.

When I was in my thirties I went to a home temple on Saturday mornings, practiced ngondro with others for two or more hours, socialized, and went home. Of course, it took time to get to the house and park. These days it would be a much bigger deal to get seven people or more to do that every week. Fortunately, we have the internet.

Nowadays, most centers' classes and practices can be accessed online. Some will require you to develop a meditation practice in their style and study Buddhism before ngondro. Others won't. If you are interested, I've included a list of centers that offer ngondro at the back of this book. People have said nice things about these various centers and their teachers to me, yet I am intimately familiar with only a few of them. You can email a center and ask about how to get to meet the main lama and the sangha.

If you aren't truly interested, I wish you well! May you find a practice that suits you.

If you have decided to do it... bravo! I salute you. Get started as soon as possible. The longer you put it off the more you will be delayed. One ngondro practitioner said, "If you do it, don't look back, just do it. Your ego will hate it, but it's powerful stuff."

Ngondro completers stress that you should first decide that you are definitely going to do it, for sure. They say that if you aren't committed to practicing most days, you probably shouldn't start. That may sound harsh, but the underlying point is if you go into it in a non-committal way, you won't follow through. The problem with stopping is that you may feel bad about yourself when your practice peters out, thinking you are lazy or flawed. (I don't see it that way.)

You Can Do It

I will share some words of advice, my own and others, about obstacles that can arise in practice in a little bit. But, first I want to say that it is easy to make too big a deal out of ngondro when you're doing it for the first time. I remember having angst about whether or not I would finish. That was more than twenty-five years ago now. I probably shouldn't say this, but, honestly, it seems kind of cute looking back on it now, like watching a child's tantrum over spilled cereal. In the long term, you will barely remember the problems you face.

You can do this. You can start and you can finish. Lots and lots of people all over the world have. If you have hard days, imagine yourself as the "future you" who has already finished at least one complete ngondro set. Let future you give present you a hug. Have a sense of humor about whatever passing thing seems so important. Enjoy the discovery process and the newness of it all.

One ngondro completer wrote:

> Try not to allow the mind to distinguish ngondro sessions as formal or rigid. Practice in the spirit of 'not-doing'—the sacredness of an ordinary act such as brushing teeth, eating, or going to the bathroom. Ngondro practice goes smoothly if it's not a big deal and is part of an everyday ordinary experience. Focus less on the mind but on the feels tone from the heart—evoking practice from the heart—feeling instead of conceptual visualization, etc.

The Ngondro Process

If you have decided to do the ngondro accumulations, the first step is to receive the reading transmission, called a *lung*, for your lineage ngondro text from a person who has been authorized to give it. A lung consists of someone reading the whole practice text to you quickly, out loud.

Some traditions require that you attend an empowerment ceremony for the central deity of the practice, or for Vajrasattva. A lama may, for example, have a system of giving the required empowerments once a year. More likely, things will not be that predictable and organized. Ask if you can start with only the reading transmission and a commitment to attend the empowerments when they happen.

It will be a huge support for you if there is a weekly in-person or online group practice session with people who are all accumulating the ngondro you are doing. It really expedites things to see how people manage a session, including prostrations and mandala offerings, right up close. After the first year, it may not be as important to you.

"Our sangha has a weekly ngondro group that all started this ngondro at the same time. Some have already completed other ngondro practices and are excellent mentors, especially for some of the intricate mechanics," a ngondro practitioner wrote.

If you don't have access to peer support, you will need to have regular check-ins with an authorized senior student to answer your questions.

What Does It Mean to "Accomplish the Ngondro"?

What is the recommended number of repetitions? How you count and how many you need to do can vary a great deal between lineages. While some of what we do in the Nyingma lineage may have leaked out into this book, what you do with your teacher in your lineage may be different. In any event, all the systems of numerical accumulations are intended to guarantee that you practice a whole lot.

One person said:

...really get to know a practice. It's not about the numbers but about the time spent. The practice unfolds as you start doing it and engaging with it. See the numbers as a guide, accept the practice as a remolding of your mind to truly accept the path and leave your old samsaric outlook and confusion behind.

Wise words.

Policies

Larger organizations will have universal policies about how ngondro is supposed to be done in their system. The policies address the main questions that will come up for you.

I have a tip for you about that. If you have, over time, developed a personal guru-disciple relationship with a teacher, they may flex the guidelines to suit your strengths, problems, situation, and personality. If you have hit a wall with a community rule related to the practice, don't be too shy about approaching the guru directly about it. They want you to keep practicing and not become alienated just because you can't do what others can. After all, there are certainly things you can do that others can't. For example, I couldn't do more than 50,000 prostrations. But I loved the practice as a whole, so I could persist and complete several ngondros. I was curious about different ngondro texts. For those reasons, I can write this book, decades later. I have a wider experience with ngondro texts than most people do.

I highly recommend approaching your teacher with an attitude of humility and positivity. No one likes a complainer. If you have an attitude, they may tell you to do things in a still more challenging way. Not to spite you, but to help you get over it. Also, do not ask questions about accumulation policies in a group setting. Do it privately.

Sequentially Versus Concurrently

Find out from your lama or center whether they want you to do the accumulations sequentially (by finishing one accumulation before starting the next), or a little bit of each in each session. Each teacher will have a unique take on this. Unless you are an athlete, it will take longer to do them sequentially because you have a physical limit to how many prostrations you can do a day. Long is not bad, though.

They could have a different policy for different people. There is no concept that people should be treated the same in Vajrayana Buddhism. You are treated individually.

I talked to one person whose lama was sold on the virtues of doing the accumulations sequentially. If that approach is not working for you, she advised, "Ask if it is permissible to 'chunk' the accumulations into sections of 10,000 or 15,000. Doing these small blocks and switching between practices helps significantly to manage resistance and build up discipline." Clearly, this person has some experience with their lama saying "yes."

On or Off the Cushion

Some lamas allow working students doing ngondro to open the practice in the morning, recite the text up to the point of the training step they are accumulating, and accumulate during breaks in their day. For example, you could quietly accumulate mantras on the train commute, or at lunchtime. In the evening, you would finish saying the remaining sections to close the practice. Others want you to do the practice "on one cushion," completing an entire text reading each time and not counting off-the-cushion accumulations. There are other ways it can be done, as well. Ask.

Alternatives to Prostrations

If you are physically unable to do prostrations, your teacher will probably have an alternative practice for you to do. One of the functions of doing prostrations is to cultivate genuine humility. In my opinion, if you have been humbled by not being able to do prostrations, in some ways it serves the same function.

The Practicalities

Your Space

I've already shared my thoughts on creating a space for your practice in your home. Here are some unique points to consider about your space for ngondro practice.

Set up your shrine, cushions, and table.

You will need the following to be ready for you each day in your space:

- A blanket folded over lengthwise, or a slick Masonite board (have a four-by-eight board cut down the middle lengthwise).

- Carpet sliders for your hands (if you are using the rug system).

- Gardening gloves with the fingers cut out (only if you will be sliding out on a slick surface).

- Volleyball or carpenter knee pads or a second folded blanket for your knees.

- An electronic counter, if you wish.
- A fan to cool you down (ideally).
- A simple mandala offering pan.
- A mandala offering cloth.
- Offering substances (e.g. saffron rice).
- An image of the specific refuge tree for your practice in front of you. Prostrate in that direction.
- A 108 or 110-bead bodhi seed or lotus seed mala.
- A 27-bead hand mala for counting prostrations.

Time Management and Scheduling

The amount of time necessary to get a satisfying number of accumulations done depends on how long your practice text is. Set a daily session length that accords numerically with the date that you plan on finishing your ngondro accumulations. Factor in a first slow year as you get up to speed and adjust to a daily routine.

I remember one tearful dharma friend telling me it was impossible for her to finish her ngondro, that her husband couldn't handle her making that kind of time commitment for her personal interests. I was shocked when I saw her, four years later, in teachings with a great Rinpoche that no one who had not finished ngondro was permitted to attend.

"What changed?" I asked.

"At first I was trying to fit practice in around my life," she said. "Then, I decided to fit life in around my practice."

That being said, in some people's lives there is no way they can do one to two hours per session. In that case, there's another way of approaching ngondro practice. Figure out how much time you realistically have in your day for practice. Then do however much ngondro you can during that timeframe. That way the practice seeps into you like a fine misty rain. Lama Tharchin Rinpoche used to use that example. The drizzle seems like nothing, but eventually, you find yourself soaking wet. That's what you want to happen with any practice.

As one ngondro practitioner wrote: "One essential part is maintaining the continuity of practice. Practice is like charging a battery, if you unplug for a full day it wears away the energy of the practice."

For most people, ngondro happens in the early morning, sometimes in the quiet pre-dawn, starting as early as four in the morning. If you can, gradually adjust yourself to rising two hours earlier than you used to. As a lazy person, I found that starting prostrations before I woke up fully did an end-run around my resistance. If your work is flexible, one possibility might be to negotiate to start your work day as late as eleven. You could also give up your gym membership, and do prostrations as your exclusive form of exercise.

I've known two people who diligently practiced in the evening. There are exceptional people who can do that.

Prostrations

As I mentioned before, prostrations are a much bigger deal in modern society than they were in traditional Tibetan society, because many of us work sedentary jobs and are much less fit. Your guide will advise you about this. For fitness buffs, they are a joyful personal challenge. But for many, they can become a distraction from the practice as a whole. Physical and mental issues can spring up around them, which can prevent people from finishing their other accumulations.

Your prostrations can be done in the refuge section, or while reciting both the refuge and bodhicitta sections, or in several other places according to the specific lineage's custom.

A practitioner wrote, "Go slow with the prostrations to build momentum, and don't stop. Do some every day even if it is not as much as you would have liked…" Don't "…become discouraged, and to really try to sink into the essence and meaning of each part."

Relationships

If you have decided that you want to embark on the path of becoming a "serious practitioner," (that always sounds so grim!) it's going to change who you are, what you are interested in, and what your values are. Here's what I recommend.

If you are in a relationship, have a heart-to-heart with your partner or spouse. I think I am saying that for the third time here because I want you to avoid my past mistakes. Talk with them about why you want to do this thing, how much time you want to put into practice, and the kind of person you want to become.

In a non-Buddhist society, it is unlikely they will share your interest. Please do not abandon your partner to run off and live at a dharma center or seek a relationship with another practitioner. It is hard not to romanticize centers, group retreats, your fellow practitioners, and Tibet. These are all human beings and their ventures whose difficulties you may not see because you don't live around them. Do not neglect or abandon your partner or spouse.

Implicit within the bodhisattva vow is a commitment to perfect six aspects: generosity, ethical self-discipline, patience, perseverance, mental stability, and discriminating awareness. Out of these six, the first three—half of the qualities we cultivate on the path of awakening—are called upon every day in our relationships. Let's practice generosity, patience, and personal discipline with our loved ones.

Psychological Obstacles

How to Accomplish a Big Goal

It is key to begin gradually with kindness to yourself and build from there. Some folks who start with great enthusiasm and throw themselves into doing huge numbers (particularly of prostrations), peter out before long.

The people who continue and meet their ngondro goals are rarely the ones only driven by "because my lama told me to" or "because I would feel ashamed if I didn't."

I believe the people who, not only finish the ngondro, but enjoy it, all hold an image of their future selves in their minds. They identify as future ngondro finishers. They see it as a heroic process that will change them for the better. It's more subtle than a writer's image of themselves holding a finished book in their hands, or a bodybuilder imagining themselves flexing shiny biceps.

I've learned one thing from coaching and supporting people in their ngondros. Practitioners who need an exceptional amount of support from me are not going to be able to sustain the practice. You need to find support within yourself.

Those self-motivated people come to love their ngondro sessions, the exercise, the imagery, the sploosh of the offerings on the mandala pan, and the muttering of mantras. At times, it can be better than a trip to a day spa.

How to Keep It Interesting

The ngondro process is, by definition, repetitive. Initially, it will be novel and captivating, but eventually a day will come when a sense of monotony will creep in. Nip it right in the bud by switching up your approach. If you feel the only way to derive meaning from the practice is to chant slowly and ponderously, do it as fast as you possibly can, instead. If you have been building a careful visualization, switch to feeling the reverberation of the sound in your body. Where does it resonate? If you have been doing the practice in English, switch to Tibetan. If you have been focusing on the meaning, focus mainly on the visualization.

Burn some new incense. Buy some new jewels for your mandala pan. Put fresh flowers on the shrine. Do some prostrations outside in the dirt. Make it fresh!

Finally, try talking to your teacher in your head. "I'm so bored, Rinpoche. Please help me!" Watch what happens.

Mental Resistance

I loved doing ngondro. But, everyone is different. There may be some part of the practice that you don't initially love. Our minds are funny things. You can convince yourself that you love something. You can say to yourself, I love this damn practice because it is so hard for me. Somehow it has managed to root out the exact thing that makes me want to throw this mala across the room!

If you are feeling resistance to completing the ngondro, and you came to the practice from a commitment you made to your teacher—particularly a magnificent awe-inspiring lama—to do it, I urge you to pause for a moment and reflect. Trust and admiration toward your external guide are key components of Tibetan Buddhist practice. But I have known many people who adored their teachers and wanted to please them by doing ngondro, who have never become a regular practitioner. You can reflect on how fortunate you are to have learned about these nine trainings. Instead of thinking that you are doing the practice for your teacher, take ownership of it as a commitment to yourself. *I am choosing to do this ngondro.*

If you realize that ngondro is not for you, why not be honest about it with your teacher? Be gutsy, and ask for an alternative more suited to who you are.

Perfectionism

I've met people who never thought they had done the practice well enough to count numbers at all. Some people did count, then started over and threw out all their previous numbers, because they felt they weren't good (in their own minds).

Listen, everyone who practices ngondro is a human being. Look around at other practitioners you know. They have just as many faults as you do, right? Ngondro is a practice for flawed, unenlightened, people like us. Please keep going.

Fear and Procrastination

In his book, *The War of Art,* Steven Pressfield proposes that the resistance that we all feel when doing difficult things, the things we must do to meet our long-term goals, can be used as a guidepost. Not a guidepost indicating we are a terrible failure, but a sign that this thing is bringing up fear for us.

Pressfield writes that the more central a goal is to actualizing our personal highest purpose, the more fear-triggered resistance will come up for us. Do you think he is right? Have you noticed this in your life? If you have, it follows that a practitioner setting out on the path toward complete awakening would encounter fear-based resistance.

You can use it to your advantage. Notice the huge brick wall of procrastination that comes up when it comes time to do your practice. Use it to serve as an alert that it is critical to follow through. The resistance we feel is like the blaring AMBER alerts Americans get on our cell phones to alert us when a child in the area has been abducted. Instead of a child, your commitment is being abducted by fear.

Adzom Paylo Rinpoche once made this same point as I was nodding off from exhaustion during a teaching. Alluding to the Buddha's encounter with "maras" trying to distract him on the very eve of his awakening, he said that as soon as we approach great accomplishment in our practice, demons will rise up with tremendous force to oppose us. Be aware of that. Don't let the "demons" win.

How To Accomplish the Ngondro Accumulations

1. Figure out the deep personal reason why you want to do it.

2. Form the intention to finish your ngondro, whether it takes six months or ten years.

3. Start slowly and build momentum. After the daily habit is rock solid, push a little beyond your comfort zone. But not too hard.

4. Don't try to do too many prostrations at the beginning. Get your body used to it by doing a small number daily for a while.

5. Keep the routine going, even if your sessions are short and accumulations are small. Aim for the same time each day.

6. Sink into the meaning of each part.

7. Be kind to yourself.

Conclusion

So Long... for Now

I know it sounds corny, but I love you. I love everyone on this beautiful orb we call Earth. I love the sun rising in the morning, I love the black beetle scratching in the dirt. I want you to experience that, too: to be able to say, "I love you" to a mailbox and mean it. To meet each day fresh, with the cobwebs of compulsive thinking at least partially cleared away. To have the frank words of dharma always on the tip of your tongue.

I am not yet awakened. Yet, if I ask myself, "Who is this who sings the ngondro in the morning?" The answer comes: "No one. Everyone. The mother of all."

As I rise stiffly from my morning cup of coffee, the "Yudron" idea visits for a while. It soon fizzles into space, like a sparkler spending itself in the night air, leaving freshness, relaxation, and an indefinable dash of spontaneous joy in its wake.

A dharma life is a beautiful life.

Join us!

Let's dedicate the merit of having read a book about Dharma together:

> Through this merit, may I quickly
> accomplish the state of a glorious teacher.
> May each and every being
> be brought to that same level!

Dakini Heart Essence Ngondro

The Khandro Tuktik Ngondro

This translation of the Dakini Heart Essence ngondro of the Dudjom Tersar lineage of the Nyingma tradition was created by Todd Creamer and myself to be sung in English along with the traditional metered melody. The Khandro Tuktik is a complete cycle of revelatory practices and instructions that came through Dudjom Rinpoche, Jigdral Yeshe Dorje in first half of the twentieth century. Chatral Rinpoche was asked to arrange it for practitioners, and it is his voice speaking in the preamble and colophon. Practicing it seriously requires a reading transmission and special instructions from an authorized teacher. I have included it here as an example of a ngondro text.

REFRESHING HAPPINESS AND EXALTATION

The Recitation Arrangement for the Foundational Practices of the Profound Path of the Dakini Heart Essence

Om Swasti. Jigdral Yeshe Dorje, by your kindness, any fears (jig) of existence and peace are completely removed, blessed by pristine consciousness (yeshe), free (dral) from elaboration. Having served at your indestructible (dorje) lotus feet, I now publish this arrangement of the foundational practices.

For those of good fortune, who desire to attain unsurpassable enlightenment in this life, the very first step is to engage in the foundational practices. There are three practices to be undertaken: the foundational practice for entering a session, the common foundational practice of the four thoughts that turn the mind, and the five special foundational practices for accumulation and purification.

1. Entering a Session:

Let the three gates settle naturally. Visualizing the guru above your head, supplicate with strong yearning and devotion:

DÜ SUM SANG GYÉ TAM CHÉ KYI NGO WO LAMA RIN PO CHÉ KHYEN NO
Essence of all the three times Buddhas, precious guide, know me—
DAK GI GYÜ JIN GYI LAB TU SOL
I pray you bless my mindstream.

Once you've supplicated, gather the guru into yourself and rest in equipoise a while. Beginning every session this way will make your continuum a suitable vessel and pacify obstacles to swift blessings.

2. Purifying the Ground of your Own Continuum: Recitation of the Four Thoughts that Turn the Mind

Join recitation with contemplation by following the instructions about the visualization.

DAK GI DAL JOR TEN ZANG DI

This fine body, free time, and fortune
CHI NÉ YANG YANG NYÉ KA WÉ
will be hard to gain again.
DA RÉ LA MÉ KUN ZANG GI
Now attain the unsurpassed
GO PANG DRUB TÉ ZHEN DÖN JA
Samantabhadra for other's sake.

DA TÉ RIN CHEN LÜ DI YANG
Now this precious body is here, yet
CHI DAK DÜ KYI DRA DANG WÉ
Due to the foe, the evil Ruler of Death,
NAM CHI NGÉ PAR MI DA YI
The time of death is uncertain,
DAK ZHEN MI TAK TSUL DI TA
view self and others as impermanent.

KHOR WÉ NÉ DIR GAR KYÉ KYANG
The states of rebirth we wander through
DÉ WÉ GO KAB MA CHI PÉ
hold no chance of happiness.
SI PÉ DÉ LA MI TA WAR
Don't look for worldly happiness.
NYA NGEN DE PÉ LAM DU JUK
Take the path that leads past sorrow.

DAL JOR LÜ DI DÖN DEN CHIR
While having this body, free time, good fortune,
NYÖN MONG DUK SUM MI GÉ PONG
abandon afflictions, three poisons, non-virtue.
GÉ WÉ LÉ LA BE PA KYÉ
Cultivate dignity, strive in good deeds.
GO SUM DAM TSIK DOM PA SUNG

Guard vows and pledges of the three gates.

Thus, give rise to a mind set on renunciation.

3. The Recitation of the Five Uncommon Foundational Practices

3.1 Go For Refuge:

DÜN KHAR PAK SAM GYE PÉ Ü
Amidst a vast wish-granting tree in the space in front,
SENG TRI PE MA NYI DÉ TENG
on lion throne, lotus, sun-moon seat,
TSA WÉ LAMA TÖ TRENG TSAL
is my root teacher, Tötrengtsal,
DOR JÉ CHANG GI CHA LUK CHEN
in the attire of Vajradhara,
TSO GYAL YUM DANG NYAM PAR JOR
with consort Tsogyal in equal union.
KU NI GEN DÜN SUNG DAM CHÖ
Body is Sangha; speech sacred Dharma.
TUK NI SANG GYÉ RANG ZHIN TÉ
Wisdom mind has the nature of Buddha.
TSA SUM GYAL WA DÜ PÉ NGÖ
They embody the Three Roots Victors,
KYAB YUL GYA TSÖ NGO WOR ZHUK
the essence of oceanic refuge sources.

Supplicate in the manner of 'the jewel which brings together all sources of refuge':

NAMO DAK SOK DRO KÜN JANG CHUB BAR
Namo Until awakening, all beings and I
KÖN CHOK SUM GYI NGO WO NYI
go for refuge with utter devotion
LAMA DOR JÉ DZIN PA LA
in the guide as Vajra Holder,
MI CHÉ GÜ PÉ KYAB SU CHI
essence of the Three Jewels.

3.2 The Mind of Awakening:

Requesting the sources of refuge to bear witness, recite:

HO KHA NYAM DRO WA MA LÜ KÜN
Ho To free all beings, infinite as space,
SI PÉ TSO LÉ DRAL JÉ CHIR
from the ocean of existence,
LA MÉ JANG CHUB CHOK GI SEM
I will fully rouse the supreme
DAK GI YONG SU KYÉ PAR GYI
Mind of Awakening beyond compare.

Finally, light rays radiate from the bodies of the sources of refuge, and immediately, upon contact, any misdeeds and obscurations of self and others everywhere are cleansed and purified. Then, like a flock of birds frightened off by a shot, all beings instantly depart for the celestial realms. The teacher, source of refuge, melts into light and dissolves into you. Rest in equipoise.

3.3 Vajrasattva Visualization and Recitation:

RANG GI CHI WOR PÉ DÉ TENG
Above, on a lotus and moon seat,
HUNG LÉ LAMA DOR JÉ SEM
from HUNG, the guide as Vajrasattva,
DUNG DOK ZHAL CHIK CHAK NYI PA
conch shell white, one face, two hands;
DOR DRIL DZIN PÉ YUM LA KHYÜ
he embraces the consort holding vajra and bell.
DAR DANG RIN CHEN GYEN GYI GYEN
They're adorned with silks and jewels.
TUK KAR DA TENG DOR JÉ TER
On a moon in the hub of a vajra, at the heart
HUNG TAR YIK GYÉ TRENG WÉ KOR
one hundred syllables surround a HUNG,
DÉ LÉ JANG SEM DÜ TSI GYÜN
from that, nectar of awakening flows.
BAB PÉ DIK DRIB NYÉ TUNG KÜN
By descending, bad deeds, darkness, faults and failings
DAK CHING DRI MA MÉ PAR GYUR
become cleansed and purified.

OM BENZRA SATTVA SAMAYA MANU PALAYA   BENZRA SATTVA TÉNOPA TIT'RA DRI DHO MÉ BHAWA   SU TO KHA YO MÉ BHAWA   ANU RAKTO MÉ BHAWA   SU PO KHAYO MÉ BHAWA   SARWA SIDDHIM MÉ PRA YATSA   SARWA KARMA SU TSA MÉ CHITTAM SHRÉ YAM   KURU HUNG   HA HA HA HA HO   BHAGAWAN   SARWA TATAGATA BENZRIA MA MÉ MUÑTSA   BENZRI BHAWA MAHA SAMAYA SATTVA AH

Recite as many times as possible and conclude with:

GÖN PO DAK NI MI SHÉ MONG PA YI
Protector, from ignorance and misconceptions,
DAM TSIK LÉ NI GAL ZHING NYAM
I've gone against and damaged my pledges
LA MA GÖN PÖ KYAB DZÖ CHIK
Teacher, protector, please grant me refuge!
TSO WO DOR JÉ DZIN PA TÉ
Foremost Vajra Holder,
TUK JÉ TSÉ WÉ DAK NYI CHEN
you embody compassion and love.
DRO WÉ TSO LA DAK KYAB CHI
Leader of beings, I go for refuge.

KU SUNG TUK TSA WA DANG YEN LAK GI DAM TSIK NYAM PA TAM CHÉ TOL ZHING SHAK SO
I openly acknowledge and let go of all impairments of the root and branch pledges of body, speech, and mind.

DIK DRIB NYÉ LHUNG DRI MÉ TSOK TAM CHÉ JANG ZHING DAK PAR DZÉ DU SOL
Please purify and cleanse all misdeeds, obscurations, faults, downfalls, and taints.

Having supplicated:

DOR JÉ SEM PA GYÉ ZHIN DZUM PA DANG CHÉ
Vajrasattva smiles with delight and says:

RIK KYI BU KHYÖ KYI DIK DRIB NYÉ TUNG TAM CHÉ DAK PA YIN NO ZHÉ SUNG SHING Ö DU ZHU NÉ RANG LA TIM PAR GYUR

"Noble child, all your misdeeds, obscurations, faults, and downfalls are purified."

Melting into light, Vajrasattva dissolves into me.

Thinking thus, rest in equipoise.

3.4 Mandala Offering:

Visualize the field of refuge in front as before. Recite:

KHAM SUM NÖ CHÜ NANG SI CHÖ
Three realms, worlds, beings, what appears and exists,
DAK LÜ LONG CHÖ GÉ TSOK CHÉ
along with body, wealth, merit, all are offered
KUN ZANG CHÖ TRIN CHEN POR BUL
as vast Samantabhadra offering clouds.
ZHÉ NÉ JIN GYI LAB TU SOL
Accepting them, please grant your blessings.
RATNA MANDALA PUJA HO

Once you have made these offerings, the field for accumulation and mandala offering, in the form of a HUNG dissolves into you. Rest in the state free from concepts of the three spheres.

3.5 Unification with the Guide

NAM DAK YE SHÉ Ö GUR LONG
Within a vast dome of pure wisdom light,
RANG NYI TSO GYAL DHA KI MÉ
I appear as the Dakini, Tsogyal.

CLEARING THE WAY TO AWAKENING

CHI WOR PEMA NYI DÉ TENG
Above my head, on lotus, sun, moon
TSA WÉ LAMA TÖ TRENG TSAL
is the root teacher, Tötrengtsal,
MAR SEL DOR DRIL KHYÜ TAB ROL
bright red, sporting clasped vajra and bell;
TSEN PÉ ZI JIN BAR WÉ KU
body, ablaze with marks and signs,
DAR DANG RIN CHEN GYEN GYI TRÉ
is adorned with silks and jewels,
ZHAB ZUNG DOR JÉ KYIL TRUNG GI
with legs crossed in vajra pose,
GYÉ DZUM Ö ZER LAM MER ZHUK
he dwells in vivid light rays, smiling.

Visualizing the support for accumulation, recite:

HUNG   ORGYEN YUL GYI NUB JANG TSAM
Hung   In the northwest Uddiyana borderland,
PEMA GESAR DONG PO LA
on a lotus blossom,
YA TSEN CHOK GI NGÖ DRUB NYÉ
you gained supreme accomplishment.
PEMA JUNG NÉ ZHÉ SU DRAK
Renowned as the Lotus Born,
KHOR DU KHAN DRO MANG PÖ KOR
surrounding you are many dakinis.

KHYÉ KYI JÉ SU DAK DRUB KYI
We follow in your footsteps.
JIN GYI LOB CHIR SHEK SU SOL
Please approach and grant your blessings.
GURU PEMA SIDDHI HUNG

Guru Pema Siddhi Hung.

The invited wisdom beings and commitment beings merge inseparably.
Next, to accumulate merit and wisdom, combine recitation with prostrations:

HRIH GYAL KÜN NGO WO LAMA LA
Hri Teacher, essence of all Victors.
GO SUM GÜ PÉ CHAK TSAL LO
I pay homage with my three gates;
CHI NANG CHÖ TRIN GYA TSÖ CHÖ
offer outer and inner offering clouds;
TOK MÉ NÉ SAK DIK TUNG SHAK
lay bare beginningless misdeeds and failings.
NAM KAR TSOK LA JÉ YI RANG
I rejoice in all virtuous deeds.
ZAB GYÉ CHÖ KHOR KOR ZHIN DU
Please turn the wheel of Dharma.
NYA NGEN MI DA ZHUK SOL DEB
Remain, not passing beyond sorrow.
GÉ WA SEM CHEN YONG LA NGO
I dedicate merit to the spectrum of beings.
LA MÉ GO PANG CHOK TOB SHOK
May the supreme unsurpassable level be attained!

Thus, make the seven-branch offering. Then with fervent one-pointed devotion, supplicate, inserting The Prayer to the Guru's Three Kayas if desired.

KYÉ KYÉ LAMA TÖ TRENG TSAL
Kye! Kye! Teacher Tötrengtsal,
NYING NÉ GÜ PÉ SOL WA DEB

I pray with heartfelt longing.
JIN GYI LOB SHIK BAR CHÉ SOL
Please bless us, quell all obstacles.
WANG ZHI KUR CHIK NGÖ DRUB TSOL
Confer four empowerments! Grant accomplishments!
Having supplicated, recite:

OM AH HUNG MAHA GURU SARWA SIDDHI HUNG

When finished, repeat the above prayer once more.
Then single-mindedly recite these words, imagining that you receive the four empowerments:

LAMÉ KU YI NÉ ZHI NÉ
From the teacher's four places,
Ö ZER KAR MAR TING JANG TRÖ
white, red, blue, and green lights emanate,
RANG GI NÉ ZHIR TIM PA YI
dissolving into my four places.
DRIB ZHI DAK NÉ WANG ZHI TOB
From four veils clearing, four empowerments are received.

Having received the empowerments, once more supplicate with fervent longing and devotion:

LA MA RANG TIM YER MAY PAR
The teacher melts into me, inseparably,
DAY CHEN Ö SEL NGANG DU GYUR

within a state of luminous great bliss.

Basking in the innate radiance of knowingness and emptiness, rest in the equipoise of suchness.

Before arising from the practice session, recite:

PAL DEN TSA WAY LA MA RIN PO CHÉ
Glorious precious root teacher,
DAK GI CHI WOR PÉ MÉ DEN ZHUK LA
atop a lotus seat above my head,
KA DRIN CHEN PO GO NÉ JÉ ZUNG TÉ
with great kindness, care for me,
KU SUNG TUK KYI NGÖ DRUP TSEL DU SÖL
grant the siddhis of body, speech and mind.
KYÉ WA KÜN DU YANG DAK LA MA DANG
May I never be born apart from the teacher,
DREL MÉ CHÖ KYI PAL LA LONG CHÖ NÉ
and enjoy an abundance of Dharma.
SA DANG LAM GYI YÖN TEN RAB DZOK TÉ
May I fully perfect the stages and paths,
DOR JÉ CHANG GI GO PANG NYUR TOB SHOK
swiftly attain the level of Vajra Holder!

GÉ WA DI YI NYUR DU DAK
Through this merit, may I swiftly
PAL DEN LA MA DRUP GYUR NÉ
accomplish the state of the glorious teacher.
DRO WA CHIK KYANG MA LÜ PA
May all beings, every one,
DÉ YI SA LA GÖ PAR SHOK
be brought to that same level!

Combine the usual prayers of dedication and aspiration, such as Glorious Copper Colored Mountain, then engage in daily activities. Between sessions, bring all appearances, sounds, and thoughts to the path as the display of the teacher's three secrets and, thereby make the activities of all three gates meaningful.

Also, as previously instructed, strive in the Four Common Thoughts to Turn the Mind, and the stages of accumulation and purification, purely repeating the words, until experiences and realizations are revealed one by one. Regarding the numbers for the stages of accumulation and purification: refuge, bodhicitta, the hundred syllable mantra, mandala offerings, the seven branches with full prostrations, and the teacher supplication verse, these all must be repeated a hundred thousand times each plus the extra repetitions. Practice with intense exertion until accumulating at least a million recitations of the teacher mantra. In this way, due to the powerful descent of blessings, special qualities will emerge effortlessly and become your support.

May all beings weary of the path of existence, climb the profound stairway to the excellent abode of the supreme level and gain the great relief of ease.

COLOPHON

For this text, *Refreshing Happiness and Exaltation: Liturgy of the Foundational Practices of the Profound Path of The Dakini Heart Essence*, I added vajra words from other sources to what was unclear in the root terma and combined them all into one clearly arranged text. I, Chatral Sangye Dorje, a servant of many vajra holders who represent Padmasambhava, wrote this at the isolated place Lha Gampo in the glorious region of Dvagpo, an open cheerful place. For those who make a connection with this practice, may it result in their reaching the highest level of the ever-excellent Padmasambhava, and Consort.

Sarwa Daka Layanam Bhawatu
May all be auspicious!

Source: Collected Works of Dudjom Jigdral Yeshé Dorjé, Vol. MA (16), pp. 541-550
Translated by Todd Creamer and Yudron Wangmo 2021

Glorious Copper Colored Mountain Aspiration Prayer

SANG GYÉ KÜN GYI NGO WO KA DRIN CHEN
Kindest essence of all Buddhas,
ORGYEN RIN PO CHÉ LA SÖL WA DEP
To the precious one from Udyan, I pray.
NAM SHIK TSÉ DI NANG WA NUP MA TAK
As life's appearances start to fade,
PÉ MA Ö DU KYÉ WAR JIN GYI LOP
bless me with birth in the Palace of Lotus Light.

Written by Jñana.

Centers to Consider

Practitioners have spoken highly of these English-speaking Tibetan Buddhist centers in Canada and the United States, as being good for beginners and ongoingly supportive of ngondro practice. I don't know the reputations of centers elsewhere in the world. Keep in mind that there is no licensing board for Tibetan Buddhist lamas. You must look into things yourself.

Abhaya Fellowship
Nyingma
Chakung Jigme Wangdrak Rinpoche
Longsal Ling
1833 Arlington Blvd
El Cerrito, CA
www.abhayafellowship.org

Chagdud Gonpa Centers
Nyingma
Various Lamas
Padma Ling — Spokane
Rigdzin Ling — Junction City, CA
Dechen Ling — Cottage Grove, OR
Ati Ling — Cazadero, CA
Amrita — Seattle, Washington
www.chagdudgonpa.org

Chicago Ratna Shri
Drikung Kagyu
Drupon Rinchen Dorjee
1038 Woodlawn Avenue
Des Plaines IL, 60016
www.chicagoratnashri.com

Clear Light Dzogchen Circle and Retreat House
Nyingma
Lama Ingmar Pema Dechen,
Lama Ngawang Tenzin/Sergio Guitierrez
Hattiesburg, Mississippi
2419976281392716
Ingmarpema@gmail.com

Copper Mountain Institute
Nyingma
Lama Carol Hoy
286 Ranchitos Road
Corrales, NM 87048
www.coppermount.org

Dharmakaya Center
Kagyu and Rime
Trungam Gyalwa Rinpoche
Khenchen Rinpoche Drupon Trinley Paljor
Dharmakaya Center For Wellbeing
191 Cragsmoor Road
Cragsmoor, NY 12566
www.dharmakayacenter.org
(Separate tracks for the public and Buddhist practitioners)

Dawn Mountain

Nyingma
Lama Rigdzin Drolma and Lama Namgyal Dorje
Houston, TX
www.dawnmountain.org

Dharmata Foundation
Nyingma
Anam Thubten
Dharmata Foundation
Dhumatala (Dhyana Hall)
235 Washington Avenue
Point Richmond, CA 94801
www.dharmata.org

Dorje Ling Buddhist Center
Nyingma
Matt Small
3200 NW Skyline Blvd.
Portland, OR 97229
www.dorjelingportland.org

The Drikung Meditation Center
Drikung Kagyu
Lama Konchok Sonam
29 Mohawk Street
Danvers, MA 01923
www.drikungboston.org

Dzokden
Kalachakra
Khentrul Rinpoche
3436 Divisadero Street

San Francisco, California, 94123
www.dzokden.org

Foundation for the Preservation of the Mahayana Tradition (FPMT)
Gelug
Centers in Ontario, California, Florida, Massachusetts, Montana, Nevada, New Mexico, New York, North Carolina, Vermont, Oregon, Virginia, and Washington
www.fpmt.org

Garchen Buddhist Institute
Drikung Kagyu
Chino Valley, AR 86323
www.garchen.net

Gar Drolma Choling
Drikung Kagyu
Khenpo Samdup Rinpoche
1329 Creighton Avenue
Dayton, OH 45420
www.gardrolma.org

Heruka Institute
Nyingma
Tulku Yeshe Dorje
www.facebook.com/herukainstitute

Kagyu Changchub Chuling
Shangpa Kagyu
Lama Eric Triebelhorn
4936 NE Skidmore Street

Portland, Oregon 97218
www.kcc.org

Kagyu Sukha Choling
Shangpa Kagyu
Lama Yeshe and Lama Pema
109 Clear Creek Drive, Suite 101
Ashland, OR
www.kscashland.org

Katog Choling
Nyingma
Khentrul Lodro Thaye
Parthenon, AR
www.katog.org

Lama Lena
Dzogchen and Mahamudra
Lama Lena Yeshe Kaytup
Tso Pema, India and U.S.
www.lamalenateachings.com

Lotus Dharma Garden Foundation
Nyingma
Loppon Jigme Rinpoche
Elk, California
www.facebook.com/LotusDharmaGarden

Mangala Shri Bhuti
Nyingma
Dzigar Kongtrul Rinpoche
Colorado and Vermont
www.mangalashribhuti.org

Mayum Mountain Foundation
Nyingma
Loppon Yudron Wangmo
Copperopolis, CA
www.mayummountain.org

Mindrolling Lotus Garden
Nyingma and Kagyu
Mindrolling Khandro Rinpoche
108 Bodhi Way
Stanley, VA
www.lotusgardens.org

Nalandabodhi International
Nyingma and Kagyu
Dzogchen Ponlop Rinpoche and others
Headquarters: Nalanda West
3902 Woodland Park Ave N
Seattle, WA 98103
They have other centers in the U.S., Canada, and elsewhere
www.nalandabodhi.org
www.nalandawest.org

Natural Dharma Fellowship
Mahamudra and Dzogchen
Lama Willa Blythe Baker and Lama Liz Monson
253 Philbrick Hill Road
Springfield, MA 03284
www.naturaldharma.org

Ngondro Gar
Nyingma or Kagyu Ngondro

Dzongsar Khyentse Rinpoche and mainly other instructors
An online program affiliated with Siddhartha's Intent.
www.ngondrogar.org

Odiyana Institute
Nyingma
Tulku Orgyen Phunstok
1524 Anacapa Street
Santa Barbara, CA 93101
www.odiyanainstitute.org

Orgyen Khandro Ling
Nyingma
Anyen Rinpoche
3300 Josephine Street
Denver, CO 80205
www.orgyenkhandroling.org

Padma Rigdzin Ling
Nyingma
Lama Jigme Rinpoche
48 Laswell Street
Henderson, NV 89015
www.padmarigdzinling.org

Padmasambhava Buddhist Centers
Padma Samye Ling
Nyingma
Khenpo Tsewang Dongyal and others
618 Buddha Highway
Sidney Center, NY 13839
www.padmasambhava.org

Palyul Retreat Center
Nyingma
Karma Kuchen Rinpoche and others
359 Hollow Road
McDonough, NY 13801
https://retreat10.palyul.org

Phurba Thinley Ling
Nyingma
Khandro Kunzang Dechen Chodron
1781 Views End Lane
Lansing, IA, 52151
www.phurbathinleyling.org

Pristine Mind Foundation
Nyingma
Orgyen Chowang Rinpoche
P.O. Box 10671
San Rafael, CA 94912-1067
www.pristinemind.org

Riwotsegya
Nyingma
Rangrig Rinpoche
133 Eilen Avenue
York, ON M6N 1W3
Canada
www.riwotsegya.ca

Sakya Monastery of Tibetan Buddhism
Sakya
Khondung Avikrita Vajra Sakya and others

108 NW 83rd Street
Seattle, WA 98117
www.sakya.org

Samden Ling
Nyingma
Lama Jacqueline Mandel
Portland, OR
www.samdenling.org

Sukhasiddhi Foundation
Shangpa Kagyu
Wisdom River Meditation Center
Lama Dondrup and associates
7110 Redwood Blvd, Suite B
Novato, CA 94945
www.sukhasiddhi.org

Tara Mandala
Nyingma/Kagyu/Chod
Lama Tsultrim Allione, Tulku Osel Dorje, and others
Pagosa Springs, CO
www.taramandala.org

Tergar International
Kagyu/Nyingma
Online Classes on Ngondro
Yongey Mingyur Rinpoche
Many groups in the U.S.
Chinese Center: Yongey Buddhist Center
682 Carlsbad Street
Milpitas, CA 95035
www.tergar.org

Three Rivers Tibetan Cultural Center
Drikung Kagyu
Khenpo Choepel and Lama Kalsang
7313 Florence Avenue
Pittsburgh, PA 15218
www.threeriverstibetancc.org

Thubten Choling
Gelug
Ven. Ngakpa Kalzang Dorje (Nyingma) in residence
5810 Wilson Avenue
Duncan, B.C.
Canada, V9L 1K4
1-250-748-6028

Tibetan Meditation Center
Drikung Kagyu
Khenpo Tsultrim Tenzin Rinpoche
9301 Gambrill Park Road
Frederick, MD 21702
www.drikungtmc.com

Tsintamani Choling
Nyingma
Lama Lakshey Zangpo
Santa Cruz, CA
www.tsintamani.org

Tubten Osel Choling
Nyingma
Sogan Rinpoche

San Francisco Bay Area, Nevada, Italy
www.tuptenoselcholing.org

Vajra Vidya
Karma Kagyu
Khenpo Lobzang Tenzin and associates
PO Box 1083
3203 Camino Baca Grande
Crestone, CO 81131
www.vajravidya.com

Vajrayana Foundation
Nyingma
Lama Sonam Tshering Rinpoche and Tulku Thadrel Rinpoche
Pema Osel Ling
2013 Eureka Canyon Road
Watsonville, CA 95076
www.vajrayana.org

Yeshe Nyingpo
Nyingma
Namgyal Dawa Rinpoche
19 West 16th Street
New York, NY 10011
www.dudjomtersar.org

Yeshe Long
Nyingma
Dza Kilung Rinpoche
6900 Humphrey Road
Clinton, WA 98236
www.kilung.org

Controversial Organizations

In the past decade, European and American Tibetan Buddhist organizational leaders have been rocked by the ultimate dilemma. What do you do when the central guru is accused of crimes of abuse, or the organization they created has come to be regarded as a high-control cult? On the one hand, they are sworn to maintain pure perception of both their lamas and their dharma friends. On the other, they are kind Buddhists who want to help people who feel utterly traumatized. What will become of the organization's altruistic projects and charities? How do they respond to lawsuits or criminal charges?

Here are examples of groups still active in the U.S. and Canada that have faced this dilemma: Balanced View, Dharma Ocean, Diamond Way Buddhism, Dzogchen Center and Foundation, Dzogchen Shri Singha, Karma Thegsum Choling, Kagyu Thubten Choling, Kagyu Triyana Dharmachakra, Kunsang Palyul Choling, New Kadampa Tradition, Rigpa International, and Shambhala International. If you find yourself interested in one of these groups, please do deep research into them to see what they have or haven't reformed since their controversy. Visit and check your gut reaction.

The responses of the boards of directors of these organizations have ranged from defensively doubling down on their denial of the allegation (while continuing the status quo and attacking the accuser) all the way to asking their leader to step down, replacing him with new lamas and new safeguards. Rarely does the public get to know the outcome of legal situations, because they are settled with the alleged victims out of court.

In any religion, there are exemplary leaders, and there are hypocrites. There are healthy organizations and there are cults. And there are leaders and organizations that have both qualities. Buddhism is no exception.

Beginner's Glossary

Fifty-two Words to Get You Up to Speed

This a reader-friendly glossary of Sanskrit (skt.) and Tibetan (tib.) words used in this book for English-reading practitioners. The words are spelled roughly as they sound, and how you will see them written in ngondro texts. To keep it simple, I have not used phonetic markers.

Abhisheka (skt.), wang kur (tib.): Empowerment. This is a ceremony performed by an authorized and qualified person. It serves several functions. It is a necessary gateway into Vajrayana Buddhist practice and a tool with the transformative power to ripen or mature your buddha-nature. Vows are bestowed that serve as training wheels to avoid subtle pitfalls in practice; crucially, to see the world and its occupants with pure perception, starting with the guru leader of the ceremony and the people who received empowerment at the same time.

Abhistana (skt.), jinlab (tib.): Transformative power. Liberating potency. Blessing. A transformative encounter with magnificence that awakens our dormant buddha-nature.

Alaya vijnyana (skt.), kun zhi nampar shépa (tib.): Storehouse consciousness. An underlying consciousness that holds karmic seeds that gradually mature until ripe, at which point they manifest as karmic consequences. The alaya is one of eight consciousnesses of sentient beings, according to an influential school of

Mahayana philosophy known as Yogacara. This consciousness carries our sense of a truly-existing ongoing self and our subconscious karmic habits and impulses.

Anuttara samyak-sambodhi (skt.), lana med par dzog pa'i jang chub (tib.): Unsurpassed complete awakening. This Mahayana term highlights the superiority of the billion-year project of attaining ultimate buddhahood so that one can generate sambhogakaya and nirmanakaya emanations to free all sentient beings from the pain, stress, and suffering of samsara, as opposed to attaining nirvana only for oneself. Vajrayana Buddhism claims to shorten the process of achieving anuttara samyak-sambodhi.

Arhat (skt.), dro chompa (tib.) An arhat is someone who has eliminated all ties to samsara (such as desire, aggression, jealousy, greed, pride, ignorance, doubt, and a sense of an ongoing self). After liberation they can continue to live in a state called "nirvana with residue." When they die, they will be free of samsara, because they attained "nirvana without residue." This is also known as parinirvana. They will not be reborn in any world.

Bardo (tib.), antarabhava (skt.). Transitional periods during the life, death, and rebirth of a sentient being. It is commonly used to refer to the periods between death and rebirth.

Bodhicitta (skt.), jangchub kyi sem (tib.). The wish to gain awakening for the benefit of sentient beings in samsara. The cultivation of boundness and equal love and compassion for all sentient beings is a necessary prerequisite. Ultimate bodhicitta is the realization of emptiness. The same word has additional meanings in the Vajrayana yogic traditions and in the Dzogchen literature.

Bodhisattva (skt.), jyang chub sempa (tib.). A person whose Buddhist practice is dedicated to attaining buddhahood for the benefit of sentient beings suffering in samsara. This is contrasted with people seeking a state of personal nirvana without returning to help others.

Buddha (skt.), sang gye (tib.): Fully awakened from ignorance. A buddha is utterly purified (sangpa) and developed (gyepa). A buddha has realized jnana—pristine wisdom—and is free from all dualistic thoughts and afflictive emotions.

Dharani (skt.), zung (tib.). Buddhist incantations with specific purposes, mostly in Sanskrit and Pali. They can be distilled versions of important texts, for use to trigger recall of what has been studied. Or, they can be recited or inscribed in charms and used for protective magic and healing. Finally, they can help with concentration.

Dharma (skt.). cho (tib.). In the context of ngondro, *Dharma* refers to the teachings of Buddhism. The word has many other meanings which are determined by context.

Dharmakaya (skt.), cho kyi ku (tib.). All buddhas' realization of the true nature of reality. Thus, it is said to be perfectly pure and formless.

Dharmata (skt.), chonyid (tib.): Ultimate truth. The true nature of all phenomena. (Literally "phenomena-ness")

Duhkha (skt.), dukngel (tib.): Suffering, pain, stress. The suffering of getting what you don't want, not getting what you do want, etc., such as birth, sickness, old age and death.

Gelug (tib.) Literally: the way of virtue). A tradition in Tibet founded in the 14th century by Je Tsongkhapa, based on an earlier tradition called the Kadampa, that stresses a deep and intensive study of the Mahayana Buddhist scriptures to cultivate insight into the doctrine of emptiness. It eventually became the most widely established tradition in Tibet, with four large monastic universities in central Tibet that attracted monks, near and far, to live, study and practice. Following thorough Mahayana training, the practitioner can opt to undertake tantric ngondro practices, various yidam practices, inner yogic practices, and Mahamudra, under the guidance of one's guru.

Ishtadevata (skt.), yidam (tib.): Meditational deity. A buddha or bodhisattva that is taken up as a heart practice by a Vajrayana practitioner. In the Sarma schools, one's own lama, one's meditational deity, and the dharma protectors are sometime referred to as the three roots of tantric practice. In the Nyingma school, yidam practice is broken down further into three types. The guru practices are focused on a guru figure such as Guru Rinpoche. These practices are the source of abhistana. The yidam practices are focused on symbolic deities that usually do not mimic the attributes of human beings, such as Vajrakilaya. These are the sources of spiritual accomplishment. The dakini practices are focused on female buddhas such as Vajrayogini. These are the sources of enlightened activity. This triad are what are referred to as the "three roots" in the Nyingma tradition.

Jnana (skt.), yeshe (tib.): Wisdom. In Mahayana Buddhism, *yeshe* is defined as the wisdom of a buddha (non-conceptual wisdom). In Dzogchen, it refers to the pristine consciousness within each person.

Kagyu (tib.). The Kagyu tradition of the present day is an umbrella term for four surviving independent lineages that descend from the Indian Mahasiddha Tilopa. The Karma, Drikung, Taklung, and Drukpa Kagyu lineage centers in English-speaking countries have commonalities. Additionally, there is the Shangpa Kagyu, formerly a secret path of practice originating from the Indian mahasiddha Niguma. Kagyu centers usually teach the basics of Mahayana Buddhism, both the practices (shamatha, vipasyana, mind-training, and tonglen), and philosophy. Outer tantric practices of peaceful singular deities, such as Chenrezig, Tara, or Amitabha are practiced. Practitioners then typically do ngondro, and more advanced Vajrayana deity practices such as Chakrasamvara, Vajrayogini, and Hevajra, the Six Yogas, and Mahamudra.

Kalyanamitra (skt.), gewa'i she nyen (tib.). A spiritual friend who supports one on the path.

Karuna (skt.), tukje (tib.): Compassion. In general Buddhism this word means compassion. In Dzogchen, it refers to the uncontrived responsive compassion of our basis.

Kusali (skt): Literally "beggar." A Buddhist practitioner who has few possessions and wanders. There is a short practice called the Kusali included in some ngondro texts, related to the Chod tradition of Tibet, founded in the eleventh century by the great female adept Machig Labdron. It involves visualizing ejecting one's consciousness into space as a wisdom dakini, followed by offering your imagined human body as a feast.

Lung (tib.): Reading transmission.

Mahamudra (skt.), chag gya chenpo (tib.) The pinnacle practice of the Sarma traditions. An advanced meditation on the nature of mind.

Mahasandhi, Atiyoga (skt.), Dzogchen (tib.): great perfection. Dzogchen is regarded as the pinnacle teaching of the Nyingma School. Brought to Tibet in the eighth century by Padmasambhava, Vimalamitra, and Vairochana, it has its own rich literature, terminology, outlook, practices, conduct, and subtle anatomy. Although traditionally practiced after ngondro and yidam practices from Vajrayana Buddhism, in the contemporary world some practices are freely available.

Mahayana (skt.), thegpa chen po (tib.): Greater vehicle. Vehicle means that which will carry the practitioner to enlightenment. A Mahayana practitioner studies and practices the Mahayana sutras and shastras with the help of a virtuous spiritual friend. There are varied ways to do that, but they all share the altruistic motivation to awaken solely to free all sentient beings from samsara.

Mala (skt), trengwa (tib). A Buddhist rosary for counting mantras or prayers.

Mandala (skt.), kyil khor (tib.): Sacred circle. The Tibetan word literally means, "center and circumference." A central principle and its surrounding field as depicted in art or metaphor.

Mudra (skt.), chag gya (tib.). In this book, *mudra* refers to sacred hand gestures that accompany Vajrayana ritual.

Ngondro (tib.): Preliminary or foundational. Literally, "what goes before." The word most commonly refers to a set of trainings like those described in this book, usually arranged as a liturgy. But, it can refer to any prerequisite practice that prepares one for another practice.

Ngowo (tib.): Essence. As a Dzogchen term, it refers to essence of one's basis, emptiness.

Nirmanakaya (skt.), tulku (tib.): Manifest body of awakening. Of the five kayas, or "bodies," of awakening, the nirmanakaya is the manifest one; visible and usually physical. It naturally arises from the dharmakaya to help unrealized sentient beings. A "supreme nirmanakaya" is the principal buddha of an eon that is fortunate enough to have one. "Diversified nirmanakayas" are objects that benefit sentient beings, such as food, water and dharma art. "Nirmanakayas of birth" are the rebirths of awakened high-level bodhisattvas and buddhas from the past.

Nirvana (skt), nyangde (tib.). The end of suffering and afflictive emotions, leading to release from samsara.

Nyingma tradition (tib.). The ancient tradition, also known as the *ngagyur*, the early translation school. This school is based on the first arrival of Buddhism from India and Oddiyana in the eighth century CE by Padmasambhava (Guru Rinpoche) and a handful of others. When a new influx of teachers, texts, and translators arrived in Tibet from India in the eleventh century, these pre-existing practice traditions known as the Nyingma (ancient) in comparison with the Sarma (new). Nowadays, a practitioner in English-speaking countries will find Nyingma centers encourage ngondro practice, followed by yidam practices, yogic practices, and Dzogchen. Some have embraced sitting meditations to accommodate contemporary preferences. Mahayana studies are usually not as strongly emphasized as they are at Sarma centers.

Punya (skt.), sonam (tib.): Merit or positive karmic force. This is the accumulation of wholesome karma that carries over into the future.

Rangzhin (tib.). As a Dzogchen term, it refers to the nature of one's basis, clarity.

Sakya Tradition. One of the main Sarma schools of Tibetan Buddhism, founded in the eleventh century. The leadership is a unique male hereditary system within a Tibetan family. Their main Vajrayana system of practice is called *lam dre*, "the path and fruition," which originally came from the Indian Mahasiddha Virupa, and is connected with the Hevajra Tantra. Sakyas are renowned for their devotion to the study of traditional texts. Contemporary practitioners visiting a Sakya center will find practices such as shamatha sitting meditation, ngondro, and simple meditations on peaceful deities such as Tara or Chenrezig, and eventual progression into lam dre.

Sambogakaya (skt.), long ku (tib.): Enjoyment body. Buddhas can emanate as visions of deities and pure realms to guide advanced practitioners. Their visionary nonmaterial spiritual bodies are depicted in traditional Tibetan art as supple, elegant, and ornamented with necklaces, bracelets, crowns, etc.

Samsara (skt.), khorwa (tib.): Cyclic existence. A continuous series of life, death and birth as an ordinary sentient being who is subject to stress, pain, and suffering.

Sangha (skt.), du de (tib.): A Buddhist community. The word *sangha* in Buddhism classically referred only to communities of monks and nuns. Sangha is now to used to refer to any community of Buddhists who study and practice together.

Shamatha (skt.), zhi ne (tib.): Tranquility, calm abiding. This is a style of meditation that involves focusing on something, be it a material object, a visualization, a sound, a smell, or a taste, or, most commonly, the breath. There is also shamatha which is not focused on an object; simply sitting and leaving your mind in its naturally calm and relaxed state, occasionally checking and reminding oneself that one is meditating.

Shastra (skt.), tencho (tib.): Discourse, commentary. Authentic traditional texts that formally explain the meaning of the Buddha's teachings.

Shunyata (skt.), tongpa nyid (tib.): Emptiness. A critical term in Buddhist philosophy for how everything lacks permanent, solid, inherent existence.

Sutra (skt.), do (tib.): Scripture. In Buddhism, these are scriptures regarded as the body of the teachings Shakyamuni Buddha (sixth to fourth centuries BCE) that he gave to his disciples after his awakening. They were memorized and passed down orally until the first century BCE when they were recorded in Indian languages. The Mahayana sutras appeared later in India, starting around the first or second century AD. They were introduced to China and other parts of East Asia, where they became influential, and where new sutras appeared. The belief that Mahayana sutras are literally the words of Shakyamuni Buddha is a religious one, strongly held by many.

Svabhavikakaya (skt.), ngowo nyid ku (tib.): The inseparability of the three kayas.

Tantra (skt.), gyud (tib.). The original authoritative texts of the Vajrayana Buddhism. Tantra, or Tantrayana, is sometimes used as a synonym for Vajrayana. More broadly, it means a thread, continuum, mindstream, or method.

Tathagatagarbha (skt.), dezhin sheg pa'i nyingpo (tib.), and **Sugatagarbha** (skt.), dewar sheg pa'i nyingpo (tib.): Buddha-nature (synonyms.) Tathagata and Sugata are both words that refer to buddha. *Nyingpo* means essence or core, sometimes translated using similar words such as "heart," "womb," "embryo," or "seed." This crucial Mahayana concept is that all sentient beings have awakening already present within us, but it is dormant or undeveloped.

Vajra (skt.), dorje (tib.): Immutable, indestructible. In the pre-Buddhist Rigveda, a vajra was an indestructible weapon wielded by the powerful god Indra. In Vajrayana Buddhism the word can refer to the qualities of emptiness, which cannot be destroyed, which are vajra-like because they are invincible, indestructible, firm, etc. Or it can refer to highly symbolic metal scepters which are held in a practitioner's right hand (along with a bell in the left) to enact mudras in ceremonies.

Vajrasattva (skt.), dorje sempa (tib.). A sambhogakaya buddha that symbolizes purity. Vajrasattva is the essence of all buddhas, traditionally depicted holding a vajra in the right hand at the heart and a bell at the left hip.

Vajrayana (skt.), dorje thegpa (tib.): The vajra vehicle. Vajrayana is also known as Mantrayana, Tantrayana, and Secret Mantra. This is a Buddhist tradition of tantric practice that developed in medieval India and spread, taking hold, most notably, in Tibet, Nepal, Mongolia, and Japan. Suitable to the subset of Mahayana practitioners who have the ability to grasp it, its practices transform consciousness through sustaining pure perception of oneself, the world, and other beings. A committed relationship with one or more lineage-holding gurus is a central feature. The practices are many and varied. They include mantra, visualization, mudra, yogas, meditations, dance, art, prayer, and ceremony.

Vidya (skt.), rigpa (tib.): Pure awareness. In Dzogchen it means that which knows, or sees, the nature of reality, free of fixation on subject and object. It has other meanings in other contexts.

Yogi (m) and **yogini** (f) (skt.), **naljorpa** (m) and **naljorma** (f): A practitioner. The word is customarily used for a serious practitioner of Vajrayana, Mahamudra, or Dzogchen. It literally means, one who is united with the natural state.

Further Reading

The Foundation Practices

Chowang, Orgyen. *From Foundation to Summit: A Guide to Ngöndro and the Dzogchen Path*. Shambhala.

Dudjom Rinpoche, Jigdrel Yeshe Dorje. *A Torch Lighting the Way to Freedom*. Shambhala.

Gyaltsap, Shechen. *A Chariot to Freedom: Guidance from the Great Masters on the Vajrayana Preliminary Practices*. Shambhala.

Kaminsky, Greg. *PRONAOS: Reflections on the Preliminary Practices of Buddhist Tantra from a Western Perspective*. Tanagana.

Khandro, Choying. *The Heart of the Cho: Volume One: Cho Foundations*. Dakini's Whisper Media.

Khyentse, Dzongsar Jamyang. *Not for Happiness: A Guide to the So-called Preliminary Practices*. Shambhala.

Mingyur, Yongey. *Turning Confusion into Clarity: A Guide to the Foundation Practices of Tibetan Buddhism*. Shambhala.

Newman, Bruce. *A Beginner's Guide to Tibetan Buddhism: Notes from a Practitioner's Journey*. Snow Lion.

Norbu, Thinley. *Cascading Waterfall of Nectar*. Shambhala.

Preece, Rob. *Preparing for Tantra: Creating the Psychological Ground for Practice*. Snow Lion.

Rinpoche, Dilgo Khyentse. *The Excellent Path to Enlightenment: Oral Teachings on the Root Text of Jamyang Khyentse Wangpo*. Boulder, Colorado: Snow Lion.

Rinpoche, Gyatrul and Khandro, Sangye Khandro. *Great Perfection Buddha in the Palm of the Hand: Instructions on the Preliminary Practices of the Namchö Tradition.* Vimala.

Rinpoche, Patrul. *The Words of My Perfect Teacher.* Yale University Press; revised edition.

Sangpo, Khetsun and Hopkins, J. *Tantric Practice in the Nyingma.* Snow Lion.

Sherab, Palden (Khenchen) and Dongyal, Tsewang (Khenpo). *Illuminating the Path: Ngondro Instructions According to the Nyingma School of Vajrayana Buddhism.*

Tharchin, Tsedrup. *The Preliminary Practice of the New Treasures of Dudjom A Commentary on the Dudjom Tersar Ngondro.* Bero Jeydren.

Sakya Trizin 42. *The Fundamental Practices: A Modern Ngondro Guide.* Wisdom. (To be released January 28, 2025)

Sherdor, Tulku and Rymar, Charlotte. *Entering The Great Expanse.* Blazing Wisdom.

Thrangu, Khenchen. *Four Foundations of Buddhist Practice.* Namo Buddha Publications.

Tromge, Jane. *Ngondro Commentary: Instructions for the Concise Preliminary Practices.* Padma Publishing.

Tulku, Ringu. *The Ngondro: Foundation Practices of Mahamudra.*

Zugchen, Lopon. *The 100-Day Ngondro Retreat: Based on the Longchen Nyingtik and The Words of My Perfect Teacher.*

Steps 1- 4 The Four Thoughts

Kyabgon, Traleg. *Karma: What it Isn't, Why it Matters.* Shambhala.

Rinpoche, Khandro. *This Precious Life: Tibetan Buddhist Teachings on the Path to Enlightenment.* Shambhala.

Shakyamuni, Buddha. *The Exposition of Karma. (Karmavibhanga).* www. 84,000.co

Step 5 Bodhicitta, Sending and Taking Practice, and the Four Immeasurables

Chodron, Pema. *Tonglen, the Path of Transformation*. Vajradhatu Publications.

Drolma, Palden (Lama). *Love on Every Breath: Tonglen Meditation for Transforming Pain into Joy*. New World Library.

Feldman, Christine. *Boundless Heart: The Buddha's Path of Kindness, Compassion, Joy, and Equanimity*. Shambhala.

Palmo, Jetsunma Tenzin. *The Heroic Heart: Awakening Unbounded Compassion*. Shambhala.

Hookham, Shenpen. *Apramanas: Practicing the Four Immeasurables (Living the Awakened Heart)*. CreateSpace.

Wallace, B. Alan. *The Four Immeasurables: Practices to Open the Heart*. Snow Lion.

Gampopa. *Ornament of Precious Liberation*. Wisdom.

Step 9 Unification with the Guide

Khyentse, Dilgo. *The Wish-Fulfilling Jewel: The Practice of Guru Yoga According to the Longchen Nyingthig Tradition*. Shambhala.

Books About Strongly Pursuing your Life's Purpose

Pressfield, Steven. *The War of Art: Break Through Your Blocks and Win Your Inner Creative Battles*. Black Irish Entertainment.

Manson, Mark. *The Subtle Art of Not Giving a Fuck*. Harper.

McRaven, Admiral William H. *Make your Bed: Little Things That Can Change Your Life… and Maybe the World*. Grand Central Publishing.

Contemporary Books On Rebirth:

Bercholz, Samuel and Thaye, Pema Namdol. *A Guided Tour of Hell, a Graphic Memoir*. Shambhala.

Drolma, Delog Dawa Delog. *Journey to Realms Beyond Death*. Padma Publishing

Guyer-Stevens, Stephanie and Pommaret, Françoise. *Divine Messengers: The Untold Stories of Bhutan's Female Shamans*. Shambhala.

Matlock, James G. and Haraldsson. *I Saw A Light And Came Here: Children's Experiences of Reincarnation*. White Crow Books.

Snow, Robert. *Portrait of a Past-life Skeptic*. Llewellyn Publications.

Tucker, Jim B. *Before: Children's Memories of Previous Lives*. St. Martin's.

Tucker, Jim B. *Return to Life: Extraordinary Cases of Children Who Remember Past Lives*. St. Martin's Griffin

Consciousness

Graziano, Michael. "A New Theory Explains How Consciousness Evolved: A Neuroscientist on How We Came to be Aware of Ourselves." *The Atlantic*, June 6, 2016.

Black Buddhists

Kyodo Williams, Angel, (Rev.) Owens, and Rod (Lama), et al. *Radical Dharma: Talking Race, Love, and Liberation*. North Atlantic.

Kyodo Williams, Angel (Rev.). *Being Black: Zen and the Art of Living with Fearlessness and Grace* (Compass). Penguin.

Vesely-Flad, Rima. *Black Buddhists and the Black Radical Tradition*. NYU Press.

Willis, Janice. *Dreaming Me, Black, Baptist and Buddhist*

Yetunde, Pamela Ayo and Giles, Cheryl A. (editors), et al. *Black and Buddhist: What Buddhism Can Teach Us About Race, Resilience, Transformation, and Freedom*. Shambhala.

Women and Tibetan Buddhism

Allione, Tsultrim. *Wisdom Rising: Journey into the Mandala of the Empowered Feminine*. Atria/Enliven Books

Allione, Tsultrim. *Women of Wisdom*. Snow Lion.

Bernard, Elisabeth. *The Sakya Jetsunmas: The Hidden World of Tibetan Female Lamas*. Snow Lion.

Gayley, Holly. *Inseparable across Lifetimes: The Lives and Love Letters of the Tibetan

Visionaries Namtrul Rinpoche and Khandro Tare Lhamo*. Snow Lion.

Gayley, Holly. *Love Letters from Golok: A Tantric Couple in Modern Tibet*. Columbia University Press.

Harding, Sarah. *Niguma, Lady of Illusion*. Snow Lion.

Harding, Sarah. *Machig's Complete Explanation*. Snow Lion.

Jacoby, Sarah. *Love and Liberation*. Columbia University Press.

MacKenzie, Vicki. *Cave in the Snow: Tenzin Palmo's Quest for Enlightenment*. Bloomsbury USA.

Michaela Haas, Veronica Newton, et al. *Dakini Power: Twelve Extraordinary Women Shaping the Transmission of Tibetan Buddhism in the West*. Snow Lion.

Monson, Christina. *A Dakini's Counsel: Sera Khandro's Spiritual Advice and Dzogchen Instruction*. Shambhala.

Shaw, Miranda. *Passionate Enlightenment: Women in Tantric Buddhism*. Princeton.

Willis, Janice D. *Feminine Ground: Essays on Women in Tibet.* Snow Lion.

Acknowledgments

I am very grateful to the following people who helped me with this book. I send my deepest thanks to Richard Darsie, copy editor, and my anonymous proofreader. Several folks read chapters and gave feedback including David Scharff, Dr. Aaron Weiss, Elizabeth Chiment, and Ani Kathy Downs. Each of them demonstrated their bodhisattva intention by helping me improve this book for the sake of readers. I would also like to thank Todd Creamer for his collaboration on the Khandro Tuktik ngondro translation, and Tibetan inputting.

I feel a deep gratitude to my primary gurus; Lama Tharchin Rinpoche, Lama Pema Dorje Rinpoche, and Adzom Paylo Rinpoche, each of whom strongly encouraged ngondro practice. I was so unbelievably fortunate to have met with them in this life.

I would also like the other members of the Mayum Mountain Foundation board of directors for their ongoing support. Shout out, as well, to the Female Teachers of Tibetan Buddhism online group, for our laughter and tears together, as we navigate the peaks and valleys of teaching dharma in the modern world.

About The Author

Loppon Yudron Wangmo is an American teacher of Tibetan Buddhism who is known as a bridgebuilder between traditional practices and contemporary ways. She directs the Mayum Mountain Foundation, a California-based source of online classes and in-person small group retreats.

Her title *loppon*, conferred by Lama Pema Dorje Rinpoche, indicates that she is a respected teacher with a deep level of expertise gained through thirty years of in-depth practice and study. She completed a traditional cloistered three-year, three-month retreat under the guidance of Lama Tharchin Rinpoche, and shorter directed isolated retreats totaling another three under the direction of Lama Pema Dorje Rinpoche. Her mentors, along with her third main inspiration, Adzom Paylo Rinpoche, placed a strong emphasis on practice.

Loppon is the author of two Buddhist novels for teenagers, in a four book series still in progress. She uses innovative ways to share the message of Tibetan Buddhism with different kinds of people.

Excavating Pema Ozer
The Buddha of Lightning Peak

She has an author website that you might want to check out:
Yudron Wangmo
yudronwangmo.com

The Mayum Mountain Foundation

Tibetan Buddhism in Our Lives

Expand your wisdom and refine your consciousness through Buddhist Practice.

At the Mayum Mountain Foundation, we aspire to be a spiritual home for those who want to integrate the practice and study of Buddhism into their lives. Our focus is on the path of personal transformation of the Nyingma School of Tibetan Buddhism. Everyone is welcome.

Mayum is a respectful word for *mother* in the Tibetan language. The *mother* is our hidden ability to find the open and free aspect of our minds, allowing limitless love and compassion to come forth. The word *mountain* means gaining stability in that. Practice is how we find *Mayum Mountain*.

We are a tax-exempt non-profit Nyingma Buddhist group based in Copperopolis, California. We provide online classes and in-person retreats and meditations. Sign up for the newsletter on our website if you want to be kept up to date about everything we are doing.

mayummountain.org

www.ingramcontent.com/pod-product-compliance
Lightning Source LLC
Chambersburg PA
CBHW030431010526
44118CB00011B/580